The Journey from Prison to Community

I0130654

The Journey from Prison to Community: Developing Identity, Meaning and Belonging with Men in the UK provides a practical guide for practitioners working with men to successfully make the transition between prison and the community.

This transition presents significant challenges, especially for those who have served many years in prison; for those who have experienced multiple cycles of release/ recall; for those whose personality traits make it harder for them to build relationships and cope with strong emotions; and for those whose lives have been characterised by trauma, chaos, crime and institutionalisation. Drawing on the authors' clinical expertise and individual lived experiences alongside the latest research in the field, the book identifies key issues in transition and explores the impact of these issues. Crucially, it provides guidance, tools and support to professionals working with men in the UK to build a crime-free, socially integrated and meaningful life after incarceration, featuring real-life stories of those who have made the transition.

This is an essential read for professionals working in a range of settings across prison and community environments, while the wide variety of professional experience represented in the book broadens its appeal to forensic and clinical psychologists, occupational therapists, probation officers, prison staff and those working in the third sector. It is also a valuable resource for qualified professionals, those in training, support roles, and managers involved in planning strategy and service delivery.

Jo Shingler is a Chartered Psychologist and Registered Forensic Psychologist currently working within STRIVE (IIRMS), a co-commissioned service between HMPPS and the NHS as part of the Offender Personality Disorder Pathway. She has worked in prisons and the community for over 25 years, specialising in psychological risk assessment, interventions and understanding and improving therapeutic relationships in forensic settings.

Jennifer Stickney is an Advanced Occupational Therapy Practitioner working part time within STRIVE an Intensive Integrated Risk Management Service (IIRMS) a co-commissioned service between HMPPS and the NHS as part of the Offender Personality Disorder Pathway and part time working within HMPPS's Future Regime Design Team, offering a health perspective to the development of the National Regime Model. Jennifer has over 25 years of experience working as an Occupational Therapist in a wide range of forensic settings.

Issues in Forensic Psychology

Series Editors
Richard Shuker
Geraldine Akerman

The views expressed by the authors/editors may not necessarily be those held by the Series Editors or HMPPS.

The Psychology of Criminal Investigation
From Theory to Practice
Edited by Andy Griffiths and Rebecca Milne

Assessing and Managing Problematic Sexual Interests
A Practitioner's Guide
Global Perspectives on Interventions in Forensic Therapeutic Communities

Global Perspectives on Interventions in Forensic Therapeutic Communities
A Practitioner's Guide
Edited by Geraldine Akerman and Richard Shuker

Trauma-Informed Forensic Practice
Edited by Phil Wilmot and Lawrence Jones

Working with Autistic People in the Criminal Justice and Forensic Mental Health Systems
A Handbook for Practitioners
Edited by Nichola Tyler and Anne Sheeran

Challenging Bias in Forensic Psychological Assessment and Testing
Theoretical and Practical Approaches to Working with Diverse Populations
Edited by Glenda C. Liell, Martin J. Fisher, and Lawrence F. Jones

The Journey from Prison to Community
Developing Identity, Meaning and Belonging with Men in the UK
Edited by Jo Shingler and Jennifer Stickney

For more information about this series, please visit: www.routledge.com/ Issues-in-Forensic-Psychology/book-series/IFP

The Journey from Prison to Community

Developing Identity, Meaning and
Belonging with Men in the UK

**Edited by
Jo Shingler and Jennifer Stickney**

Routledge
Taylor & Francis Group

LONDON AND NEW YORK

Designed cover image: Drawing by Nick

First published 2024
by Routledge
4 Park Square, Milton Park, Abingdon, Oxon OX14 4RN

and by Routledge
605 Third Avenue, New York, NY 10158

Routledge is an imprint of the Taylor & Francis Group, an informa business

British Library Cataloguing-in-Publication Data
A catalogue record for this book is available from the British Library

Library of Congress Cataloging-in-Publication Data
A catalog record has been requested for this book

ISBN: 978-1-032-31121-0 (hbk)
ISBN: 978-1-032-31115-9 (pbk)
ISBN: 978-1-003-30817-1 (ebk)

DOI: 10.4324/9781003308171

Typeset in Bembo
by Taylor & Francis Books

Drawing by Jason

All the proceeds from this book will be donated to Coffee Connexions, a charity founded in 2022 to support those transitioning from prison to the community with mental health challenges in gaining work skills and employment on release.

Logo designed and created by Nick.

Charity number: 1198951

Contents

Illustrations

Figures

Table

Boxes

Acknowledgements

We would both like to thank the people who gave up their time to read drafts of our chapters, provide feedback and guidance, and help with editing, referencing and proofreading. They are Geri Akerman, Poppy Arnold, Natasha Balsamo, Nicola Bowes, Peter Dawson, Kate Herrity, Emma Holmes, Flora Fitzalan Howard, Camille Mangelinckx and Emma Nicklin. Your feedback and advice has been invaluable, and we both really appreciate it. We would also like to thank our publishers, Emilie Coin, Khyati Sanger, Ceri McLardy and Tori Sharpe, who have all been so supportive and constructive throughout our journey. Finally, we want to thank the men we have worked with over the years who have taught us so much about the pains of release and how they can be ameliorated. We would particularly like to thank those people whose stories illuminate the chapters.

JSh: I would like to pay tribute to my family (S, B and F) who have all sat by while our holidays and weekends have been dominated by book chat. That they find the whole process incomprehensible (especially when they realised this was not going to be the next "Harry Potter") yet remained supportive and encouraging (or possibly just tolerant?!) is all I need. I would also like to say thank you to Jenny, my co-editor. I could not have stuck with this without you. I have learned an immense amount from you, and think there is something really special about the interface between Psychology and Occupational Therapy that can support people in their journey from prison to the community. I am glad we have embodied that in this volume. I would also like to acknowledge our fabulous work team. It is because of the clinical and theoretical creativity within the team, and the supportive atmosphere that encourages us all to reflect and discuss issues, that we had this idea in the first place. You are the best bunch to work with and I am so grateful that I found you all. Finally, I would like to pay tribute to the late Ruth Mann. I would not have had the skill or confidence to have thought I could possibly have an idea for a book, pitch it to a publisher, let alone actually complete it, without her teaching, support, guidance and most importantly friendship. Those planning chats in that odd holiday cottage in Chipping Sodbury (for a book that never materialised) were not wasted after all.

JS: My experience as an Occupational Therapist is that we tend to be *doers* rather than writers. Whilst *doing* is key to our profession, by writing we can share our knowledge, experience and skills with others. By not writing we prevent this sharing of knowledge and limit how we promote our profession. Being on this journey of writing and editing this book and working closely with Jo, I have experienced the joy of writing about what we do, reflecting on the skills Occupational Therapists bring to supporting the transition of individuals from prison to the community. Through this experience and reading others' publications I have learnt so much and developed as a professional. I hope this book inspires other Occupational Therapists to research, write and publish, to continue to promote the value and importance of Occupational Therapy in this field of work.

This book feels like an enormous accomplishment, which I would not have been able to achieve without the unwavering support, love and tireless encouragement from my husband and children, my parents and sister over the last year: thank you. I would also like to thank: the wonderful teams I work in for all your skills, guidance, support and encouragement, you are amazing; Kate Herrity for your time, advice and sharing of information. I appreciate this so much; Emma Holmes, for your encouragement through every step of this book journey. Finally, I would like to acknowledge Jo, my wonderful co-editor. The relationship between Occupational Therapy and Psychology is an invaluable partnership from which I have benefited in working with you both clinically and when writing and editing this book. It has been an incredible experience and I feel so proud to have been on this journey with you.

Dusty Book

I'm on the edge of discovering my new self
Don't wanna live my life like a Dusty Book on a shelf
You'll know the one that no-one reads and always passes by
I felt like that Dusty Book and wanted so much to die
My pages were stained, all tattered and torn
Now slowly recovering I feel reborn
The journey I'm taking to replenish my style
My Dusty Book I am reading but it's gonna take a while
The first few chapters I've torn them out
The shame and the guilt, you'll know I have no doubt
It takes a lot of courage to read your Dusty Book
So if you ain't done it yet
Just pick it up and HAVE A LOOK!

By Liam

Contributors

Geraldine Akerman, Oxford Health NHS Foundation Trust, UK

Geraldine is a Forensic Psychologist employed by the NHS working in HMPs Grendon and Springhill, and Aylesbury. Geraldine has worked in prisons with men who have committed sexual and other violent offences for 24 years. She has published papers on the subjects of Therapeutic Communities, sexual offending, compassion-focused therapy, co-authored by those in custody. Geraldine is a visiting lecturer at the University of Birmingham, where she was awarded her PhD, and at Cardiff Metropolitan University. Geraldine is the former Chair of the Division of Forensic Psychology.

Nicholas Blagden, University of Derby, UK

Nicholas Blagden is Professor in Criminological Psychology at the University of Derby, former Head of the Sexual Offences Crime and Misconduct Research Unit at NTU, co-founder and trustee of the Safer Living Foundation and Chartered Psychologist. He currently sits on the HMPPS Correctional Services Advice and Accreditation Panel and NOTA's Policy and Practice Committee. He has a track record of publishing in high-quality journals and has authored and co-authored multiple books. He is also a registered psychotherapist.

Christabel Budd, Occupational Therapist, NHS, UK

Christabel Budd is an Occupational Therapist employed by the NHS with an interest in sensory modulation and its application in our everyday life.

Jenny Devine, HMPPS, UK

Jenny Devine works as a Registered Forensic Psychologist for His Majesty's Prison and Probation Service in the United Kingdom. She has worked for HMPPS since 2008, engaging in work across prisons and the community.

Alan Hirons, Leeds Beckett University, UK

Alan qualified as an Occupational Therapist in 1999 and completed the MSc Working with Personality Disorder – Extending Expertise and Enhancing Practice in 2014. After 23 years in the NHS working primarily in Leeds Personality Disorder Services, Alan is commencing a new career as a Senior Lecturer in Occupational Therapy at Leeds Beckett University.

Hannah Jenner, Occupational Therapist, NHS, UK

Hannah is an Occupational Therapist currently working within STRIVE (IIRMS), a co-commissioned service between HMPPS and the NHS as part of the Offender Personality Disorder Pathway. Hannah has worked within Forensic Services for over 8 years.

Joe Lowenstein, Consultant Clinical Psychologist, UK

Joe is a Consultant Clinical Psychologist. He has worked within forensic clinical services for the last 10 years. He is an Advanced Schema Therapist with a special interest in trauma and personality issues.

Samantha Macmillan, Assistant Psychologist, UK

Samantha Macmillan has an MSc in Forensic Psychology from NTU and a BSc in Psychology. She is currently an Assistant Psychologist within the Central London NHS Trust.

Kellsey McCann, Assistant Psychologist, UK

Kellsey McCann has an MSc in Forensic Psychology from NTU and a BSc in Psychology. She is currently an Assistant Psychologist within the Cambridgeshire and Peterborough NHS Trust.

Charlotte Purvis, Principal Clinical Psychologist, UK

Charlotte Purvis is a Principal Clinical Psychologist with significant experience working with individuals, across the lifespan, who present with complex trauma, personality difficulties and serious offending. Charlotte has expertise within secure mental health inpatient, community and probation settings. Charlotte has worked in the OPD pathway in Dorset for the last five years.

Sue Ryan, Consultant Clinical & Forensic Psychologist, UK

Sue Ryan is a Consultant Clinical & Forensic Psychologist, CAT Practitioner and EMDR Therapist, at Merseycare NHS Trust in the OPD Pathway. She has a particular interest in how services and teams can remain compassionate and enabling, to better support individuals within forensic services to make safer life choices.

Jo Shingler, Chartered Psychologist, Registered Forensic Psychologist, UK

Jo Shingler is a Chartered Psychologist and Registered Forensic Psychologist currently working within STRIVE (IIRMS), a co-commissioned service between HMPPS and the NHS as part of the Offender Personality Disorder Pathway. She has worked in prisons and the community for over 25 years, specialising in psychological risk assessment, interventions and understanding and improving therapeutic relationships in forensic settings.

Millie E. Smith, HMPPS, UK

Millie is a Facilitator employed by HMPPS working in the Therapeutic Community HMP Grendon on the Extended Assessment Unit. Millie has begun researching Therapeutic Communities during a MSc in Criminology and Criminal Justice at the University of Oxford. Previously, Millie worked in open conditions at Springhill as part of the Pathway's Enhanced Resettlement Service.

Jennifer Stickney, Advanced Occupational Therapy Practitioner, UK
Jennifer is an Advanced Occupational Therapy Practitioner working part time within STRIVE an Intensive Intervention Risk Management Service (IIRMS) a co-commissioned service between HMPPS and the NHS as part of the Offender Personality Disorder Pathway and part-time working within HMPPS's Future Regime Design Team, offering a health perspective to the development of the National Regime Model. Jennifer has over 25 years of experience working as an Occupational Therapist in a wide range of forensic settings.

Ian, Jason, Liam, Mark, Nick, Rob, Sam and Wayne are all men with lived experience of making the transition between prison and the community.

Foreword

This book is a rare thing: a book about the post-prison resettlement process written from a psychological perspective. As a psychological criminologist (or a criminological psychologist), straddling the fields of psychology and sociology, I am often amused by what subjects are assigned to which discipline. For instance, sex offending is something that has been essentially given over to psychology with almost all of the important, recent social scientific research on that topic done by those with psychology backgrounds. On the other hand, resettlement after prison is largely seen as the domain of sociological criminology. After all, so much of reintegration involves the pragmatics of employment, housing, economics, neighbourhood factors, and so forth. Usually, these divisions make no coherent sense and the assignment to strict disciplinary silos only serves to limit the imagination of the research. For instance, surely there are cultural, social and structural factors at play in sex offending that are missed by a purely psychological focus. Sometimes, it takes a brave disciplinary defector to shake up a field and develop ideas that are genuinely original and generative. There could be no better example of this sort of boundary crossing and its potential for transformative change than this remarkable collection.

This is not to say psychologists have not studied "rehabilitation". Far from it. Rehabilitation (especially inside prisons) is nearly entirely "owned" by the field of psychology. Almost all accredited interventions are based in the principles of cognitive-behavioural therapy and aimed at changing attitudes and patterns of thinking thought to be related to offending. However, when individuals are actually released from safe confines of the "treatment programme" and face the barrage of challenges in the "real world", the psychologists are typically escorted out of the room and replaced by those with a better understanding of social and structural factors.

After all, the transition from the total institution of prison to society is surely the sociologist's ultimate example of "setting people up to fail". Individuals are removed from wider society because they are struggling to cope in various ways. Incarcerated with hundreds of peers with similar struggles, they become socialised into institutional norms that, albeit highly adaptive in the world of the prison, are seen as highly deviant in nearly any other environment. Next, they are released back into the world accompanied by an intense stigma that will limit their chances of finding work, securing housing, reintegrating with family, or pursuing educational opportunities. At the same time, they are the subject of justice system scrutiny and surveillance far beyond what the rest of us would tolerate, policing what they consume, where they go, and with whom they associate. The process appears to be a sort of recidivism "machine" invented by a mad man, and thus rightly the struggle of the formerly incarcerated is an absolute staple of sociology (see e.g., Morenoff & Harding, 2014; Western, 2018). Indeed, the structural obstacles these works reveal have been known for nearly a century and should be taken as one of the exceedingly few, undisputed facts of criminology.

As essential as this work is, what it is often missing, however, is the human being inside of this recidivism machine. This is where this book feels so incredibly rich and original with contributions like Stickney and Lowenstein's (wonderfully titled) chapter "They spoke to me like I was a human, so I behaved like a human". Here, the contributors transcend the usual structural factors impacting reintegration – housing, employment, family – and remind us also that "mattering" matters as well. "Mattering" may even matter more than any other factor. Borrowing from Rosenberg and McCullough's (1981) work on self-esteem, Stickney and Lowenstein define "mattering" as a person's need to feel significant to others, to feel noticed, appreciated, understood.

In fact, by that definition, this entire collection, with its emphasis from start to finish on "lived experience", personal testimony and foregrounding the perspective of the person returning from prison, can be seen as a work of "mattering" – of recognising the humanity and moral worth of the people at the heart of this research. In short, this collection is, in my view, a demonstration of the best of what psychology can and should be. Our field has, for far too long, viewed resettlement purely from the perspective of 'risk' – a Faustian bargain the field struck, selling our soul for a chance at relevance and sitting at the grown-up table inside the justice system. The accounts in this book vividly demonstrate the inadequacy of framing 'risk' as somehow residing inside of individuals in these incredible circumstances. This collection is based on a humanistic psychology that rejects what Ian (in his outstanding afterword) calls the "them and us" narrative plaguing criminal justice. This redemptive psychology perfectly suits the task of understanding reintegration experiences and offers a way forward not seen in traditional sociological accounts that can feel so lacking in hope or potential for escape. With luck, it will inspire a new generation in both psychology and sociology to work together around this extraordinarily challenging issue.

Professor Shadd Maruna
Queen's University Belfast

References

Morenoff, J. D., & Harding, D. J. (2014). Incarceration, prisoner reentry, and communities. *Annual Review of Sociology, 40,* 411.

Rosenberg, M., & McCullough, B. C. (1981). Mattering: Inferred significance and mental health among adolescents. *Research in Community and Mental Health, 2,* 163–182.

Western, B. (2018). *Homeward: Life in the year after prison.* Russell Sage Foundation.

Preface

Jo Shingler and Jennifer Stickney

In 2001, Shadd Maruna noted that "the question of how to improve the process of ex-offender re-entry or reintegration will be among the most important issues facing the country in the next few decades" (p. 17). As practitioners working in the community to support men coming out of prison, we firmly believe that over 20 years later, we still need to see the sorts of improvements to which Maruna was referring. We see men who have demonstrated enormous change whilst in prison, with regard to insight into their offending behaviour, being able to recognise and reduce the impact of their risk factors and show empathy for and understanding of the effects of their offending on their victims. However, these men too frequently struggle within days or weeks of release, often ending up being recalled back to prison within a few months. We have seen men who have done well in the community, who have found jobs and homes of their own and who have started to build relationships with their communities, suddenly begin to struggle, disengage and begin a downward spiral that also has led to recall. Whilst some may seek to attribute blame to the "recall happy" probation service for this, we work with and alongside compassionate and brave probation officers who have done literally all they can to avoid initiating a recall. Alongside this, some (not all) of the men we work with who have been recalled have recognised that their recall was inevitable and ultimately "saved them" from the impact of their escalating behaviours. In fact, some men have deliberately taken ("noncompliance") steps that they know will result in recall in order to draw a line under their disintegration in the community. Ultimately, resettlement is a complex and multifaceted process that requires greater understanding and investment.

The hiatus in our personal and professional lives caused by the COVID-19 lockdowns provided an unexpected reflective space for us to take more notice of the challenges experienced by people coming out of custody, as well as to look at how we as professionals could better support people making that transition. In the space created by lockdown and in the absence of traditional services to support people on release, we heard personal accounts of prison/community transitions that we wanted to bring to life. We wanted to give people a voice and enable them to share their experiences. The stories we heard during COVID-19 also highlighted that release plans are frequently not sufficiently robust to support the complexity of people's needs in the community following prison. We have thought and reflected on these issues, between ourselves, with our colleagues, and with the men themselves, to try and understand why the process and maintenance of release and resettlement is so difficult to navigate. We agree wholeheartedly with Farrall (2004) who suggests that the factors leading up to offending that tend to be the focus of interventions in prison are distinctly different from the factors that predict and support successful resettlement. Therefore, this book is an attempt to identify the challenges that occur throughout the resettlement journey and discuss how practitioners, both in custody and the community, can best approach and respond to these challenges.

We also felt strongly that we wanted to give the people we work with a voice and a space to tell their stories of release: their successes, the difficulties and challenges they have experienced and their perspectives on how they and others can be helped and supported in their journey to successful resettlement. The accounts people have given of what they need, of how they have struggled, of the ways they feel they have been let down and why, and of what needs to be in place to support success have been real, authentic and with recognition of their personal fallibility and accountability. We have been moved by the generosity of people in sharing sometimes painful experiences for no reward other than making a contribution and helping others. It would not have been possible to write this volume without them. Most names have been changed and pseudonyms used except where people have actively wanted their own names to be used: some people have felt a sense of pride and ownership in having a named contribution. Ian, Jason, Liam, Mark, Nick, Rob, Sam and Wayne have all given permission for their words and names to be included in this volume and we cannot thank them enough for their contributions. All of the other names have been changed to protect privacy.

Relatedly, we want to mention our use of terms in this volume. Individual authors have chosen their own terms, although we have encouraged everyone to remain true to the ethos of this book, which is, as far as possible, a collaboratively produced volume about the prison community transition. We have been fortunate in working with a group of authors who share our ethos and approach to criminal justice work. For our part, we have largely chosen to use "individuals", "people in prison" or "people on probation". We have avoided contractions and acronyms, as we feel they risk dehumanising people. We have veered away from "service user" because we feel it lacks acknowledgment of the voluntary nature of many community services. We have been concerned that the term "service users" implies an obligation or a lack of collaboration. It communicates a sense of someone "using" services rather than engaging and participating in their own unique journey. We have also avoided the term "client", as this reflects someone who pays for services and this does not represent the experience of people engaging with criminal justice services. Ultimately, we want to develop collaborative and humanising relationships with the people we work with, with joint aims to achieve outcomes that are meaningful to the individual and achievable within the parameters of risk management, and we want our language to reflect this.

In summary, this book focuses on the prison/community transition, an area that we feel has been neglected in the field. Prison and probation is full of transitions and discussing and reflecting on how these are managed is essential to support people to get the best out of services. This book is a clinicians' guide produced by professionals and those who use our services, for professionals. The development and production of the book has been informed by the voices of the people with whom we work, as they are the people who know most what they need, alongside academic literature and professional experience. We also want to draw attention to the complimentary partnership between Occupational Therapy and Psychology that is central to this book. The collaboration of these professions provides greater value than the sum of each profession working in isolation.

We are honoured to have so many experts in research and practice from a range of professional backgrounds contributing to this volume. We clearly explained our vision of the book to each contributor and we are delighted that people produced work consistent with this, in particular the value given to individual stories of transition and co-production. Each contributor approached the brief differently, but we feel that all of the perspectives included throughout this volume provide a valuable insight into the complexity of the transition.

We have divided this book into three parts. Part I focuses on stages of the prison community transition. We start with Geraldine Akerman and Millie E. Smith discussing how people can be prepared for release in prison, and the special role that open prison conditions plays in supporting this transition. We are fortunate to have original data from a study exploring the transition between therapeutic communities and open prisons to enrich this chapter. Jo Shingler and Jennifer Stickney go on to look at the specific challenges of the first few days and weeks of release, how people navigate the emotional overload of release and what they need in those early days to optimise success. Finally in this section, Jo Shingler, alongside Nick and Wayne, two men with lived experience, explore the pains of recall to prison, and how they can be avoided and ameliorated.

Part II focuses on specific issues in the transition journey. We recognise that we cannot possibly cover all the relevant challenges faced by people as they manage their resettlement and reintegration journey, but we have been guided by our clinical experience, by the literature and by the experiences of men making the transition to identify what we feel to be key priorities. This section starts with Charlotte Purvis and Jenny Devine exploring trauma within this population, how the process of release itself can be traumatising or retraumatising, and how trauma responses might show themselves in difficulties with resettlement. They go on to emphasise the importance of practitioners taking a trauma-informed approach to understanding people's behaviour in the community. Following this, Jennifer Stickney, Christabel Budd and Mark look at the complex and enlightening area of sensory issues, and how having a greater understanding and awareness of sensory issues can support reintegration success. This is an area of growing interest within the criminal justice field. Mark's lived experience brings light to the nature and extent of struggles people can experience in the community and provides guidance on how to better support people using a sensory lens. In the third chapter in this section Sue Ryan and Sam go on to address the issue of substance misuse and how this can so often be a trigger or a pathway to deterioration in the community, even for those who have been substance-free in prison. Sue takes a case-study approach to bring creativity and reflection to this topic. Next, Jennifer Stickney, Alan Hirons and Hannah Jenner look at the practical aspects of release: how the learning and development of practical daily living skills is so often overlooked, yet so crucial for successful reintegration. In the final chapter of Part II, Nick Blagden, Kellsey McCann and Samantha Macmillan, who also report new and exciting research data, discuss specific issues relevant to resettlement for men who have convictions for sexual offences. This group is particularly marginalised and vilified within society so arguably, resettlement is even more challenging for them.

Part III closes the volume by turning attention to professional issues in the resettlement process. Firstly, Jo Shingler and Charlotte Purvis address the crucial area of developing and navigating supportive and meaningful professional relationships with men as they prepare for release in prison and step out into the community. There is a plethora of literature focusing on professional and therapeutic relationships, and in this chapter the authors draw on this to focus attention specifically on transition issues. Finally, Jennifer Stickney and Joe Lowenstein address another less well-known, but equally enlightening and important area, that of hope and mattering in the transition process. Understanding the importance of mattering, how to communicate to people that they matter, and how to support people to develop a sense of mattering can make a significant difference to people struggling with the emotional and practical demands of resettlement.

We are lucky enough to have our volume bookended by two impressive and valuable authors, who are also kind, generous and decent human beings. Shadd Maruna fittingly provides a foreword, given that *our* foreword is opened by a quote from his volume "Making Good". "Making Good" has changed approaches to desistance and resettlement irreversibly and undoubtedly for the better. Ian C provides our afterword. Ian has many years of lived experience within services. Whilst he no longer requires any additional support, he has remained in touch with us, offering valuable advice on topical issues. Ian has truly "made good" and is living and thriving in the community. His generosity and willingness to give back and make a contribution to this volume speaks to his success.

References

Farrall, S. (2004). Social capital and offender reintegration: Making probation desistance focused. In S. Maruna & R. Immarigeon (Eds). *After crime and punishment: Pathways to offender reintegration* (pp. 57–82). Cullumpton, Devon: Willan Publishing.

Maruna, S. (2001). *Making good: How ex-convicts reform and rebuild their lives.* Washington: America Psychological Association.

Part I
Stages in transition

1 One more step along the road to freedom

Geraldine Akerman and Millie E. Smith

Introduction

It has long been known that times of transition can be unsettling, bringing confusion and worry (Micklethwaite & Earle, 2021). For those in custody, moving from one establishment to another can generate anxiety. The transfer to open conditions is a particularly important transition that marks progress through a prison sentence, and a significant step along the road towards release and freedom. This transfer does, however, encompass challenges. This chapter considers the process of transition from a closed to an open prison and the role of this transition in preparing people for community life. Discussion is situated in the context of existing literature, pointing to present knowledge about the comparisons between open and closed prisons in England and Wales and those in Scandinavia, and around the particular pains of open imprisonment. Consideration is given to the impact of imprisonment on identity, and how this alters across prisons and throughout a sentence.

A range of lived experience is provided in this chapter via the voices of men in prison who have completed the transition from closed to open conditions. Experiences have been collected by informal discussion and formal research conducted by the second author as part of a master's degree (Smith, 2022). Experiences highlighted by those in prison are discussed in relation to existing knowledge around trauma and identity. We consider the difficulties encountered by specific groups, exploring the distinct experiences of those serving indeterminate sentences, and those that transition into open conditions from a democratic therapeutic community. Finally, we make suggestions as to how we may assist men to make the transition from closed to open prison, in order to maximise their chances of a successful journey along the road to freedom.

Understanding open prisons

Open prisons present less physical security than closed, and house those who are nearing or working towards their eventual release (Prison Reform Trust, 2015). In England and Wales, people in prison must undergo a risk assessment to be eligible for transfer to open conditions. Ministry of Justice guidelines

DOI: 10.4324/9781003308171-2

requires those in prison to have sufficiently reduced their risk of harm and their risk of absconding; be able to show that they can be reasonably trusted in open conditions; and be considered as someone for whom open conditions are appropriate (Ministry of Justice, 2020[1]). Generally, people spend at least two years in an open prison, enabling preparations for resettlement. Open prison also enables those serving indeterminate sentences to work toward a successful parole hearing before they can be released into the community.[2] Those held in the open estate have much more freedom to move around the establishment with limited restrictions, and additional access to education and voluntary and paid employment both in the establishment and the community (Ministry of Justice, 2011; Prison Reform Trust, 2015).

Release on Temporary Licence (ROTL) is a distinct feature of open conditions, providing the mechanism by which people in prison are authorised to leave the establishment to undertake activities that have a clear rehabilitative or resettlement purpose. Examples may include temporary release to attend places of training or employment, to spend time with family, or on compassionate grounds to attend a funeral and so on. ROTL offers those in open conditions a valued opportunity to spend time and reassimilate themselves to the community while still serving their sentence. This enables individuals to be tested under strict conditions and supervision prior to release (Grayling, 2014), with research finding a 99% ROTL compliance rate (Potter & Gunderson, 2015).

Comparing open prisons

There is limited literature comparing the experiences of open conditions with closed prison, with existing discussion focused primarily on Scandinavia. Media representations portray life in Scandinavia's open minimum-security prisons as comfortable, rehabilitation oriented and with generous welfare state provisions. As in England and Wales, Scandinavia's open prisons have lower security with limited outer perimeter control, more trusting attitudes toward those in prison from staff, and greater opportunities for autonomy, freedom of movement, and time spent in the community than in typical closed prisons.

Mjåland, Laursen, Schliehe, and Larmour (2021) compared experiences of imprisonment in closed and open prisons in England and Wales, and Norway, discussing their findings in the context of differing neoliberal and social democratic penal philosophies. In both settings, issues such as health, safety, and control were identified as key differential areas. When exploring these areas, those in open prisons in both jurisdictions reported worrying much less about their health, safety, and lack of control than those in closed prisons. Those in open prisons also reported feelings of greater autonomy and trust. Further, whilst individuals were found to experience similar kinds of problems and frustrations in both types of prison, they were found to be significantly less severe and acute in open prisons.

However, some similarities between open and closed prisons persisted, with those in both settings missing little luxuries, and wishing that time would go faster (Mjåland et al., 2021). The only area in which open prisons were found to be more problematic in both jurisdictions was feeling that you are losing contact with family and friends, and feeling that you need to be careful about everything you say and do. These results suggest that feelings of being out of touch with community life and feelings of being under scrutiny are problematic for people in open prisons. However, overall, the results indicate that open prisons are experienced as safer, less restrictive, and less degrading than closed prisons in both England and Wales and Norway. Unsurprisingly, men rated their overall experiences more positively in open than closed prisons. This comparative research highlights the aspects of open conditions that are experienced positively or negatively, how these persist across jurisdictions, and what may be important in supporting the wellbeing of those across prison estates.

The pains of freedom

The improved material conditions and increased autonomy and involvement in the community afforded by open conditions are understood to reduce the overall intensity of the pains of imprisonment (Pakes, 2020; Marder, Lapouge, Garrihy & Brandon, 2021). Open prisons are therefore considered as more psychologically survivable (Liebling, 2012) than closed. This reduced intensity of the prison experience is positioned as an attempt to reverse the negative impacts of closed imprisonment and better support the re-entry of individuals by offering them greater freedom and autonomy before their release (Shammas, 2014; Statham, Winder and Micklethwaite, 2021).

However, whilst such increased freedom and autonomy is longed for, transitioning to this from a closed prison can present particular pains that must be managed. Sykes (1958) described the pains of imprisonment as the deprivation of liberty, goods and services, contact with people outside, autonomy, and security in terms of violence and being at risk from other people in prison. The literature has discussed experiences of open conditions to be characterised by distinct pains of freedom (Shammas, 2014). Shammas (2014) considered this in the realms of an open prison in Norway, and discussed the feelings of anxiety, boundlessness, ambiguity, relative depravation and individual responsibility brought by the freedom of open conditions. As such, whilst the autonomy and freedom of open conditions is clearly longed for and valued, it comes with often unexpected and unpalatable tensions. The freedom of the changed environment and regime can feel boundless and ambiguous, inflicting anxiety. Those that have been held in closed conditions for lengthy periods can become reliant upon the routine of regimes for the structure of their day. Being held in highly structured regimes and being dependent upon the orders and decisions of others can lead to a lack of agency and inability to make decisions for oneself (Cohen & Taylor, 1981), meaning the less secure environment and structured regime of open prisons can be especially challenging.

Statham, Winder and Micklethwaite (2021) considered that such pains of freedom underpinned the difficulties that both staff and people living in prison experience in adapting to this more flexible and less restrictive regime. For staff, difficulties of maintaining control in an environment of reduced physical security were apparent, whilst residents had to learn "how to sit with the cage door open, while not flying away" (p.745). Here, both people living and working in prison are found to experience difficulties coping with less security and confusion around whether open prisons exist to provide freedom or containment. They must contend with the Prison Service's attempts to balance priorities of upholding the security of the establishment and protecting the public whilst assisting with individual resettlement needs (Liebling & Arnold, 2004). Pennington and Crewe (2015) highlight the challenges of this balancing act and reflect on the high levels of public scrutiny of open prisons and their staff, particularly if an individual absconds, generating pressure for decision makers to be more risk averse. Consequently, it is clear that both staff and residents in open prison settings must be supported in adapting to and managing the tensions presented by the simultaneous aims of containment and freedom inherent to open conditions.

Further, with this reduced physical security, the need for *dynamic* security[3] increases, reliant upon respectful relationships and people in prison feeling comfortable to approach staff before problems escalate (United Nations Office on Drugs and Crime, 2015). Considering this reliance, Jarvis, Shaw and Lovell (2022) report that those arriving in open conditions are often mistrusting toward staff and other people in prison; thus, the necessity for positive, pro-social and trusting environments and relationships in the open estate is clear.

People in prison have reported feeling overwhelmed by the lack of physical containment resulting from the porous boundaries of open prison (Statham et al., 2021). Blurred lines between the prison and the community create ambiguities around the space and role of the establishment, and the levels of individual freedoms they provide. Those in open conditions, whilst aware of their improved position in relation to closed prison, are said to experience a relative deprivation in their longing for more permanent freedom and involvement in the community than temporarily experienced whilst in open. This reveals the frustrations those in open conditions experience in being one more step along the road to their freedom, but with more still to go. With this in mind, it is crucial that those moving to open conditions are prepared for the less familiar and visible boundaries, rules and regimes of the establishment, and the expectations of them prior to their arrival, to help offset some of this confusion.

Further, in reducing the level of physical security, cell searches, use of force, mandatory drugs tests and so on, open prisons rely on incentives for compliance. Lammas (2015) discussed how open prisons maintain control by giving those within them something to lose and then threatening to take it away. Here, the freedoms offered by open conditions are revealed to be contingent on compliance, revealing their precariousness. The feeling of having a lot to lose has been found to be ever present, with increased freedoms positioned against a lack of clarity as to what is expected of individuals, inflicting further anxiety and revealing further pains (Statham et al., 2020). Statham et al. (2021)

described how open conditions felt tinged with frustration, suspicion and limitation, presenting an experience of the soft power (Crewe, 2011) and need for personal responsibility inherent in open conditions. As such, those in open conditions must adhere to more ambiguous rules with starker consequences, and heightened fears around antisocial behaviour. These changes to penal power and responsibility in open conditions whereby more freedom is promised, but more accountability to authority presides, has been described by Neumann (2012) as resulting in an 'imprisonment of the soul' (p. 139), that is tantamount in pain to that experienced by those in high-security establishments. Constant fear of failure and uncertainty is exhausting, a view further supported by Hampton (2012). Appell (2018) conducted informal research with men in one open prison in England, finding them to encounter difficulties managing their hopes for more freedom in open conditions, and navigating their bureaucracies.

Changes in identity

Alongside challenges with individual autonomy and freedom, progression through prison sentences and between establishments impacts upon identities. Discussion of prisons as stripping individuals of their identities (Crewe, 2009; Warr 2020) and imposing new carceral identities reveal the implications of individuals developing a prison self that is attuned to surviving conditions of confinement, but not succeeding in the community. Liem and Kunst (2013) developed the notion of 'post-incarceration syndrome' whereby individuals are 'over-adapted' to the prison environment in ways that make life after release more difficult. Liem and Kunst (2013) noted the high psychological, financial, and vocational needs of people exiting prison following long-term confinement, all of which had been greatly exacerbated by so many years in prison.

Maruna and Roy (2007) describe how in the early stages of change, it is crucial for individuals to disconnect from their criminal risk factors to allow emerging identities to form and strengthen. Whilst Maruna and Roy (2007) explain this to involve a distinct knifing off of parts of a previous antisocial identity, Perrin and Blagden (2016) suggest more of a drip-by-drip process whereby changes are made incrementally. Whilst identity changes are in process, individuals may not have strong enough resolve or sufficient resources to overcome temptations that lead to antisocial action. Here, the state of flux between incarceration and release found in open conditions provides a test for the developing prosocial identity. The opportunity to break ties and reconstruct the identity is a helpful one but requires a safe and dynamically containing environment away from temptations and away from those who are participating in rule breaking. This reveals open prisons as a potential major crossroads for men who are at a crucial point in their journey towards release. One respondent in Statham et al.'s (2020) study of men in open prison suggested that 'if you don't build a wall round you then people will prey on you' (p.739), asserting the requirement to protect the psychological sterile space and be assertive against those who try to breach it. They also revealed it is hard to bring yourself back from antisocial involvement if you get in too deep, reasserting the need for robust boundaries early on and distance from those who do not fit with the emerging identity.

Open conditions and indeterminate sentences

Looking at specific groups, Pennington (2015) demonstrated how the pains of freedom in open conditions can be particularly acute for those serving indeterminate sentences. For this group, Micklethwaite and Earle (2021) describe the transition from closed to open conditions to be a major life event and highlight the failure of existing research literature to pay adequate attention to this. The move to open conditions is positioned as uniquely significant for those on indeterminate sentences, solidifying their journey toward release after lengthy periods in closed conditions, with an undetermined stretch of imprisonment ahead. Crewe, Hulley and Wright (2020) describe this move as disturbing the equilibrium that those in prison establish and maintain in closed conditions. That said, Pennington and Crewe (2015) note that those released on a life sentence are three times less likely to reoffend if released from an open rather than a closed prison. As such, particular attention should be paid to those who transition to open conditions whilst progressing through an indeterminate sentence, for whom 'success' in the open estate is crucial.

The challenges experienced across the transition from a closed to an open prison are clear. The freedom and autonomy provided by the open estate, whilst welcome, inflict tensions upon those in open conditions. Their intensity is potentially heightened for those serving indeterminate sentences, as discussed above. Additionally, those who make the transition from a supportive, therapeutic environment may find it particularly difficult to adjust to the new environment of open conditions.

The transition from a therapeutic community to an open prison

The experiences of those that had transferred from a closed therapeutic community (TC) to an open prison were explored by Smith (2022). This research paid particular attention to the impact of the change of environment and culture on participants' identities and sense of self, and their self-management and use of therapeutic tools. The research aimed to identify what helped or hindered the transition from closed TC to open prison, and what could be done to better support those going through it. The results can directly inform practice in terms of how to better support men in the transition to open conditions.

Participants of this research were men currently in open conditions serving lengthy or indeterminate sentences for violent offences. They had spent between 5–21 years in prison, and had spent between 20–108 months in a TC. The men had been transferred to open conditions between 4–27 months ago. Interviews investigated experiences of the transition, challenges encountered, and support received. Experiences of leaving therapy, and the use of therapeutic tools in open prison were also reflected upon. So too were individual experiences of community, peer support, trust, and identity through the transition. Two key areas are discussed below, which help us to understand the experience of the transition to open prison, *liminality of space and self*, and *pains of the transition*.

Liminality of space and self

Liminality was experienced in a range of areas. Firstly, a *liminality of progress* was felt in the transition from a TC to open prison. Participants reflected that the transfer signified both their progress in being one more step along the road to freedom, but with their continued imprisonment presenting them with further steps to go. Participants spoke of the importance of gaining the Category D security status[4] that deems them of sufficiently low risk to move to open conditions, and the significance of the transfer in affirming their journey toward the end of their sentence, with Joel[5] remarking:

> Throughout your sentence you're always hearing about D cat D cat D cat D cat, so now that you're at that step it's like another step forward.

Joel also spoke of feeling as though he was headed in the right direction:

> Yeah, I'm definitely stepping in the right direction. I know the ropes yeah, and I'm definitely going in the right direction.

This confirmed the transition to open conditions to be a significant step forward along the road to freedom. Liminality was however, heard in participants' acute awareness of there being many more steps to go, revealing the experience of being closer to freedom but still not truly free. Joel discussed these steps very clearly:

> I would say like urm, in terms of steps like 1–5 let's say, I'm probably at like step 2, at the moment I'm not getting home leaves because they're just sorting stuff out with probation so once I get that that'll be step 3, and then building stuff on the outside when I go home and stuff will be step 4, and 5 being ready to like, get out, like know where I'm gonna live, having a place to rent, do you know what I mean.

This highlighted how the move to open conditions was found to make eventual release more tangible and realistic through the provision of resettlement preparations, demonstrating lived experience of the resettlement aims of the open estate. Participants discussed the need not only to make practical preparations, but also to readjust from prison to daily routines and socialising:

The end goal is to obviously you know, get yourself a job, get yourself
into proper society, you know, get into that routine.

(Frank)

What I need to do is get out, and get working, get mixing in with people

(Harry)

Such points resonated with earlier discussions around the need for those in
open conditions to spend time socialising themselves out of prison cultures and
regimes ahead of their eventual resettlement in the community. With this
preparation, participants presented as motivated to make their release a reality,
and confident in their ability to succeed in this, with Toby remarking:

Cos everything's there now, set for me now, to be out there and succeed
in whatever I do, and I have no doubt that I will do.

This demonstrated the utility of spending time in open conditions prior to release
in setting the foundations for success in the community, and building confidence.
Further to this, those in open conditions spoke of them as providing a valued
opportunity not only to assimilate but also to test themselves in a less securitised
environment and validate their readiness for freedom to themselves and others.
Frank reflected open conditions as a step toward and test before release:

This is the step before you're getting out. So, if you can't manage in here
you're not gonna be nothing in the community, you're gonna fail in the
community.

Toby spoke to the particular utility of this when serving an indeterminate
sentence and needing to prove a readiness for release to the Parole Board in
order to eventually secure freedom:

I look at that as help, and of benefit as well, because at the end of the day,
the more evidence I can produce, to the judge again, the better chance I
have at getting release, you know what I mean.

Participants were seen to be building and validating their narratives through the
transition and experiencing this as a point in which to test and prove their
capacities to keep these going. Liminality prevailed, with an awareness of the
need for further progress prior to release being at the forefront of their minds.
Some revealed their fears around sustaining their progress, revealing the precariousness of progress and desistance through the transition:

But also like, I think about meself and think like, how long's this gonna
last before I end up fuckin flippin?

(Frank)

This confirmed the need for those in open conditions to maintain their narratives and progress despite difficulties. Participants revealed their experiences of being subjected to the earlier discussed 'soft power' (Crewe, 2011) and responsibilisation of open conditions, alongside their awareness of the uncertainty of their capacities to maintain their projects of the self under such pressures. Reece reflected on the overwhelming pressures of bureaucratic processes and soft power, and how the need to succeed was day to day, expressing a sense of relentlessness:

> There's no get up, there's no release from it, there's no, there's no down time from it, it's just on to the next, you know, staff get a holiday, I haven't had a holiday for 5 years, and I know I'm in prison and I don't deserve a holiday, but it's like you're constantly there with your face against the glass 'go, go, go, go, go, go, go.' There isn't any down time.

Here, the utility of the TC experience in enhancing their capacity to deal with prison pressures was asserted as central to the ability to successfully transition to open conditions:

> That's what the TC has helped me with this transition, it's helped me navigate situations that I definitely would've solved with violence, one million percent, and I'm only being honest wit ya.
>
> (Frank)

Alongside this liminality of progress, whereby participants found open conditions to be a step along the road to freedom but with many more uncertain and difficult steps to go, open prisons were discussed as being a *liminal space*: whereby individuals are positioned physically between confinement and freedom. They can feel and see their proximity to release whilst continuing to be confined in prison, albeit a markedly different one. Progress toward release was found to be suspended in the context of continued incarceration, with freedom confronted by and dependent upon an institution of confinement. Relating to the above point around the pressures of open, participants spoke of their impatience to be out of the prison environment and away from these stresses:

> It's more just looking forward to being able to breathe. It's all done, like it's hard to explain. It's hard to explain. There's always something to deal with in jail. There's always something to deal with, there's always this hurdle that hurdle, you're always fighting something like, when you go home you've just got your own space you're done, do you know what I mean?
>
> (Joel)

Joel's contribution above reflects the confusion and frustration emerging from the increasing proximity to but continued isolation from the community, inflicting a state of flux between being imprisoned and free. An eagerness for civilian life was noted, with participants trying to align their position in prison with their excitement around their progression towards the community. Within this, Toby spoke of his readiness for freedom:

> Cos I know, in me heart, that I'm ready. I'm ready for out there.

Alongside the difficulties of remaining in prison, the unique environment of the open estate was consistently discussed as difficult to deal with. Many experienced feelings of shock and unfamiliarity during the transition from a highly securitised to an open space:

> it's a bit mind blowing you know, when you come from closed conditions and you just open, open all of sudden, you're free... I say free, you're free to walk about.
>
> (Dylan)

This disorientation of the open and rural environment of the prison as a stark contrast to the environment of their lengthy periods in closed conditions contributed to a nervousness and anxiety around the transfer:

> When I came over I got me trolley I went to reception, didn't half feel nervous you know, just like shock as well, if I'm honest you know.
>
> (Frank)

The shock and anxiety of the unfamiliar and open prison space was compounded by confusion around the ambiguous parameters of the prison, resonating with earlier discussions around the problems encountered with porous boundaries:

> Even where you can go and where you can't go, like, urm, the boundaries of the prison, are you allowed there? Do you know what I mean? Things like that.
>
> (Joel)

In the midst of liminal progress and liminal space in the transition to open conditions, participants were also positioned between the state of 'prisoner and free citizen'. This had a profound impact on their identities, with a *liminality of identity* experienced across the transfer and time in open. Discussions revealed an experience of being suspended between the old prison self, and the new free self. Participants noted the impact of progress on how they perceived themselves, enabling a conception of themselves beyond being in prison:

> I know there's a purpose in life ... in my life, for the time being I mean, unfortunately my life is in prison but, my life is out there, and that's what I'm working towards.
>
> (Toby)

Discussions highlighted how those in open felt that they were doing something different this time, with a need to sustain this:

> Well, you know, I know that the next time I go out there it's gotta be for keeps.
>
> (Toby)

> I'm trying me best to just do the right thing for once in me life.
>
> (Frank)

This reiterated the move to open conditions to be a step along the road to freedom, with a need for those completing this journey to maintain their desistance projects. In this process of identity reconstruction and in their narratives of desistance, participants spoke of the centrality of their experience in the TC in providing them with insight into their histories and how they have impacted upon their behaviours:

> In terms of myself, oofh, erm, I got a greater understanding of like where things come from, the way you act and where that comes from. Mmm, and how things early in life can affect you later in life.
>
> (Joel)

Changes were however, conveyed with a continued sense of liminality, with alterations to identities continuing to be a work in progress:

> So of course, the old me can kick in anytime, but it's how I deal with it, do you know what I mean?
>
> (Frank)

Ultimately, participants reflected on how their identity had been altered through the TC process and that this remained intact through the transition to open conditions. However, such alterations were not the creation of an entirely new self, but rather a process through which they could bring out their best identity (Maruna, 2001; Stevens, 2012) This resonated with Maruna's concept of best core self and across participants, reiterating the experience of the TC as enabling the real self to emerge:

> I wouldn't like, change, it's a weird word that, change, I don't think, I mean obviously I've changed because I do things differently now, but I, I'm still, I've always felt that I've just been this person, just, but it's took this long for him to come out, but I've always been me, it's just like… different, you know, it's weird.
>
> (Toby)

It was, however, clear that participants had to readapt their emergent selves for the context of an open prison, reflecting discussions around the difficulties encountered by adjusting to a prison space whilst trying to maintain identity reconstructions:

> Because I'm back in mainstream prison, I'm a different kind of person with a different head on.
>
> (Toby)

This was felt to be particularly difficult given the levels of antisocial attitudes and behaviours prevalent in the mainstream open estate, contrary to the pro-social TC:

> People doing really short terms, just coming in and having a party, smoking weed, thinking 'fuck it I don't care,' and just that atmosphere sort of dragging you in a bit.
>
> (Harry)

Here, participants described the therapeutic tools gained in the TC as central to their projects of renewing themselves, revealing a *liminality of practice* of therapeutic techniques in a non-therapeutic environment. Therapeutic tools were unanimously described as central to the ability to progress to and succeed in open conditions. Participants reflected changes not only in identities but in coping strategies, expressive tendencies, and empathy for others, continuing the theme of the altered self:

> Using coping strategies, therapeutic mechanisms, I have to, on a daily basis, I have to.
>
> (Reece)

> Now, I know, I mean, the greatest gift that you can do is speak to someone. That's the greatest tool, out of it all, really, is, asking, or you know, letting people know that you need help.
>
> (Toby)

> I give people a lot more time now, I, I'm not so, massively judgemental to people, to people as I was before.
>
> (Harry)

Further, the transition was revealed to present an occasion to test whether the tools and identities gained in the TC would remain once leaving its doors. Open conditions were found to give those from a TC an opportunity to implement and solidify their TC tools outside of this unique environment, remarking on the benefit of being able to reflect on their progress:

> Being able to put into practice what you've learned over there, and seeing it in real life, being able to reflect and seeing how I was whilst I'm here now, that's a really positive thing.
>
> (Frank)

Many welcomed the opportunity to put therapeutic learning into practice in the 'real world' and saw this as a route to further progress. They stated the value in having a chance to 'test' how ready they were to put their skills into practice, and whether this was sufficient for survival of open conditions and ultimately, the community:

> If you can't do it here, you're not gonna survive outside, and ye lying to yeself.
>
> (Frank)

This revealed the transition to open conditions to provide a chance not only to be tested in terms of risk and reintegration but in terms of the use of therapeutic tools and behaviours outside of a TC. Discussions revealed how therapeutic tools were used almost subconsciously, suggesting the learning and techniques of the TC to be embedded in the renewed self:

> So, it's just, when I need to use it, it just kicks in, it just automatically just kicks in.
>
> (Toby)

Participants asserted the value of deploying therapeutic tools not only for their self-identity, but also in showing their progress to others:

> It's just more time for me to evidence you know, and every time there's a situation or a live issue, I can then show – here's my skills, this is what I learned, this is how I'm applying it now, do you know what I mean?
>
> (Reece)

This revealed the benefit of having the opportunity to test and demonstrate therapeutic tools in an open prison, with participants using these to overcome difficulties and considering this to be of benefit in validating their progress to others. It also highlights the ongoing preoccupation with being under scrutiny discussed earlier.

Pains of transition

Findings from the research also revealed that the liminality of progress, space, identity and practice encompassed in the transition from TC to open prison inflicted distinct pains, conceptualised as the 'pains of the transition'. These included a *relative deprivation of autonomy, deprivation of security*, and *deprivation of therapeutic relations* in comparison to that experienced in the TC. Each relates to earlier explored pains of freedom experienced in open conditions, and will be discussed in turn.

Whilst those coming from a TC had experienced significant progress in their processes of change across their identities and narratives of desistance, and found benefit from the opportunity to test these in the open environment, they did encounter a *deprivation of autonomy* whereby their ability to continue this progress was frustrated by the processes of the open prison. Participants expressed frustrations around their continued imprisonment and an impatience for their freedom, with periods of stagnation in open conditions particularly challenging:

> Yeah. It's just dealing with that, because, it can be frustrating to take, because I want to take that step, and other people sort of, are less inclined to sort of let me do it because of, erm, you know, risk management.... and, I am aware, that that is necessary, absolutely I get it, and they're right, but, sometimes when you're sitting there and waiting for weeks, it can be frustrating, and I have to catch myself, I do sort of erm, build up a bit of tension over that.
>
> (Harry)

Periods of awaiting ROTL were found to be particularly frustrating, whereby they were unable to make the most of the opportunities for time in the community that are so central to the open prison experience:

> The frustrations of going up to OMU and all that, police checks, being boarded[6], you're not getting boarded, OASys. It's just bollocks, you know, it's so frustrating you know.
>
> (Dylan)

A need for purposeful activity and support during this time as posited as crucial, with Toby speaking of how

> Something needs to be in place for, you know, for times of like, when people say for instance now, that I just feel as if they're stagnating, you know what I mean, sitting on the huts, you know, waiting to be boarded.

Here, the environment of open conditions and increased prevalence of contraband was found to present TC graduates with a *deprivation of security*, confronting them with antisocial behaviours and criminogenic risk factors opposed to the learning and developments acquired through the TCs during a crucial time in their progress, inflicting anxiety and fear upon them:

> Am I going to go onto one of the huts where everyone's smoking weed and everyone's got phones?
>
> (Frank)

> If you come across and get put on one of them huts where they're sat smoking crack on a night time, music blasting on a night time, you're thinking "fuck me, this is a warzone" you know, I mean, they don't refer to it up there as a council estate for nothing.
>
> (Dylan)

Additionally, those from the TC expressed difficulties not only of the less secure space, but of the less therapeutic space, revealing the *deprivation of therapeutic relations* experienced in the transition to open conditions. They spoke of having developed close relationships with peers and staff over their time in therapy, and the difficulties of being in an environment that was less open and community minded. Dylan spoke of the differences between the TC and open, whereby there was much less interrelating amongst residents:

> I don't know, I think… it's, I think it's different here because in (the TC) I'm living with 43 people, and they know a lot about your life, and to a certain extent, you'll know a lot about their life, they'll tell you a bit about themselves, and erm, over here, you don't really get to find anything out about people's lives, because they're too, sort of erm. paranoid, you know, because over here you have totally different clientele.
>
> (Dylan)

This deprivation of the therapeutic relations of the TC posed a challenge whereby individuals had to try and assimilate themselves to a changed and non-therapeutic social milieu in which many other residents of the prison were not accustomed to the same types of relations or pro-social attitudes:

> Well, you know, it's like, they've got like, very pro-criminal attitudes, you know what I mean, it's difficult.
>
> (Reece)

This reiterated how open conditions require those moving from TC to readjust themselves to a changing carceral environment whilst attempting to continue their narratives of change and developments of desistance. The stigma attached to those that have completed a TC was found to intensify tensions amongst the 'mainstream' population, leading to feelings of frustration and isolation:

> They don't understand it over here, they just see people as nonces and grasses from over there, it's got a lot of, really bad name over here.
>
> (Dylan)

This deprivation of *therapeutic relations* was found to require acclimatisation to the non-therapeutic milieu of open conditions, without the unique structures of support inherent in a TC. For those that had been used to the uniquely secure, positive and enabling environment and relationships of the TC, this move was distinctly challenging. Frank spoke of how the 'bubble has been burst now', in describing his experience of moving from a TC, explaining the

TC to provide a 'totally different environment' to that of open conditions. Reece reflected upon how this is particularly challenging for those that had spent a long time in the TC:

> I think the longer that you've spent over there, doing therapy in that environment, I think, people that have relied on that you know, it's, to come here can be a bit of a shock.

Difficulties relating to the deprivation of therapeutic relations persisted across those with staff. Staff in open prisons were discussed as having a different role and approach to those in a TC. Dylan spoke of the different types of relations with staff in open compared to TC conditions:

> It's just different. You get to know the staff over there, over here you don't really get to know them over here, you know, and I don't think they want you to know them, it's just, they're doing their job.

Participants spoke of the difficulties adjusting to the decreased levels of support, reflecting on the benefit of their increased ability to express themselves and seek support in an environment where support was no longer integral to the structure of the prison. Here, open conditions were discussed as requiring individuals to be proactive:

> Cat D's about being proactive yourself, nothing's given to ya, you have to go up and go and get it.

(Toby)

Some found it difficult to adapt to this looser and more remote social support, compared to the all-encompassing TC:

> I was running around and asking people for help, like me personal officer, going up to OMU, and they probably got sick of me but I was that anxious I needed to talk to people.

(Frank)

Here, constructed circles of support were crucial to experiences of this difficult transition. Participants affirmed the value of building positive relations with trusted members of staff, and others that had moved to open conditions from a TC. They spoke about seeking out others that had been through the TC and transferred to open prior in order to gain knowledge and share common ground. Participants were found to construct circles of support that mirrored the structures and community found in TCs, to aid their adaption to and success in the less supportive environment of the open prison:

You have that peer support network there, we have our meetings and stuff which is kind of, it's a little bit of an extension to (the TC).

(Reece)

Discussions reasserted the need for positive prosocial environments and relationships to ensure the continuation and realisation of narratives of desistance post prison.

Implications for practice

The experiences of people transitioning from a TC to an open prison provide a useful insight into the challenges they face, and into what could be done to support transition for this group. It could be argued that those transitioning from a TC are a unique group, whose challenges are similarly unique, but we would argue to the contrary. Whilst there are some issues specific to this group, more generally, they are articulate and reflective men who have learned, through their TC experiences, to make sense of themselves and their surroundings, and to understand their reactions to people, places and change. We therefore argue that these men are ideally placed to inform us about how to better support people in general making the transition to open conditions. Therefore, the practice implications discussed below are drawn from this project and from informal discussion sessions with men in open prison, and are relevant to supporting the transition to open prison in general, as well as for those who have spent time in a TC.

Firstly, it is clear that those transitioning to open conditions would benefit from more support prior to their arrival. People in prison need to be fully informed and aware of the expectations, processes and environment of open conditions prior to their transfer. The results described above highlight the precariousness some men feel in relation to their place in open prison. Similarly, Hampton (2012) found that there was a fear amongst men in open prison of talking to staff about difficulties with others, through fear of being labelled a 'grass' or fear of being associated with trouble and being returned to closed conditions. This reveals the pervasiveness of feelings of precariousness and being under scrutiny. Some of these pains of transition could therefore be eased by better orientation for individuals when they first arrive in open conditions, including clearer expectation of prisoner/staff roles (Hampton, 2012). Many men throughout discussions with the authors highlighted the importance of having realistic expectations about open conditions, the regimes they run and the period of time required before accessing ROTLs. Accordingly, providing information outlining the regimes and processes involved in open conditions to those awaiting transfer would be of benefit in helping them to set appropriate expectations. Further, induction processes could be supplemented with additional information and the use of a mentor to check in with new arrivals to ensure they are settling in. In summary, orientation to procedures and expectations both before arrival in open and in the early days and weeks, could have significant benefits.

Secondly, more emotional support would be of benefit alongside increased practical assistance. It is clear that additional interactions and opportunities to build good relationships with staff would go a long way in helping those moving into open conditions feel supported. Here, opportunities to have contact with staff from the open prison prior to transfer has been found to be of distinct benefit by way of beginning relations and helping ease the transition. Overall, discussions with both authors and with Hampton (2012) reveal that those in prison want, and would benefit from greater levels of emotional support throughout.

Relatedly, providing those in prison with space to reflect on their experiences in open conditions would also help. Despite clear difficulties in open conditions across those in prison, research does suggest that having greater freedom within open establishments provides more space for 'emotion zones' (Danks & Bradley, 2018, p. 13), potentially providing an ideal space for the thoughts, feelings and identity changes surrounding the transition from closed to open to be discussed and processed. Professionals need to make use of such 'emotion zones' to acknowledge of the pains of transition, the liminality of space and self, and validate that experience as normal and understandable. This alone could be significant in supporting transition. As acknowledged by the participants above, there can be an expectation that the move to open prison is entirely positive, and any negative feelings or challenges are evidence of weakness, unsuitability for open and consequently evidence that the person should be moved back to closed prison. People feel a pressure to succeed and sense of being under scrutiny. These experiences need to be named and validated, to allow people to express how challenging they are finding open prison, rather than feeling they have to put on a brave face. If professionals were able to validate and empathise with the pains of transition and the experience of liminality, this could be significant in supporting people to feel understood, to feel able to reach out for support and advice, and to learn to cope and adjust.

In particular, there may be benefits to those transitioning from a TC to open in having contact with staff who have a fuller understanding of what their time in a TC may have entailed. Relatedly, TC graduates spoke of the necessity of being housed with others that had been through therapy in order to have a safe space and opportunity to build a prosocial community away from the more challenging mainstream population. Here, the use of a peer mentor scheme, or informal group may be particularly beneficial amongst those that have been used to more proactive supportive relations.

Thirdly, the results suggest that reminding people of their strengths and abilities may help support the transition. TC graduates described drawing on their learning from the TC experience to support them to cope. People who have not been through the TC experience may still have learned and developed, and skills and coping resources can sometimes be sidelined during the stress of a transition. Professionals should encourage people to remember their skills and strengths, and coach them in applying them in a new and challenging environmcnt. Rclatedly, professionals need to give people as much choice and autonomy as possible in their time in open conditions. This not only improves psychological wellbeing, but also shapes up the skills of choosing and deciding; skills that are essential for successful resettlement in the community.

Finally, professionals should prioritise discussion of and working towards building prosocial, non-prisoner identities amongst men in open prison. The liminality of identity was challenging for the men who took part in the research; in the move towards the community, it is the strengthening of the community identity that is paramount. The point of transition to open prison is an ideal time to facilitate discussion and reflection about this.

Conclusion

This chapter has revealed the transition from a closed to an open prison presents both progress and challenge in an individual's movement through and towards the end of a sentence, and ultimately freedom. The impact of the transition from closed to open conditions, and some of the inherent difficulties involved have been discussed. In particular, the altered pains of imprisonment present in open conditions, and the distinct pains of freedom have been posited as central to the experience of the transfer to open. The impact of these upon the identities of those moving through different prisons and towards release are highlighted, with ramifications upon individual journeys of desistance. Given the discussed difficulties presented by the move to open conditions, particularly but not exclusively for those on indeterminate sentences, and those that arrive from a TC, practitioners on both sides of the transfer are presented with a responsibility to best support those we work with in order to facilitate their success. Through discussions, it was apparent that simple and manageable changes could be made to enhance experiences of the transition to open conditions, with potentially significant benefits by way of better facilitating success. As this 'step along the road' is into a prison that we hope will be the individual's last, we must ensure individuals are adequately prepared for, supported through and successful in this move.

Notes

1 Those who are moved to open prison are seen to have reduced their risk sufficiently so as to be held in less secure conditions. This is generally at the end of a sentence and to help prepare for release. In the case of serving a life sentence, the decision is made by the Parole Board and sanctioned by the Secretary of State. For those serving a determinate sentence, it can be decided by a prison governor.
2 Those serving indeterminate sentences must pass the 'test for release' which requires the Parole Board to be satisfied that confinement is no longer necessary for the protection of the public, before they can be released into the community.
3 Dynamic security involves that which is developed through the relationships between staff and prisoners such that there is mutual respect, thus providing a safe environment.

4 An individual needs to be given Category D security status in order to move to open prison.
5 Pseudonyms have been used throughout this chapter to protect the identities of participants.
6 'Boarded' refers to the process by which an individual's application to access ROTL is subject to a local risk assessment and subsequently authorised by the Governing Governor.

References

Appell, C. (2018). *Preparing men for open conditions*. Unpublished document.
Cohen, S., & Taylor, L. (1981). *Psychological survival: The experience of long-term imprisonment*. Middlesex: Penguin Books Ltd.
Crewe, B. (2009). *The prisoner society: Power, adaptation and social life in an English prison*. Oxford: Oxford University Press.
Crewe, B. (2011). Soft power in prison: Implications for staff–prisoner relationships, liberty and legitimacy. *European Journal of Criminology*, 8(6), 455–468.
Crewe, B., Hulley, S. & Wright, S. (2020). *Life imprisonment from young adulthood: Adaptation, identity and time*. London: Palgrave Macmillan.
Danks, K., & Bradley, A. (2018). Negotiating barriers: Prisoner and staff perspectives on mental wellbeing in the open prison setting. *Journal of Criminal Psychology*, 8(1), 3–19.
Grayling, C. (2014). Prisoners: Temporary release. (House of Lords). Retrieved from https://publications.parliament.uk/pa/ld201314/ldhansrd/text/140310-wms0001.htm.
Hampton, E. (2012). *Coping with imprisonment: Exploring bullying, safety and social support within prison settings* (Doctoral dissertation). University of Birmingham, Birmingham, UK.
Jarvis, D., Shaw, J., & Lovell, T. (2022). Service user experiences of a psychologically enhanced resettlement service [PERS] in an English open prison. *The Journal of Forensic Practice*, 24(3), 241–252.
Lammas, V. L. (2015). A prison without walls: Alternative incarceration in the late age of social democracy. *Prison Service Journal*, 217, 3–9.
Liebling, A. (2012), "Can human beings flourish in prison?" PPT Lecture, London, retrieved from: https://www.artsevidence.org.uk/media/uploads/evaluation-downloads/can-human-beings-flourish-in-prison—alison-liebling—may-2012.pdf.
Liebling, A., & Arnold, H. (2004). *Prisons and their moral performance: A study of values, quality, and prison life*. Oxford: Clarendon Press.
Liem, M., & Kunst, M. (2013). Is there a recognizable post-incarceration syndrome among released "lifers"? *International Journal of Law and Psychiatry*, 36(3–4),333–338.
Marder, I., Lapouge, M., Garrihy, J., & Brandon, A. (2021). Empirical research on the impact and experience of open prisons: state of the field and future directions. *Prison Service Journal*, 233(4), 3–9.
Maruna S. (2001). *Making good: how ex-convicts reform and rebuild their lives* (1ˢᵗ Ed.). Washington D.C.: American Psychological Association.
Maruna, S., & Roy, K. (2007). Amputation or reconstruction? Notes on the concept of 'knifing off' and desistance from crime. *Journal of Contemporary Criminal Justice*, 23(1), 104–124.
Micklethwaite, D., & Earle, R. (2021) A voice within: An autoethnographic account of moving form closed to open prison conditions by a life-sentenced prisoner. *The Howard Journal of Crime and Justice*, 60(4), 529–545.

Ministry of Justice (2011). Prison Service Instruction 40/2011: categorisation and reca-tegorisation of adult male prisoners. Retrieved from https://www.gov.uk/governm ent/publications/security-categorisation-policy-framework.

Ministry of Justice (2020). Security categorisation policy framework. Retrieved from https://assets.publishing.service.gov.uk/government/uploads/system/uploads/attachm ent_data/file/1011502/security-categorisation-pf.pdf.

Mjåland, K., Laursen, J., Schliehe, A., & Larmour, S. (2021). Contrasts in freedom: Comparing the experiences of imprisonment in open and closed prisons in England and Wales and Norway. *European Journal of Criminology* 1–22.

Neumann, C. E. B. (2012). Imprisoning the soul. In J. Dullum & T. Ugelvik (Eds.), *Nordic prison practice and policy-exceptional or not? Exploring penal exceptionalism in the Nordic context* (pp. 139–155). Abingdon, Oxon: Routledge.

Pakes, F. (2020). Old fashioned Nordic penal exceptionalism: the case of Iceland's open prisons. *Nordic Journal of Criminology*, 21(2), 113–128.

Pennington, S. (2015). *The experience in open prison conditions and absconds by prisoners sentenced indeterminately to Imprisonment for Public Protection (IPP) (Master's thesis) Home-rton College*, University of Cambridge, Cambridge, UK. Retrieved from: www.crim. cam.ac.uk/alumni/penology/theses/Sara%20Pennington.pdf.

Pennington, S., & Crewe, B. (2015). Open prisons: A governor's perspective. *Prison Service Journal*, 217, 12–14.

Perrin, & Blagden, N. (2016). Movements towards desistance via peer-support roles in prison. In L.S. Abrams, E. Hughes & R. Meek (Eds.). *The voluntary sector in prisons: Encouraging personal and institutional change.* New York: Palgrave Studies in prisons and penology. London: Palgrave Macmillan.

Potter, C., & Gunderson, C. (2015). Open prisons: A policy-maker's perspective. *Prison Service Journal*, 217, 10–12.

Prison Reform Trust (2015). Inside Out: release on temporary licence and its role in promoting effective resettlement and rehabilitation. Prison Reform Trust.

Shammas, V.L. (2014). The pains of freedom: Assessing the ambiguity of Scandinavian penal exceptionalism on Norway's Prison Island. *Punishment and Society*, 16, 104–112.

Smith, M. (2022). *Exploring prison transitions: From democratic therapeutic community to open resettlement regime* (Master's thesis). Pembroke College, University of Oxford, Oxford, UK.

Statham, B.M., Winder, B., & Micklethwaite, D. (2021). Success within a UK open prison and surviving the 'pains of freedom'. *Psychology, Crime and Law*, 8, 729–750.

Stevens, A. (2012) "I am the person now I was always meant to be": Identity recon-struction and narrative reframing in therapeutic community prisons. *Criminology and Criminal Justice*, 12(5), 527–547.

Sykes, G (1958). *The society of captives: A study of a maximum-security prison.* Princeton, NJ: Princeton University Press.

United Nations Office on Drugs and Crime. (2015). *Handbook on dynamic security and prison intelligence.* Retrieved from: https://www.unodc.org/documents/justice-and-prison-re form/UNODC_Handbook_on_ Dynamic_Security_and_Prison_Intelligence.pdf.

Warr, J. (2020) "Always gotta be two mans": Lifers, risk, rehabilitation, and narrative labour. *Punishment and Society*, 22(1), 28–47.

2 "I can see freedom but I can't have it"

Supporting people in the immediate aftermath of release

Jo Shingler and Jennifer Stickney

The prospect of release from prison is understandably accompanied by excitement, euphoria and anticipation: the desire to get through the gates, breathe the air of freedom and start living life again; the anticipation of being able to do what you want when you want, eat what you want, go to bed and get up when you want; the hope that "this time will be different" (Visher & Travis, 2003). Sadly, these hopes and expectations are often not realised as people struggle to adjust to life in the community. The experience of imprisonment in itself is likely to undermine community re-entry (Ashforth, Kreiner, & Fugate, 2000; Hulley, Crewe, & Wright, 2016; Visher & Travis, 2003), notwithstanding the actual challenges of release. In particular, experiences in the initial period of release are significant in determining success (Gwynne, Yesberg, & Polaschek, 2020; Visher & Travis, 2003), but little is known about interventions that support successful community re-entry (Göbbels, Willis, & Ward, 2014; Gwynne et al., 2020).

In this chapter, we will identify and elucidate some of the issues people face in the early days of release, drawing on our experiences as community practitioners and the experiences of the men we work with. We do not think that this is an exhaustive list, but the themes and issues that we have included are those that in our shared experiences have most challenged people's ability to cope. They are also issues that have been found in the broader literature to be particularly problematic. We will then discuss how best to support people to navigate these challenges, again drawing on professional and personal experiences, as well as the extant literature.

The experience of release: Anticipation vs reality

The mismatch between the anticipation and reality is reflected in Jake's experience of release to an Approved Premises after serving 13 years in prison. Jake expected release to be accompanied by enjoyment and a sense of freedom with fewer restrictions. His reality was immediately being pressured by expectations: after being welcomed he was given five letters, each for a different appointment in the following 24 hours. He felt overwhelmed and infantilised, with too much to do in too little time. He felt he could not be trusted to

DOI: 10.4324/9781003308171-3

manage even 24 hours without professional contact. He felt fearful of letting people down and failing. He experienced disabling feelings of pressure and fear and an absence of anticipated joy. Sadly, Jake's experience is not uncommon, and is reflected in studies of prison-community transition. Phillips and Lindsay (2011) described how optimism and hope at the prospect of release was quickly followed by practical barriers and urges to use substances. This in turn was followed by a sense of being overwhelmed, giving up and returning to old avoidance coping strategies. Maruna (2001) described how persistent offenders felt unable to face life in the community, believing they belonged in prison.

There is good evidence that the first few days and months following release from prison are the most vulnerable for those who have served long sentences (Pratt, Piper, Appleby, Webb, & Shaw, 2006; Robinson, Tucker, Hargreaves, Roberts, Shaw, & Challis, 2022). People on post-release supervision are at increased risk of all-cause mortality (Farrell & Marsden, 2008); people in the first month of release are at high risk of suicide (Pratt et al., 2006). Canton (2022) described release as an "acute existential shock" (p. 1) for people having served long prison sentences.

Coping resources can be undermined by things people either did not anticipate, or expected to navigate easily. Martin reported being overwhelmed when his family member stopped off in a supermarket on the drive from prison to the hostel. The number of people, the unpredictability and unfamiliarity of the situation combined with his own sense of "being different" all overcame him in the moment and he had to wait outside the store. Martin also reported being unprepared when in his first week he had the usual dream about prison life that he had regularly whilst incarcerated. He awoke, terrified, in his bed in the hostel, having no idea where he was or how he had got there. This was a shock to him, and the experience of a familiar dream in an unfamiliar setting disoriented him. These experiences had lasting effects on Martin's emotional resilience and confidence in his ability to adjust to community life.

Relatedly, people are often unprepared for social and technological changes that have been absorbed into our daily lives over the decades they have been incarcerated. A man described humiliation at not knowing how to use contactless payment, and having to loiter in a shop to watch others before he felt confident to pay. Being unfamiliar with elements of modern life that we take for granted can make people feel that they do not fit in in the community, that they somehow stand out as odd or incompetent, and this will give them away as someone who has just come out of prison.

People also commonly experience structural challenges that can undermine resettlement efforts (Visher & Travis, 2003; Petersilia, 2003; Maruna, 2001). Many people are released with no other money than the prison discharge grant.[1] Therefore, there is an urgency to organise access to benefits in the first few days of release. This urgency is exacerbated by the fact that many people do not have any identification, and may not have a bank account. These things can rarely be arranged for people prior to release. The wait to access funds via the benefits system can be up to a month, leaving people with very little money if the person has no family or friends to support them or no access to private savings. Lack of money negatively affects the ability to feel part of the community. It also means people are unable to meet their immediate needs, further reinforcing their sense of being someone who is dependent and incapable and increasing the risk of obtaining money by illegitimate means. Lack of money is evidently a significant obstacle to desistance (see Burnett, 2004). To add to this pressure, prison is deskilling: for many people, the skills needed to meet basic needs are at best rusty, at worst non-existent (Liem & Kunst, 2013 and see Chapter 7). Rob's reflection a few days following release sums up his struggles to cope:

> I have had such a hectic day; I just want to lock myself away for a very long time… I am thinking how easy it is being in prison, sometimes I just want to head back there.

Finally, the Approved Premises (AP) itself can be a factor in hopeful expectations being disappointed. An AP is a multi-occupancy hostel, run by the Probation Service. Many men who have served long custodial sentences (mainly those who are considered a high risk of harm within the community) are required to live in an AP for at least three months. APs are designed to provide a transition between prison and the community. They are staffed twenty-four hours a day; people are provided with a furnished room, often food is provided, and the "service charge" residents are required to pay is well below market prices for rent. The benefits of an AP in supporting the transition from institutional to independent life and in risk management can be significant (Petersilia, 2003). However, many people experience APs as an extension of their custodial period, or as more confining than custody (Padfield, 2013). They describe not really being free, but feeling controlled by AP rules and by the requirements of their licence conditions (see below for further discussion of the licence). AP life has different rhythms and interactions to other community-based accommodation. Residents' accounts suggest that deprivations experienced when incarcerated can continue on release, through limited access to services, goods and social relationships (Sykes, 1958). APs can feel unsafe. They commonly house young men, which can affect the resettlement of older people. Men who have served time for sexual offences (see Chapter 8) can feel especially vulnerable in APs, where other residents have access to the internet and could easily identify them. There is less control over substance misuse and behaviour in general in an AP than in custody. Men who are recovering from addiction can feel vulnerable, if surrounded by others who are actively using and dealing drugs. For example:

> I came out of prison determined I could get my life back on track, sort my drug problems out and use the help around me to stay out. I didn't have the nicest start to arriving at the AP, I felt a black cloud over me as I arrived – as though people remembered me from last time I was there and

didn't expect for me to be different. It was a horrible feeling, I felt so stressed and overwhelmed. As I was moving into my room at the AP someone offered me Valium. I took it without thinking. Something to help calm me down. It was my choice, I took them. I am not blaming anyone for this, but it was the start of my journey back into serious drug use. Within just a few hours of release I was using again. The AP was not the right environment for me to go to on release, surrounded by people that use in an area where there are drug dealers on every corner. I was never going to make it at this AP, too many things against me.

(Neil)

Here, Neil expresses his intention to remain drug free, but the emotional stress of release combined with the environmental challenges in the AP undermined his intentions.

In summary, the expectation and anticipation of freedom is often an illusion. The reality of the early days of release is often overloaded with stress, worry and a sense of impending doom (an existential crisis, as noted above by Canton, 2022; see also Harris, Edgar & Webster, 2020). People struggle to adjust emotionally and physically to a new environment after years in prison, with a sense of being overwhelmed commonly reported (Liem & Kunst, 2013; Richards & Jones, 2004). The absence of joy, the feeling that incarceration is prolonged in an AP, the physical and structural barriers that people face on release and a sense of inadequacy and emotional overload can all combine to mean that the great promise and hope of freedom does not materialise.

Scrutiny and the illusion of freedom

A "liminal state" of being neither one thing nor another (e.g., Woods, 2019), or having "semi-freedom" (Fitzalan Howard, 2019, p. 191) seems to be characteristic of people's experiences in the early days and weeks of release. The feeling of both being free and constrained can start at the very moment of release: the necessity to make the transport to the station on time, to catch the train or bus on time, to arrive at the approved accommodation on time. This process can feel pressured and conflictual: having to prove you can cope; a sense of being technically free but with the knowledge that your time and decisions are not your own, and failure to comply (even by accident) having the potential to send you straight back to prison; being free but feeling under scrutiny (see Rennie & Crewe, 2023). One man, on the walk from the prison gates to the bus stop, described a feeling of rising fear, that people around him would notice him and judge him for having been in prison. He felt watched from the moment he was no longer physically confined. There is evidence that a feeling of being watched is related to impaired reflective skills (Muth, Schwarz, Kunde, & Pfister, 2017). Impaired reflective abilities are likely to be prevalent amongst people in the immediate aftermath of release: the presence of post-release anxiety (Western, Braga, Davis, & Sirois, 2015); experience of trauma (Willmot, 2022); and the potential of generally impaired cognitive skills (Andrews & Bonta, 2010) will all limit reflection and result in increased vulnerability to an unsettling sense of invisible scrutiny.

In addition to perceptions of scrutiny, there is also the reality of scrutiny by criminal justice agencies, in the form of supervision by the probation service.[2] Those serving standard and extended determinate sentences have fixed periods of community probation supervision. People serving indeterminate sentences (life sentences; indeterminate sentences for public protection: IPP) are subject to an indefinite period on licence during which they are at risk of recall to prison (see Chapter 3). The purpose of licence conditions is to protect the public, prevent re-offending, and to support successful community reintegration. Licence conditions must be "proportionate, reasonable and necessary" (Parole Board, 2018) to enable risk management and enable supervising probation officers to build up confidence in someone's compliance and ability to live an offence-free life. Some people experience licence conditions as reassuring and containing external controls (Edgar, Harris, & Webster, 2020; Rennie & Crewe 2023). Sometimes licence conditions enable victims to feel safe in their own homes and whilst going about their daily lives. Our purpose here is not to explore the costs and benefits of probation supervision on licence, but to reflect on the impact licence conditions can have on people trying to rebuild their lives in the community. From that perspective, licence conditions can be experienced as punitive and restrictive. They can extend the sense of incarceration and not being in control of one's own life (Harris et al., 2020; Shingler, Sonnenberg, & Needs, 2020). They can make people feel excluded from community life in that they are marked as different from "normal citizens" by virtue of the restrictions upon them (Uggen, Manza, & Behrens, 2004). Licence conditions can create a state of constant anxiety and inhibit communication with professionals for fear of disclosures leading to recall (Harris et al., 2020). They can create a sense of being "set up to fail" (Padfield, 2013). Living under a licence is often experienced as just more prison, but with the glimpse of an inaccessible freedom. As Martin put it, "I can see it [freedom], but I can't have it".

Edgar et al. (2020) identified practical problems resulting from licence conditions, including making it hard for people to find work and maintain family ties (see also Rennie & Crewe, 2023). For example, Martin found that requirements to sign in at the AP at specific times meant that he was unable to visit his family. Aaron was offered employment but unable to accept it as his sign-in and curfew times clashed with the working requirements of the job.

Licence conditions can, at times, increase risk (Edgar et al., 2020). For example, Colin was required to disclose new and developing intimate relationships to his probation officer, which he did as required. Colin's relationship broke down following disclosure, and the disclosed information about Colin's offending was widely shared by the ex-partner. This increased his vulnerability to harm in the community as well as increasing his risk to others. Relatedly, Freddy was unable to adhere to a licence requirement to attend group drug-rehabilitation meetings. Discussion and exploration of the reasons for this revealed that the group setting triggered significant social anxiety that prevented him from gaining any therapeutic benefit from the group. It also led to increased likelihood of drug misuse to cope with the anxiety: drug misuse was directly linked to his violent crime. A flexible and supportive probation officer removed the mandatory condition to attend groups, leading to (1) stabilisation on a heroin replacement, (2) increased engagement with psychological therapy to manage anxiety, and (3) ongoing "clean" drug tests.

The mere presence of the licence and the knowledge that they are vulnerable to immediate recall can have a significant effect on people and their ability to reintegrate successfully into society (Harris et al., 2020; Padfield, 2013; Rennie & Crewe, 2023). Western (2018) described people living under licence as being in an "environment of surveillance [which] is primed for the possibility of violation" (p. 130). There is consistent evidence that people in prison, including those who have been recalled, feel they lack control over their lives and destinies (Shingler et al., 2020; Fitzalan Howard, 2019). There is similar evidence that people on licence feel more vulnerable and less able to build or rediscover a sense of self (Nugent & Schinkel, 2016; Rennie & Crewe, 2023). Having a strong prosocial identity is central to successful desistance (Maruna, 2001; Nugent & Schinkel, 2016) and it seems that the presence of a licence (broader risk management benefits of a licence notwithstanding) could actively interfere with this. A discussion with Mark about the process of applying for his IPP licence to be removed went like this:

JSH: What difference would it make to you if your licence was removed?
MARK: None, it wouldn't make any difference
JSH: What do you mean?
MARK: I would still do the same things, I would carry on doing the right things what I'm already doing. But I'd be doing them because they are the right things to do and it's my choice to do them. Not because of the licence.

This exchange illustrates Mark's feeling that his licence is impeding his sense of self as a person who does the right things because they are morally right. The presence of the licence means he feels people think this is his sole reason for compliance. The crucial issue of identity and how this affects the resettlement is discussed in more detail below.

Identity: Who am I and what is my place?

The experience of prison can be deeply transformational (Hulley et al., 2016), and the incarceration experience is fundamental in understanding the experience of release (Visher & Travis, 2003). Prison can be experienced as harshly impersonal (Visher & Travis, 2003), or violent and intimidating (Butler, 2008; Shingler et al., 2020). Constant exposure to violence can leave people with lasting symptoms closely mirroring those of Post-Traumatic Stress Disorder

(PTSD), including intrusive, distressing and recurrent dreams about prison (see Martin's example, above); hyperarousal and hypersensitivity to threat; feeling unsafe; struggling to trust and connect with others; emotional numbing, detachment and coldness (Hulley et al., 2016; Liem & Kunst, 2013). Even if PTSD type symptoms do not overtly manifest themselves, prison is an environment in which you always have to watch your back and where you can never relax or show vulnerability (Butler, 2008; Jarvis, Shaw, & Lovell, 2022; Shingler et al., 2020). It is inevitable that people develop an image or identity to survive in this environment. This identity can interfere with successful transition into the community (Jarvis et al., 2022; Hulley et al., 2016; Schinkel, 2014), as illustrated by Nick:

> In prison you have to survive, and on long sentences endure, get through it. And no matter how real you are, you put up defences, carry yourself in a certain way. But that prison face or identity is not needed in the real world and years later, you, if you're anything like me, will feel a little lost, even lonely.

Harry coped with a sense of vulnerability in prison by putting on weight, building up muscle in the gym, shaving his head, growing facial hair and isolating himself. He created an intimidating physical image which encouraged others to leave him alone. When he was released, he found the image that had kept him safe in prison was an obstacle to successful reintegration. He felt isolated, lonely and unaccepted in an unfamiliar world, and unsure of how to make a life for himself.

Relatedly, prison is an institution, where the daily routine of life is controlled by the authorities and the requirement for autonomy is limited (Liem & Kunst, 2013). In prison, compliance is rewarded; independence and challenging institutional practices is not. Callum described how he decided to cope with prison by controlling what he could control, namely remaining alone in his cell, reading and listening to music. In these circumstances, the skills needed to manage daily life slowly erode; one's identity as a person who makes decisions and structures their own life diminishes.

It has also been found that many people cope with long-term imprisonment by deliberately focusing only on their prison world and shutting out community links: prisoners in Schinkel's (2014) study described "keeping your head inside the walls" (p. 73) as a way of coping with the losses incurred by imprisonment. Similarly, Codd (2008) reported that people chose to avoid contact with family during their sentence: some found visits too distressing; others believed that cutting contact would protect loved ones from the prison experience and the shame of being connected to someone in prison. Martin made a conscious decision not to have family visits when he realised that a recall was going to stretch into years rather than months. Callum cut contact with friends to protect himself from the fear of being rejected and to protect his friends from the burden of having to support him in prison. Schinkel (2014) also described the lack of control over communication with the outside. She reported the emotional pain caused by unanswered phone calls, for example, and concluded "it is not within their control to maintain contact, only to cut it off" (p. 73). Michael described reaching emotional crossroads in prison and reaching out to family members, only to be rejected and criticised in a way that triggered traumatic childhood memories. He had no avenue to repair this relationship when the recipient declined any further contact with him.

Whilst understandable, the decision to shut out the outside world has consequences for release. Firstly, it can reduce the chances of success in the community. People coming out of prison with family support find developing prosocial identities easier; they resettle more quickly and more successfully than those with no or little social support (HMIP, 2016; Codd, 2008; Visher & Travis, 2003). Having family support contributes to the sense that you are accepted by the community as a non-offender; it gives people a sense of meaning and value (Hlavka et al., 2015). Nick's observations support this:

> If you have family, people who love you, they can help you with a feeling of belonging, giving you back a sense of where you fit in, who you are.

The reality for many is that they are released with only statutory support in place.

Secondly, the taking on of the "prisoner" role and the shutting out of other roles men may have taken in their pre-prison lives (e.g., "father", "partner", "employee") makes return to those normative and prosocial roles more challenging (Ashforth et al., 2000; Visher & Travis, 2003), given the different demands and expectations of these roles. Role transition requires preparation (Ashforth et al., 2000) and prison generally does not provide this. The skills needed for successful navigation of community life (confidence, initiative, asking for help and advice) are the antithesis of what is needed for successful prison life (compliance, humility and "keeping your head down", see above). We discussed above how some of the biggest challenges experienced soon after release were totally unexpected: this may be partly explained by poor preparation for role transition. John described prison as a bubble that protected him from realising the impact of his offence on the community. Release had a significant and detrimental effect on his mental health as he described seeing people everywhere that triggered intense shame at what he had done and left him questioning whether he should be punished further. As Schinkel (2014) notes, "Limiting their horizons in prison meant that they now had a difficult time coping with the complexities and demands of life outside" (p. 80).

To summarise, "the very coping mechanisms that aim to alleviate some of the pains and problems of imprisonment might, as a secondary effect, be deeply transformational and in some sense debilitating" (Hulley et al., 2016, p. 787). That is, coping strategies and identity development that enable survival or even success in prison are maladaptive for community life. Therefore, people who have served long sentences find they are coming out of prison as very different people, but also into a very different community to the one they left behind.

These things can leave people feeling lost and overwhelmed almost immediately. Life in the community feels unfamiliar and uncertain compared with prison (Rennie & Crewe, 2023). Nick's reflections sum this up:

> [People think] I must have loved it so much in prison I wanted to come back. Ridiculous, right? Well swap the word "love" for "missed" and you'd be getting warmer... How can you not feel loss for something that's been your whole life pretty much for years, decades? If you were punched in the face every day at lunch for 15–20 years then one day not, you'd miss it, it would seem strange, you'd be a little lost without it. Not because it was nice but because that's what happened day in, day out for years. You might even find yourself looking for someone to punch you to feel "normal".

People can struggle to find a place in the community after many years in prison. Nick had served over 20 years of pretty much continuous incarceration, and only knew himself in the community as a young person who offended and used drugs. On release, he did not know how to be, or where his place was, given the changes in both him, and in the world. He reflects:

> As a result of being lonely, or alone, I gravitated to the wrong people. For me at the time, they were like a pair of old slippers, comfortable in that I understood their humour, they mine. That I was rough around the edges in language or demeanour was normal to them. And as much as I didn't feel a stranger, I knew I didn't want this. I don't judge them, how can I? But I'm not that person. I don't want to be a part of that life or world.

It is easy to see how, despite not wanting that life, the loneliness and isolation overwhelmed Nick's good intentions to desist. Nugent and Schinkel (2016) note that the decision not to offend cannot always survive the absence of a non-offending identity or the absence of people with faith in your ability to desist. Therefore, answering the fundamental question of identity, "who am I and where is my place?" is essential to successful community reintegration.

Supporting people in the immediate aftermath of release

In this section, we will discuss the specific clinical and structural strategies we rely on for maximising the chances of successful transition from prison to the community. As above, we do not claim that this selection is exhaustive, more that it has professional and experiential meaning and resonance and support in the broader literature.

Planning and preparation

Careful planning of the release process has been demonstrated to facilitate successful community re-entry (Hopkin, Evans-Lacko, Forrester, Shaw &

Thornicroft 2018; Scoones, Willis & Grace, 2012; Willis & Grace, 2008). Yet Edgar et al. (2020) found that many people felt unprepared for release and this lack of preparation contributed to their recall. Participants identified problems like not having had home leave, not having a job or anywhere to live or being released to a new area where they knew no-one. Therefore, the process of planning for release needs to start well in advance of people leaving prison. Reaching into prisons enables people to begin to build relationships with professionals and build up a level of trust. This is essential if people are to reach out for help when they are struggling (Harris et al., 2020). It provides opportunities for positive therapeutic relationships to develop; it allows professionals to better understand a person's needs and consequently plan how these needs can be met (Hancock, Smith-Merry & Mckenzie, 2018). Having individualised plans that are personally meaningful encourages engagement, thereby strengthening commitment to change (Göbbels et al., 2014).

Reaching into prisons enables professionals to structure expectations and discuss plans when people are in an environment they know and understand. People may hate being in prison but many are adept at coping. This can mean that they are more able to think, plan and reflect, and they may be more open to discussions about the sorts of challenges they may face in the community. Identifying potential problem areas and making provisional plans for managing and averting difficulties can be easier when people are not tackling the daily challenges they face in the community. There is evidence that pre-release planning needs to be accompanied by appropriate support in the community (Hopkin et al., 2018) and continuity of care by community services is central to success in the first few days and weeks of release. AP staff can support orientation to the community by making contact with people before release, providing information about the layout of the AP, the rules and regulations, the local amenities and services, and building relationships. Many APs provide information packs prior to release. Our service also provides "welcome packs", which include basic toiletries, tea and coffee, a notebook or diary, a stress ball, a mug printed with a quote chosen by the individual, and a personally relevant item (e.g., a sketch pad). This ensures some basic needs are met, as well as providing a practical message of care and support.

For some people, spending time in an open prison can support the process of adjusting to community life (Edgar et al., 2020; Jarvis et al., 2022; and see Chapter 1). A period of time in open conditions can allow for gradual exposure to the emotional and sensory demands of the community but without the pressure of having to survive. From open prison, people can apply for "Release on Temporary Licence" (ROTL). ROTL can be either a single day, usually to a local town, or overnight, usually to the area in which the person plans to resettle. ROTLs help prepare people for resettlement by enabling them to experience a range of normal daily community stresses whilst returning to the safety net of prison to support learning and reflection. People can focus on just being in the community rather than necessarily having to do anything (see "slowing things down"). It can also provide people with an opportunity to try out basic practical skills in which they may lack confidence, or which they may not have developed if they have been in prison for many years (see Chapter 7).

For people who are released directly from closed conditions and do not have access to ROTLs, this process can be more challenging. In these circumstances, reaching into prisons is even more important. Regular pre-release meetings, in person, via phone or videolink, can help people prepare for the reality of release. Preparing people to be caught off guard, and *normalising* this experience can help people cope more effectively when it happens: supporting people to understand that it is very common to feel overwhelmed and it does not mean that they are failing. Open discussion about how they have changed and about how the world has changed is also important, alongside *validating* their sense of not knowing how to navigate this new world as a different person. The essence of validation is to communicate that one's responses "make sense and are understandable within [the person's] current life context or situation" (Linehan, 1993, p. 222). We commonly hear, "I'm [40] years old; I should be able to cope with this". This communicates a sense of being a failure, of being inadequate, and of being inferior to fellow community members. A validating response would be to say "You have been in prison for 20 years, and everything has been done for you. How can you possibly know how to do it?" As Tom put it recently, "When everyone else was learning this stuff, I was drunk or in prison". He was successfully validating himself in this, recognising his lack of skill as being a result of his previous life choices, circumstances and dysfunctional coping strategies resulting from years of trauma. Self-validation is enormously helpful, and we can support and reinforce it. If people continue to have unrealistic expectations of their ability to navigate the world, then we can gently and supportively validate their lack of skill, or their emotional reaction as being entirely normal and understandable in their own context. The next step is to support people to learn the skills they need to navigate the world and Chapter 7 focuses on precisely this issue.

When there are several different agencies involved in a person's release it is essential that all agencies communicate with each other and with the person to devise a collaborative and supportive release plan. Whilst collaborative working takes place through processes such as Multi Agency Public Protection Arrangements (MAPPA), these meetings generally exclude the person at the heart of the discussion (Padfield, 2013; Taylor & Yakeley, 2019). This leaves the person reliant on feedback from professionals to understand their risk management plan. Release plans should ideally be co-created between professionals and individuals in order to frame expectations and begin to build self-efficacy. A good plan should identify risk management priorities and how these will be translated into meetings with professionals. This allows the individual to know what meetings they need to attend, the name and/or role of each professional, and the provisional aims of the meeting. This can support the mental preparation for release, the practical planning for the first few days and reduces the likelihood of feeling overwhelmed.

Slowing things down and creating psychological space

> Take it slow. That's my advice. Find your feet. Learn the rhythms of the new
> world outside. It seems fast, and that's the trap, it seems it.
>
> (Nick)

Throughout the first part of this chapter we have discussed the common experience of being emotionally overwhelmed on release, as well as the strong pressure people feel to succeed, and show they are succeeding. A sense of "spinning" (Richards & Jones, 2004, p. 13) or being on a treadmill that is moving too quickly (Jarvis et al., 2022) has been described by people at different stages of resettlement. Slowing things down is central to supporting the resettlement process, giving people time to think, process information, plan and be realistic about what can and cannot be achieved. The urge to rush ahead and achieve milestones such as employment, independent accommodation and an intimate relationship is understandable given how many years have been wasted to imprisonment (see Uggen et al., 2004). Slowing things down is about supporting reflection and effective problem solving, and enabling people to adjust emotionally and physically to the community. It is also about allowing emotions to be experienced and processed rather than suppressed in a rush of activity. Phillips and Lindsay (2011) noted that whilst people could identify effective coping approaches pre-release, the emotional burden of release overwhelmed their coping resources and pulled them back into old (largely avoidance, largely substance misuse) patterns. Supporting people in understanding how to apply effective coping strategies, communicate effectively and navigate complex community systems to slowly support the first few days in the community can make a significant difference. Martin specifically identified his tendency to rush through tasks, as if to make up for lost time, as a contributory factor in a previous recall. Discussion of and reflection on this tendency (and a validation of the understandable desire to make up for lost time) enabled us to notice and challenge when he started to rush, thus building his insight and ability to self-manage this process.

As noted above, planning and preparation is key to supporting a more measured approach to the first few days and weeks in the community. This means noticing changes in presentation as people approach their release date. In many cases, people become increasingly focused on what release will look and feel like. Many have not experienced the outside world for several years and feelings of anxiety, panic and excitement can be tangible. Our role is to support people in identifying, naming and understanding these feelings. Reflecting on changes in people's talk enables understanding of their emotional state. From this we can provide validation and support, as well as collaborative intervention to contain these thoughts and feelings. Listening to concerns enables plans to be put in place to address practical problems alongside providing space in which people can express and process their emotions. Callum spoke about his traumatic and distressing experiences in prison, including witnessing violence, feeling out of control and feeling unimportant and forgotten. Discussion of his urge to "get on with living" identified a process of racing thoughts and pressure to know what "living" meant and how he could achieve this. Validating his trauma and acknowledging the need to take time to recover allowed him to recognise and validate his experience for himself. He was then able to discuss how resettlement plans might need to prioritise taking the first few weeks slowly, to help him process and manage the experience of prison, and to enable him to "just be" out in the community, without the pressure to achieve multiple goals.

Whilst planning and preparation is crucial to effective resettlement, at times plans need to be guided and supported. It is common to find plans are idealistic (Uggen et al., 2004). People want to achieve every important milestone within the first few weeks of release which adds significant pressure to an already pressured and emotionally charged situation. Guided support to develop clear and realistic goals, prioritise these and set parameters to release expectations can enable people to slow thinking down and reduce impulsivity. Release can be overwhelming, and the emotional reaction can result in plans being forgotten or abandoned. It is therefore important within the first few days following release that plans are reviewed, revised (if necessary) and confirmed.

Crucial to the process of slowing things down and creating psychological space is building the working relationship (see Chapter 9). Clinicians' roles need to be clear, so individuals know who does what and when, yet flexible to support the changing needs of each person. Individually meaningful and relevant plans are essential (Göbbels et al., 2014). People need a supportive, stable space where they feel safe to identify when they are struggling and ask for help, and to feel heard, without fear of recall (Jarvis et al., 2022; Harris et al., 2020). When people are experiencing significant emotional turmoil in the early days of release, a trusted professional can be the "stronger, wiser other" (Sainsbury, 2011, p. 103) that models and supports emotion regulation and enables emotional containment. As mentioned previously, reaching into prison provides a vital connection to the community, and opportunities to build and develop relationships in preparation for release. The combination of existing and established trusting professional relationships, clearly defined and understood professional roles within appropriate boundaries, individualised plans with an element of flexibility can feel containing (Shingler et al., 2018). Psychological and emotional containment is particularly important in the first few days following release when life can feel chaotic and impossible to manage.

Finally, the maintenance and communication of hope for people when things get tough is central (Nugent & Schinkel, 2016). A sense of hopelessness pervades incarceration experiences (Jarvis et al., 2022; Shingler et al., 2020) and holding on to hope for people can be the key to success (Maruna, 2001). Finding meaningful activity, supportive relationships and suitable accommodation within the confines a person's licence can make resettlement a constant struggle. If we can be a voice that maintains hope and belief in the person's desire for identity desistance, we increase their chances of success. This issue is discussed in more depth in Chapter 10 of this volume.

Building identity desistance

Building or rediscovering a coherent, prosocial identity is central to successful life in the community (Maruna, 2001); as Nick says, "… it boils back down to who do you want to be out there?" Nugent and Schinkel (2016) describe three levels of desistance that are needed for successful life in the community. "Act desistance" is the process of not committing further offences. "Identity desistance" is the internalisation of the new identity as a person who does not offend. "Relational desistance" is the recognition of change and the acceptance of the new identity by others – those close to the person (family and friends), those in the wider community who have contact with the person (employers, professionals in relevant agencies) and society as a whole.

An important role for community workers is to support people who have achieved (or are currently enacting) "act-desistance" to move on to build "identity" and "relational" desistance. We are explicit from the outset that we see our role as supporting people in identity rediscovery or development. We bring issues of identity to the fore and encourage discussion and reflection on identity. We support people to explore elements of their identity, and which parts have the most meaning and value for them. For example John described how he chose to spend a day on ROTL when a prison mix-up meant that he was unable to meet a family member as planned. He had very little money, so impulsively went into an art gallery that offered free entry. He described being immensely moved by this experience. He compared the emotional connection and peace he experienced in the gallery with the stress and apprehension of being in a riverside area which was full of people eating and drinking alcohol, with a recognition that his old self would have wanted to be drinking with them. We construed this as being a potential thread of his new identity, "Perhaps you are now the sort of person who goes to look at art? Perhaps that can be who you are now?" This gave him another element to talk about and reflect on when planning for his future.

If appropriate, we engage in specific exercises in which people reflect on their values, what is important to them, what roles they take or would like to take in their lives, what sort of parent, partner, friend, employee they would like to be. This is consistent with the Good Lives Model of rehabilitation (Ward & Brown, 2004) in which people are encouraged to reflect on how to meet basic needs in a prosocial way. We also engage people in specific exercises to reflect on their old identity ("who I was"); their current sense of self ("who I am"); and the sort of person they would like to be, and what it will take to get them there ("who I want to be"). This sort of "wise intervention" has been shown to be effective in supporting people to make and sustain change (van Gelder, Hershfield, & Nordgren, 2013).

For some men who have spent many years (sometimes decades) in prison, community support workers may be the only contact they have in the outside world. However, whilst this professional support can be crucial, ongoing contact with criminal justice staff can also maintain a sense of identity as an offender (if you are not an offender, why do you have to see a probation officer?). The need to step away from language that holds people in their "offending" identity is now more commonly recognised and enacted by criminal justice workers and agencies (Willis, 2018; HMPPS, 2021): the decision by His Majesty's Prison and Probation Service to drop the label "offender" from their official criminal justice language is a healthy step in the right direction. However, changing language does not change the stigma of contact with criminal justice professionals and agencies (see Uggen et al., 2004 for discussion of stigma). These seemingly irrelevant issues can hold people back from fully enacting their pathway to identity desistance. Therefore, meeting people outside of a criminal justice environment, if risk assessments allow, can be a gateway to identity and relational desistance. Frank, after successfully gaining and keeping his own tenancy, and gaining and maintaining paid employment, disliked attending the probation office for his appointments. For us, this was a clear message that his sense of identity was moving away from that of an "ex-offender" and towards "community member", and we validated and hopefully strengthened this process by meeting with him in his home, or in the community. Additionally, our decision to support Mark to access services in a local village hall, as the probation office had so many negative associations for him, strengthened his sense of being validated and accepted as a member of the community. Our experience has been that whilst it may sound trivial, the process of meeting someone in their own environment as a person in the community can be transformational in their journey towards identity desistance.

In addition to spending time reflecting on and discussing issues of identity, a key practical solution is that of obtaining valid, non-criminal-justice-related identification. For many, the only easily available forms of identification are their prison or probation licence, or letters from criminal justice agencies: all reminders of the "offender" identity. Therefore, acting quickly to support people to obtain non-prison related identification is an essential part of the resettlement process. Luke placed high priority on owning a citizenship card and supporting him to apply for this within a few days of release was central to his success. When the card arrived, he was excited, proud and joyful. The citizenship card symbolised hope for his successful resettlement and a sense of belonging to the community (Baumeister & Leary, 1995). This was his starting point to building social bonds, free of stigma.

In order to strengthen identity desistance, we support people to take steps towards building social capital.[3] Ideally pre-release, we discuss with people what interests they have, what they feel they are good at, and what they enjoy. These discussions support people to reflect on their non-offender "roles" (Ashforth et al., 2000). We find that people often struggle to answer these questions because so much of prison-based conversation is about risks, deficits and problems (Shingler et al., 2020). A series of discussions with Michael, who had spent over 20 years in prison enabled the development of a loose timetable for him on release, incorporating voluntary activities at a furniture recycling centre, as well as a creative woodworking group. This enabled him to see himself as someone who wanted to volunteer, contribute and create. It also enabled him to see himself through our eyes, as someone who could achieve this, thus taking a step towards building relational desistance. Finding meaningful and purposeful structure to daily life increases community contacts and increases opportunities for relational desistance (Maruna, 2001). The more people you meet and engage with, the greater the opportunities for some of those people to see you in your new identity. It supports identity desistance as people see *themselves* as someone who volunteers, learns or contributes to their community. It also builds skills needed to be successful in paid work. Supporting people to find paid employment further contributes to the development of identity desistance (see Hlavka et al., 2015). It opens the door to discussions about disclosing an offence history in a way that supports identity desistance. This involves (1) giving clear and concise information about the offence; (2) making a decision about what is proportionate to disclose based on the nature of the work or volunteering setting; for example in a setting with a limited public facing role, people might only disclose the "title" of their offence and the length of their sentence; (3) providing historical and personal context to the offence, followed by what is different now and how the individual is able to manage their risks (see Canton, 2022). For example, someone might explain that their offence was committed in the midst of drug addiction, and go on to explain that they are now abstinent, and/or working with substance misuse services. Steve was adamant that he would never engage in disclosure for fear of people seeing him for his past self rather than his current self. With careful support and gentle encouragement he agreed to make a disclosure in an attempt to gain volunteering work. He was offered the volunteering work which led to paid employment. The impact of this was a strengthening of both his identity desistance (he saw himself as a valued employee who earned his own money) and his relational desistance (he felt part of the community). Of course, disclosure of a criminal conviction is a very sensitive area and needs to be managed with care and thought. We encourage people to engage with "Unlock"[4] who provide comprehensive training and support for people around offence disclosure.

Conclusion

The first few days and weeks following release from prison can feel overwhelming and fraught with practical, emotional and relational stress. Prison commonly leaves people poorly prepared to navigate the challenges of community life. Equally, people can have unrealistic expectations of their own skill and ability to navigate the challenges ahead. This is not to be demeaning or pejorative, rather to reflect the common experience that the hoped for joy and liberation of release does not materialise in the way that was expected. Additionally, hearing the resettlement challenges experienced by people who are at their most vulnerable can be a difficult experience for the clinician: the stigmatisation and marginalisation that people can experience feels unfair and unjust. Our job is to reframe experiences and find practical and psychological solutions to assist progress. Clinical supervision and team support is essential to provide a strong foundation from which clinicians can absorb and proactively support people through life stress.

As clinicians working in the community, we continue to learn how to identify, understand and support people through the resettlement process. Good planning and preparation for release is essential. This needs to start in prison and be truly and genuinely co-produced. Structuring expectations, normalising the challenges, and validating the fear, anxiety and sense of inadequacy that release can bring are all essential. Supporting people to slow down, take one step and one day at a time is central to successful resettlement, as well as to providing psychological and relational containment. Finally, there is the role of identity in successful resettlement. The building of identity desistance is a crucial element of community support in the early days of release and as people continue their resettlement journey. The provision of effective, individualised aftercare following release from prison is likely to be more effective than laborious monitoring and enforcement (Canton, 2022) and this is our aim for every person we work with: the development of a plan that involves them and is individually relevant, meaningful and supportive.

Notes

1 The discharge grant was £76 at the time of writing.
2 For details on types of custodial sentences and how post-custodial supervision fits into them can be found at https://www.sentencingcouncil.org.uk/sentencing-and-the-council/types-of-sentence/custodial-sentences/
3 Social Capital is a concept that recognises the value of social networks, where people with shared values form relationships enabling that society to function effectively.
4 https://unlock.org.uk/

References

Andrews, D. A., & Bonta, J. (2010). *The psychology of criminal conduct.* London, Abingdon, Oxon: Routledge.

Ashforth, B., Kreiner, G., & Fugate, M. (2000). All in a day's work: Boundaries and micro role transitions. *The Academy of Management Review*, 25(3), 472–491.

Baumeister, R. F., & Leary, M. R. (1995). The need to belong: Desire for interpersonal attachments as a fundamental human motivation. *Psychological Bulletin*, 117(3), 497–529.

Burnett, R. (2004). To reoffend or not to reoffend? The ambivalence of convicted property offenders. In S. Maruna & R. Immarigeon (Eds). *After crime and punishment: Pathways to offender reintegration* (pp. 152–180). Cullompton, Devon: Willan Publishing.

Butler, M. (2008). What are you looking at? Prisoner confrontations and the search for respect. *The British Journal of Criminology*, 48(6), 856–873.

Canton, R. (2022). After-care, resettlement and social inclusion: The role of probation. *Probation Journal*, 69(3), 373–390.

Codd, H. (2008). *In the shadow of prison: Families, imprisonment and criminal justice.* Cullompton, Devon: Willan Publishing.

Edgar, K., Harris, M., & Webster, R. (2020). *No life, no freedom, no future: The experiences of prisoners recalled under the sentence of imprisonment under public protection.* London: Prison Reform Trust.

Farrell, M., & Marsden, J. (2008). Acute risk of drug-related death among newly released prisoners in England and Wales. *Addiction*, 103(2), 251–255.

Fitzalan Howard, F. (2019). The experience of prison recall in England and Wales. *The Howard Journal of Crime and Justice*, 58(2), 180–201.

Göbbels, S., Willis, G. M., & Ward, T. (2014). Current re-entry practices in sex offender treatment programmes: desistance facilitating or hindering? *Journal of Sexual Aggression*, 20(3), 354–366.

Gwynne, J. L., Yesberg, J. A., & Polaschek, D. L. (2020). Life on parole: The quality of experiences soon after release contributes to a conviction-free re-entry. *Criminal Behaviour and Mental Health*, 30(6), 290–302.

HM Chief Inspector of Prisons for England and Wales (HMIP) (2016). Life in prison: Contact with families and friends. Retrieved from https://www.justiceinspectorates.gov.uk/hmiprisons/wp-content/uploads/sites/4/2016/08/Contact-with-families-and-friends-findings-paper-2016.pdf.

Hancock, N., Smith-Merry, J. & Mckenzie, K. (2018) Facilitating people living with severe and persistent mental illness to transition from prison to community: A qualitative exploration of staff experiences. *International Journal of Mental Health Systems* 12 (1), 1–10.

Harris, M., Edgar, K., & Webster, R. (2020). 'I'm always walking on eggshells, and there's no chance of me ever being free': The mental health implications of imprisonment for public protection in the community and post-recall. *Criminal Behaviour and Mental Health*, 30(6), 331–340.

Hlavka, H., Wheelock, D., & Jones, R. (2015). Ex-offender accounts of successful re-entry from prison. *Journal of Offender Rehabilitation*, 54(6), 406–428.

Her Majesty's Prison and Probation Service (HMPPS) (2021). The target operating model for probation services in England and Wales. Retrieved from https://assets.publishing.service.gov.uk/government/uploads/system/uploads/attachment_data/file/1061047/MOJ7350_HMPPS_Probation_Reform_Programme_TOM_Accessible_English_LR.pdf.

Hopkin, G., Evans-Lacko, S., Forrester, A., Shaw, J., & Thornicroft, G. (2018). Interventions at the transition from prison to the community for prisoners with mental illness: A systematic review. *Administration and Policy in Mental Health and Mental Health Services Research*, 45(4), 623–634.

Hulley, S., Crewe, B., & Wright, S. (2016). Re-examining the problems of long-term imprisonment. *British Journal of Criminology*, 56(4), 769–792.

Jarvis, D., Shaw, J., & Lovell, T. (2022). Service user experiences of a psychologically enhanced resettlement service [PERS] in an English open prison. *The Journal of Forensic Practice*, 24(3), 241–252.

Liem, M., & Kunst, M. (2013). Is there a recognizable post-incarceration syndrome among released "lifers"? *International Journal of Law and Psychiatry*, 36(3–4),333–337.

Linehan, M. M (1993). *Cognitive-behavioural treatment of borderline personality disorder.* New York: The Guilford Press.

Maruna, S. (2001). *Making good: How ex-convicts reform and rebuild their lives.* Washington: America Psychological Association.

Muth, F. V., Schwarz, K. A., Kunde, W., & Pfister, R. (2017). Feeling watched: What determines perceived observation? *Psychology of Consciousness: Theory, Research, and Practice*, 4(3), 298–309.

Nugent, B. & Schinkel, M. (2016). The pains of desistance. *Criminology and Criminal Justice*, 16(5), 568–584.

Padfield, N. (2013). Understanding recall 2011. *University of Cambridge Faculty of Law Research Paper* (2).

Parole Board. (2018). Licence conditions and how the parole board use them. Retrieved from https://www.gov.uk/government/news/licence-conditions-and-how-the-parole-board-use-them.

Petersilia, J. (2003). *When prisoners come home: Parole and prisoner re-entry*. Oxford: Oxford University Press.

Phillips, L. A., & Lindsay, M. (2011). Prison to society: A mixed methods analysis of coping with re-entry. *International Journal of Offender Therapy and Comparative Criminology*, 55(1), 136–154.

Pratt, D., Piper, M., Appleby, L., Webb, R. T. & Shaw, J. (2006) Suicide in recently released prisoners: A population-based cohort study. *The Lancet*, 368, 119–123.

Rennie, A., & Crewe, B. (2023). 'Tightness', autonomy and release: The anticipated pains of release and life licencing. *The British Journal of Criminology*, 63(1), 47–68.

Richards, S. C. & Jones, R. S. (2004). Beating the perpetual incarceration machine: overcoming structural impediments to re-entry. In S. Maruna & R. Immarigeon (Eds). *After crime and punishment: Pathways to offender reintegration* (pp. 201–232). Cullumpton, Devon: Willan Publishing.

Robinson, L., Tucker, S., Hargreaves, C., Roberts, A., Shaw, J. & Challis, D. (2022). Providing social care following release from prison: Emerging practice arrangements further to the introduction of the 2014 Care Act. *The British Journal of Social Work*, 52(2), 982–1002.

Sainsbury L. (2011). Attachment theory and the therapeutic relationship in the treatment of personality disorder. In P. Willmott & N. Gordon (Eds). *Working positively with personality disorder in secure settings* (pp. 93–114). Chichester, UK: Wiley.

Schinkel, M. (2014). *Being imprisoned: punishment, adaptation and desistance*. London: Palgrave Macmillan.

Scoones, C. D., Willis, G. M., & Grace, R. C. (2012). Beyond static and dynamic risk factors: The incremental validity of release planning for predicting sex offender recidivism. *Journal of Interpersonal Violence*, 27(2), 222–238.

Shingler, J., Sonnenberg, S. J., & Needs, A. (2018). Risk assessment interviews: Exploring the perspectives of psychologists and indeterminate sentenced prisoners in the United Kingdom. *International Journal of Offender Therapy and Comparative Criminology*, 62(10), 3201–3224.

Shingler, J., Sonnenberg, S. J., & Needs, A. (2020). Psychologists as 'the quiet ones with the power': Understanding indeterminate sentenced prisoners' experiences of psychological risk assessment in the United Kingdom. *Psychology, Crime and Law*, 26(6), 571–592.

Sykes, G (1958) *The society of captives: A study of maximum security prison*. Princeton, NJ: Princeton University Press.

Taylor, R., & Yakeley, J. (2019). Working with MAPPA: Ethics and pragmatics. *British Journal of Psychiatry Advances*, 25(3), 157–165.

Uggen, C., Manza, J., & Behrens, A. (2004). Less than the average citizen: Stigma, role transition and the civic reintegration of convicted felons. In S. Maruna & R.

Immarigeon (Eds). *After crime and punishment: Pathways to offender reintegration* (pp. 261–293). Cullompton, Devon: Willan Publishing.

van Gelder, J. L., Hershfield, H. E. & Nordgren, L. F. (2013). Vividness of the future self predicts delinquency. *Psychological Science*, 24, 974–980.

Visher, C. A., & Travis, J. (2003). Transitions from prison to community: Understanding individual pathways. *Annual Review of Sociology*, 89–113.

Ward, T. & Brown, M. (2004): The good lives model and conceptual issues in offender rehabilitation. *Psychology, Crime and Law*, 10(3), 243–257.

Western, B. (2018). *Homeward: Life in the year after prison*. New York: Russell Sage Foundation.

Western, B., Braga, A. A., Davis, J., & Sirois, C. (2015) Stress and hardship after prison. *American Journal of Sociology*, 120(5),1512–1547.

Willis, G. M. (2018). Why call someone by what we don't want them to be? The ethics of labeling in forensic/correctional psychology. *Psychology, Crime and Law*, 24(7), 727–743.

Willis, G. M., & Grace, R. C. (2008). The quality of community reintegration planning for child molesters: Effects on sexual recidivism. *Sexual Abuse*, 20(2), 218–240.

Willmot, P. (2022). Childhood maltreatment and its links to offending. In P. Willmot & L. Jones (Eds.). *Trauma-informed forensic practice* (pp. 15–31). Abingdon, Oxon: Routledge.

Woods, S. (2019). Between somewhere and nowhere: Navigating the liminal space of prisoner reentry. Syracuse University honors program capstone projects. Retrieved from https://surface.syr.edu/cgi/viewcontent.cgi?article=2122&context=honors_capstone.

3 Recall, recovery and re-release

Jo Shingler, Nick and Wayne

My name is Nick and I'm a life sentenced prisoner currently on my second recall. Ah, I'm sure I hear you say, "Why are you back in then?" and you know what, you'd be right. I myself, reaching a point where release was at last a real and near possibility, witnessed other lifers I knew, finally, after all those years get out, only to see them back, often within weeks or months. I didn't get it. I asked, "Why?" and in nearly every case it was a minor breach of the hostel or licence conditions, usually drugs or drink related, but no crime to speak of. I was never sure what to think. I admit I often believed there was more to it, had to be, it didn't make sense. Not only the fact it was a small reason most times to be sent back to prison, but why would you? Why would you serve all that time, all those long and lonely years, finally to be given the amazing gift of your freedom back, to be back in within months as if you've learned nothing? Well I asked them that and before I knew it I was asking myself the same questions, "How or why am I back in?" as if more than 22 years wasn't enough. Like I must have loved it so much in prison I wanted to come back. Ridiculous right?

Nick's account of his experiences illustrates the pain of recall for many men serving long and especially indeterminate sentences as they navigate the challenges of release from prison and resettlement in the community. Recall rates are increasing (Fitzalan Howard, Travers, Wakeling, Webster & Mann, 2018; Padfield & Maruna, 2006), but as Nick suggests, the evidence indicates that this increase is not a consequence of rising reoffending rates amongst people on licence. This implies that other failures in supervision or resettlement are relevant. There is evidence that recall is emotionally painful (Croft & Winder, 2018; Digard, 2010; Edgar, Harris & Webster, 2020; Fitzalan Howard, 2019) and that it can undermine hope, self-efficacy and relationships between recalled men and supervising probation officers. These factors mean that there are special and challenging considerations when responding to the immediate aftermath of recall and supporting people to work towards re-release. In this chapter, we will review the literature on the process and experience of recall, and reflect on the reasons for recall, as described above. We will then go on to discuss clinical approaches to working with recalled people, in particular focusing on (1) ways to reduce the likelihood of recall; (2) supporting people post-recall; and (3) supporting people to approach the prospect of re-release.

DOI: 10.4324/9781003308171-4

Whilst people serving all types of custodial sentence are liable to be recalled, recall is especially salient for those serving indeterminate sentences, so a great deal of this chapter focuses specifically on that group.

What is recall and how does it work?

People released from custody before the end of their sentence are generally subject to a period of supervision on licence by the probation service. People serving standard and extended determinate prison sentences are released with a fixed period of supervision, during which they must abide by the conditions of a licence. During this period, people are liable to be recalled (returned to prison) if they breach the conditions of their licence[1] and if their behaviour indicates an increased risk of serious harm to the public and this risk cannot be safely managed in the community (Fitzalan Howard et al., 2018). The purpose of the licence is to "protect the public, to prevent re-offending, and to secure the successful reintegration of the individual back into the community. A licence is not a form of punishment and must be proportionate, reasonable and necessary" (Parole Board, 2018). People serving determinate sentences can be recalled either for a fixed period of 14 or 28 days, or on a "standard recall". A standard recall means that decisions about re-release are taken by the Parole Board. If the Parole Board is not satisfied that risk can be effectively managed in the community, a person on a standard recall can remain in custody until the end of their sentence (see HMIP, 2020 for more information). People serving Extended Determinate Sentences are not eligible for a fixed-term recall: the only option for them is a standard recall.

People serving indeterminate sentences (life sentences, and Indeterminate Sentences for Public Protection (IPP)) are liable to be recalled at any time during their period of probation supervision, for the rest of their lives.[2] Indeterminate sentenced prisoners can only be recalled on a standard recall (a fixed-period recall is not an option for them). Given there is no end date to an indeterminate sentence, there is similarly no date on which their recall will end and they will be re-released. For example, Edgar et al.'s (2020) sample of recalled IPP prisoners had spent on average 18.25 months in prison post-recall. Decisions about re-release of indeterminate sentenced prisoners are always made by the Parole Board.

There is good evidence that recall rates are increasing in England and Wales (Fitzalan Howard et al., 2018; HMIP, 2020) and Scotland (Weaver, Tata, Munro & Barry, 2012). Rennie and Crewe (2022) reported that since 2017, the number of mandatory lifers being recalled to prison from the community had increased. Edgar et al. (2020) reported a 13% rise in IPP recalls over the 12 months preceding September 2020. They also reported that in the five years prior to June 2020, the number of recalled IPP prisoners had grown by 184%. Between January and March 2020, for the first time, the number of IPP recalls (181) was higher than the total number of releases (174; Edgar et al., 2020). Between January and March 2022, recalls were 5% higher than in the same period in 2021 (Ministry of Justice, 2022).

There is also growing consensus that the rising rate of recall is related to changes in criminal justice policy and priorities (Canton, 2022; Padfield & Maruna, 2006), rather than to increases in reoffending by people on licence. Fitzalan Howard et al. (2018) noted that increases in recall rates could be partly attributed to: (1) changes in how licence conditions are enforced in the community; (2) a growing prison population (more people in prison means more people on licence, which means more people at risk of recall); (3) probation supervision being extended to more people, including those serving shorter sentences; and (4) the introduction of extended sentences. Weaver et al. (2012) suggested that more complex and onerous conditions of conditional release were harder to comply with, leaving people more vulnerable to recall. They also suggested that wider criminal justice policy decisions had an impact on recall rates. Relatedly, HMIP (2020) noted that recall rates increased following publication of reports into high-profile, serious further offences committed whilst on licence. They also noted that changes in policy direction contained within the Recalled Prisoners Framework (RPF, Ministry of Justice, 2019) preceded increased recall rates. The RPF placed "renewed emphasis on public protection as being at the heart of recall" (p. 14). HMIP (2020) described a review of recall decisions, which concluded that whilst recall decisions were generally appropriate, ineffective support was available for people before and after release. Deficits included poor pre-release work, inconsistent access to interventions and services, and inadequate risk management planning. This suggests that more could be done to support people in the community in order to avoid a situation in which recall is necessary.

Reviews of the reasons for recall also support the view that increasing recall rates are not attributable to increasing rates of offending on licence. Fitzalan Howard et al. (2018) identified the primary reason for recall in their sample was non-compliance (43% of all recalls). Of the recalls, 12% were for failing to reside as directed, and 9% were for failing to maintain contact with their probation officer. Only 23% were recalled following further criminal charges. Therefore, the number of people being recalled following further charges was far outweighed by those being recalled for reasons of compliance. Edgar et al. (2020) found that the most common reason for recall amongst released IPPs was non-compliance, followed by new offences or charges, and then by failing to reside as required. Similarly, HMIP (2020) reported that between April 2019 and March 2020, 73% of recalls involved non-compliance with licence conditions. This could include failure to inform the probation officer about a new relationship, making contact with victims, or any breach of the individual's licence. This is consistent with the observations of people in prison, as seen in the introductory paragraph. In essence, the picture of recall is that it imprisons people "not for what they have done but for what they might do in the future" (Prison Reform Trust, 2018, p. 2). The length of time taken to review recall decisions for standard recalls can mean that people are re-imprisoned for months or even years, having committed no further offences. This picture begins to provide some explanation for the detrimental effects of recall, as discussed in the following section.

How is recall experienced?

Studies examining the experience of recall have found that some people reported recall as helpful, in that it prevented a descent into serious crime or drug addiction (Edgar et al., 2020). It was also seen by some as an opportunity to deal with problems that had inhibited success on release (Fitzalan Howard, 2019). As Wayne explained, "I was a mess, both mentally and physically. I knew things were out of control, I had planned my end. I know I would not be here now if I had not been recalled". Therefore for some people, recall has benefits. However, the (albeit limited) literature generally indicates that recall has detrimental and painful consequences. Recalled prisoners describe serious problems with their mental health, loss of family relationships, and the undermining of plans for desistance. In particular, recall is reported as feeling unfair and lacking in legitimacy (Croft & Winder, 2018; Digard, 2010; Edgar et al., 2020; Fitzalan Howard, 2019; Padfield, 2013). It is often experienced as a disproportionate response to misdemeanours on licence, especially by those serving IPP sentences (Edgar et al., 2020) and Extended Sentences (Digard, 2010; see also Fitzalan Howard, 2019). People who are recalled for issues of compliance seem to feel the sense of unfairness particularly keenly. Again, Edgar et al. (2020) reported that this unfairness was particularly salient for those serving the (now abolished) IPP sentence when they compared themselves with people who had received determinate sentences for very similar (or more serious) original offences. People serving determinate sentences are not subject to the same indefinite threat of recall as people serving IPPs and life sentences, so it makes sense that recall feels more painful for this group. Additionally, recall is one of the few remaining criminal justice sanctions in which the individual has no immediate right to reply: recall decisions are not taken by a judge, recall can be initiated on the basis of suspicions that are never proven in court, and the individual does not get a contemporaneous opportunity to see and challenge the evidence against them (see Padfield, 2013). It can be months before people get the opportunity to challenge recall decisions in front of the Parole Board. The absence of a voice in the recall process likely adds to perceptions of unfairness (Digard, 2010; Padfield, 2013; Parsons, 2019). In addition to this absence of voice, the act of being recalled (i.e., literally removed from society) may communicate to people that they have no value or significance in the community. This is likely to reinforce early maladaptive schemas that speak to a sense of worthlessness and defectiveness (e.g., Young, Klosko & Weishaar, 2006).

Relatedly, for some people, the act of recall communicates a clear message that those in authority do not believe have changed, leading them to feel pushed back into their old identities (Fitzalan Howard, 2019). Padfield (2013) found that the written reports about the recall created hopelessness and resentment: such reports seemed to focus entirely on risks and negative attributes (seen as a way of justifying the recall) and neglected to mention progress and efforts towards change. Feeling helpless and despairing about change is unlikely to support a journey towards identity desistence (Nugent & Schinkel, 2016). Recall potentially undermines identity desistance by communicating to the person that they are a risk and are not safe to be part of the community (Digard, 2010).

The literature indicates a general lack of clarity around recall. Padfield (2013) found that people either did not know the details of their recall and what they had to do to be re-released, or they seriously misunderstood the process. Edgar et al. (2020) found that IPPs were unclear about their licence conditions, with some seeming vague and arbitrary, and not making a sensible contribution to managing their risk or supporting their resettlement. For example, Aaron had learning difficulties and an autistic spectrum condition. The Parole Board directed his release but with twenty seven licence conditions which he strug-gled to understand. He was recalled after eight weeks in the community as a result of his failure to comply with his licence conditions, an outcome that was generally seen as inevitable, by both the professionals working with him and by Aaron himself. Padfield (2013) describes "many painful uncertainties" (p. 31), including uncertainty about the timing and process of re-release, that add to the emotional burden of recall. A lack of information and support exacerbates feelings of unfairness, both in the community prior to recall, and in prison post-recall. It seems that in the absence of a clear rationale for decisions, people are inclined to draw their own conclusions about their recall. Some make sus-picious attributions, for example that recall makes their probation officer's life easier (Rennie & Crewe, 2022), reduces their caseload, or frees up space in the probation hostel (or Approved Premises (AP); Digard, 2010); or that it is due to their ethnicity (Fitzalan Howard, 2019).

Recall can create significant emotional pain and loss (Fitzalan Howard, 2019); it can be experienced as traumatic (Croft & Winder, 2018) and can trigger anxiety, depression and panic attacks (Edgar et al., 2020). People talk about the loss of protective factors such as pro-social partners or families, independent secure accommodation, and pro-social roles such as being a father. Recall can engender feelings of hopelessness and undermine self-efficacy: people describe giving up and resigning themselves to a life in prison (Digard, 2010; Edgar et al., 2020). People who have been recalled describe an "unobtain-able, impossible future" (Fitzalan Howard, 2019, p. 188) in which they have no control and no hope. There was a general sense in Fitzalan Howard's study that the recalled men felt passive in the face of an uncaring and harsh system, with their futures being entirely in the hands of others. Recalled men seemed to have no sense of agency, something that is known to be associated with desistance from crime (Maruna, 2001).

There are additional, perhaps more concrete, but no less distressing con-sequences to recall. People can be separated from photographs of their children, bank cards, citizenship cards, bus passes. Such items may seem insignificant, but they can be challenging to obtain on release, and can signify a sense of belonging in the community. One probation officer described their experience with the loss of personal belongings post-recall:

Such matters cause such stress and worry; there is also the issue of them not having anyone to collect something on their behalf. The odd time I have collected something and kept it at work (but this is not something encouraged) until that person gets released or posted it to the prison, the gratitude expressed has been significant.

Croft and Winder (2018) identified additional consequences, including the impact of the speed of recall; the panic and stress people felt at leaving behind possessions, with no way of knowing if they would be safe; and the fear they felt at the impact of their recall on their friends and families. As Mark describes,

No one expects to be recalled back to prison, but if you do something you shouldn't have done it will happen. When it does happen, it happens really quickly, much quicker than when you were first arrested.

Similarly, Wayne reflects "I had caused a lot of damage to the relationships I had in the community before I was recalled. I lost everything, all my belongings, my flat, my friends". These experiences reflect the speed of recall and the extensive and damaging consequences. Interestingly, both of these men believed there was legitimacy in their recall. It is likely that the negative emotional overload would have been enhanced if, in addition to these consequences, the recall felt unfair or was not understood.

Finally, research indicates that recall interferes with relationships between recalled people and their community probation officers. Recalled prisoners describe losing motivation to engage with community supervision, feeling hopeless, demoralised and angry (Edgar et al., 2020). Fitzalan Howard's (2019) participants described similar negative feelings, including anger, frustration and grievance, some of which were directed at a specific person who was seen as responsible for their recall (see also Croft & Winder, 2018). Digard (2010) similarly reported recall triggering deep mistrust in community probation officers, which for some progressed into animosity. For example, Darren believed his recall was unfounded and unfair as he had followed the requirements to disclose a forming relationship and get professional support. He was unable to recognise the impact of a chaotic relationship that was destabilising him and increasing his risk. His anger at professionals following his recall interfered with his ability to reflect on different perspectives of the events leading to recall, and affected his willingness to work towards re-release for some months.

Both the act and the *threat* of recall can result in reluctance to be honest about difficulties. There is fear that opening up about struggles or mistakes will provide evidence of increasing risk which then triggers the recall process (Edgar et al., 2020; Padfield, 2013). Similar fears have been reported in people transferring to open prison conditions (Jarvis, Shaw & Lovell, 2022). Fitzalan Howard (2019) described two forms of intended disengagement reported by recalled participants. "Active defiance" was the plan to limit or actively refuse further contact, for example by intentionally avoiding re-release before sentence expiry date, in order to avoid being under probation supervision. Fitzalan Howard construed this as a potential route into taking back control of their lives, given the lack of agency experienced by recalled people. The other form of disengagement reported by Fitzalan Howard was "feigned compliance", becoming a "yes man", or "going through the motions" rather than actively and meaningfully engaging with the process of supervision. This is similar to Digard's (2010) findings, that people reported intending to comply formally (with the letter of the licence) but not substantively (i.e. without proper engagement in the process). Digard found that participants felt determined to resist any attempts by their probation officer to build a working relationship or engage in rehabilitative activity. For some, this was a response to feeling that recall had been a direct consequence of being open with their probation officers (Croft & Winder, 2018 and see above).

Recall is also a challenging process to manage for staff (Edgar et al., 2020). Community probation staff have to tread a difficult balance, especially when supervising people who are assessed as presenting a high risk of serious harm to the public (Weaver et al., 2012). HMIP (2020) found that probation officers were fearful of being blamed for not initiating recall, if the person went on to commit a Serious Further Offence (SFO). Such fears and observations of organisational responses to SFOs are liable to affect recall decision making (Canton, 2022; Edgar et al., 2020).

In summary, recall is challenging for both people being supervised in the community, and those working with them. Recall undermines compliance with community sanctions, as a result of the perception of recall as being profoundly unfair and lacking in legitimacy. Recall is also very likely to undermine relationships with both existing and future professionals, as people feel hostile and angry, and fear being open about difficulties, in case openness results in recall. Therefore, recall should be used only as a last resort, when risk is unmanageable in the community (Edgar et al., 2020). In the next section we will discuss what community workers can do to navigate the challenging and complex issues around recall. Edgar et al. (2020), Fitzalan Howard (2019) and Padfield (2013) all make a number of structural and procedural recommendations for the Ministry of Justice and His Majesty's Prison and Probation Service (HMPPS) regarding the process of recall and re-release, the use of licence conditions et cetera, and these would seem likely to significantly improve the transparency, legitimacy and speed of the recall process. We will not repeat these recommendations. Rather we will focus on steps community workers can take to reduce the risk of recall, to support individuals to cope post-recall and plan for their re-release.

Working with recalled people

What can professionals do to reduce the likelihood of recall?

There is a general view that more support, both in prison to prepare for release and when in the community, could have a significant effect on recall rates.

Edgar et al.'s (2020) study identified that people serving IPP sentences wanted more help with meeting basic needs in the community (e.g., with obtaining identification, organising finances, finding work and accommodation) as well as more mental health support. Canton (2022) described the woeful absence of practical support available to those on release, and how basics like money and safe accommodation are essential if already deprived and marginalised people are going to make a success of release. Ensuring plans are in place pre-release for people to have quick access to benefits, find somewhere to live, and make contact with essential services (such as General Practitioners, mental health support and substance misuse services) is central. Chapters 1, 2 and 7 reflect in more detail on effectiveness in preparing for release.

Supporting people to plan and prepare for the emotional demands of release is equally important (Padfield, 2013; and see Chapter 2). Orienting people to the emotional pain of release, the sense of feeling overwhelmed and unable to cope (Phillips & Lindsay, 2011), could prove vital if people are to have the best chance of coping effectively in the community. This was true for Nick, who wrote:

> I can't say I found any one single thing too tough to cope with or deal with on its own, but more than once found myself in tears, upset more than I should be, thinking about it as I have. I think it's the difference of it all, the "newness", the sudden change of one environment to another like the shock of hot and cold.

After reflecting on his first experience of being in the community after more than two decades in prison and being recalled after around five weeks, Nick gives this advice for those approaching release:

> Take it slow. That's my advice. Find your feet. Learn the rhythms of the new world outside.... It's taking your time, not rushing into a game you don't understand, yet thinking "it will be alright". Take time to learn where you fit into this new freedom.

Some people might benefit from coaching or support in developing good coping skills; others need support to apply existing coping strategies. It is also important to recognise that support is still needed as people achieve key milestones, such as finding employment or their own accommodation (Maruna, 2001). Digard's (2010) participants reported being potentially more vulnerable at these times. They reported being on such a high at their success that their licence conditions and risk management strategies took a back seat.

Forming trusting professional relationships is central to reducing recall (Croft & Winder, 2018). Edgar et al. (2020) reported that recalled IPPs recognised that seeking professional support could have averted recall. Nick advises:

> Use the help and support offered to you and if things are tough, say that they are tough. There is no weakness in that.

However, people are often understandably reticent about speaking up about difficulties in case disclosures themselves provide evidence to initiate recall, as discussed above. This is what makes the development of trusting professional relationships so important. People on licence need to feel confident to seek support when they are struggling, rather than hide their struggles out of fear of recall. It is also important to have frank and open discussions about the sorts of changes in someone's functioning that would genuinely cause sufficient concern to warrant recall. This is likely to be different for every person, as each person's risks and needs are unique. Ideally, reaching into prisons prior to release provides an opportunity for people to get to know the professionals who will be working with them in the community (Padfield, 2013; see Chapters 2 and 9 of this volume) and begin to develop an understanding and trusting relationship. Padfield (2013) described a deep sense of resentment when people felt their licence was designed by someone who did not know them. This is consistent with other studies that report a lack of legitimacy in professional decisions when the individual in focus does not feel known by said professional (Shingler, Sonnenberg & Needs, 2020). Getting to know and build a relationship with someone confers greater moral authority to set licence conditions, and therefore increases the likelihood of compliance.

Open acknowledgement and discussion of the pains of serving an indeterminate sentence could help to support people and reduce the likelihood of recall. The emotional and psychological pain of indeterminacy is well documented (Jacobson & Hough, 2010; Jewkes, 2005; Shingler et al., 2020), especially in relation to the IPP sentence (Edgar et al., 2020; Jacobson & Hough, 2010). Being able to talk openly about the impact of the sentence, and have those fears acknowledged and validated is an important step in building professional relationships that can protect against recall (see Canton, 2022). The constant state of fear around recall can in itself make people more vulnerable. It can interfere with good decision making; inhibit open discussion of difficulties (see above); and drive people to self-isolation, which tends to compound negative feelings and potentially increase vulnerability to risk-related coping strategies.

Finally, clarity about the nature, extent and meaning of licence conditions before release could make a significant difference. Men need to know what is expected of them and why, without surprises in the first few days of release. Padfield (2013) found that short or no notice of licence conditions (i.e., finding out about a condition once in the community) created anger and resentment. People also felt aggrieved that they had not had a voice in decisions about licence conditions – they felt powerless. Therefore a "checklist" for practitioners devising licence conditions pre-release should include:

- Are they understood?
- As far as possible, does the person have a say in the development of licence conditions?

- Do they understand the role of each licence condition in supporting their resettlement?

(Padfield, 2013).

How can professionals support people post-recall?

Possibly the single most valuable thing to do is to connect with people immediately and personally post-recall. As Wayne described,

> I found the consistent support offered to me by [community services] every 4–6 weeks, writing, video calls and visits the most helpful. This felt like a contact support. It helped me understand the process of recall. The continuity of support helped me feel connected to the community.

Fitzalan Howard (2019) reported that even for people who described recall as painful, the presence of support was "powerful and meaningful" (p. 193) when it existed. The importance of consistent community support is reflected in Wayne's experience above. People report feeling abandoned, unimportant and unsupported after recall (Fitzalan Howard, 2019), so connecting with them quickly and personally could begin to ameliorate this. One thing that can be especially helpful is to write to or email people as soon as possible after recall (that usually means as soon as they have arrived at a prison where they are likely to be for some weeks, to ensure that correspondence reaches them). Nick wrote the following in response to a letter received following his emergency recall:

> 3–4 days into a recall, sat on my bed, head in bits, I received a letter. That letter was from the team working with me. The failure was mine but far from dropping me and moving on they told me how sorry they were at my recall but assured me how they were every bit as much still behind me and would be if I wanted to try again. I can't tell you how much that meant, or how much I needed it at that moment.

This reflects both the importance of connection, of reaching out quickly post-recall, and the importance of communicating a sense of hope and expectation for the future: that things can be different, we can all learn from this experience, reset and try again. Edgar et al. (2020) reported that recall undermined motivation, so engaging early and with a sense of hope can be helpful. Similarly, Wayne described how:

> The positivity of professionals was helpful when my negativity was so strong. The consistency of this helped me to start to understand that there was a future for me and this contact with community professionals helped me with planning.

This reinforces the view that it is the contact, the maintenance of a connection and the communication of hope that is so important in the early days post-recall. In terms of the method of communication, this is usually by letter or email initially (see Chapter 9). However, telephone contact can also be offered post-recall, as soon as the person feels able and willing to use the telephone. Prison visits can also be part of the process of learning from the recall and planning for re-release.

In addition to contact post-recall to offer support and hope, it is also important to explain clearly the reasons why recall was initiated and to listen to the person's perspective. This will usually be a task for the person's community probation officer. It is clearly too late to change the decision, but the process of giving the person the opportunity to express their views can support re-building of damaged relationships. Padfield (2013) found that resentment was heightened when people felt their probation officer had not bothered to contact them after they had been recalled. Additionally, research suggests that people are often completely ignorant or mistaken about the reasons for their recall and the processes that need to be gone through to be considered for re-release. Staff in prison can be similarly ill-informed and unable to advise people appropriately (Padfield 2013). Fitzalan Howard et al. (2018) found that whilst community probation officers felt men had a good understanding of the reasons for recall, the majority of recalled men did not share this view. As noted in the previous section, if people (who may already be primed for mistrust) are not given clear information about a recall decision, they may assume the worst and make hostile attributions about professionals' reasons for recall (Canton, 2022). Therefore, an essential element of the post-recall support process is to carefully explain the reasoning behind recall and ensure people fully understand this. We have engaged in this process with a man who was angry at the decision to recall him, and blamed his community probation officer for what he felt was an unfair and hasty decision. A lengthy process (starting within weeks of recall and continuing for a year) enabled the man and his probation officer to voice their opinions and feelings about the recall, to hear each other's perspectives, and to begin to repair their working relationship. This was facilitated with the support of the prison through a series of telephone calls, videolinks and visits. Whilst this situation remains challenging and painful, our practice here followed principles of procedural justice: giving the man a voice, and also clearly explaining recall decisions so motives and reasoning were clear and transparent (Tyler, 1990; Fitzalan Howard, 2019).

Finally, we can support people effectively post-recall by being more aware of the emotional burden of recall. Digard (2010) reported that in many cases, prisons did not treat recalls as new arrivals, so they often were not subject to the sorts of additional monitoring and support available to this group. People are especially emotionally vulnerable post-recall: Padfield (2013) reported a finding by the Prison Ombudsman in 2011, that 29 of the 208 prisoners (14%) who took their own lives in that year were recalled prisoners. Given the emotional pain of recall, especially in relation to feelings of hopelessness, despair and "giving up", this is problematic and change is needed. Prison workers need to engage with recalled men to support them at what could be a particularly vulnerable time. Professionals need to recognise losses incurred by recall, and empathise and validate the experience (Fitzalan Howard et al., 2018). Whilst recall may have been necessary, this does not mean it is without loss. Professionals need to listen to individual stories of recall and give men a voice in expressing their loss (Fitzalan Howard et al., 2018).

How can professionals prepare people for re-release after recall?

Even though recall is emotionally painful, people have communicated to us that our ability to hold hope for them and continue to think about a future in the community has been central to their ability to recover. Therefore, involving people in plans towards re-release as soon as is practical is important. Fitzalan Howard (2019) found that people felt even more hopeless and out of control when considering how to get to re-release, so building confidence and self-efficacy by identifying and analysing reasons for recall, identifying gaps in support and putting in place practical and psychological support networks could help here. Relatedly, Edgar et al. (2020) suggested that having a clear plan for what needs to be done to achieve re-release was needed, but often absent, post recall. Having a co-produced plan can reduce feelings of hopelessness and help people gain some level of self-efficacy. This process needs to be properly collaborative, involving the recalled person fully and meaningfully to learn from the experience of recall and reflect on what needs to be done differently next time. Nick described how, "I've learned something from previous times about where I did struggle, perhaps why and what support I feel I need this time". Genuine commitment to and engagement in collaborative working post-recall can encourage involvement in the planning of the journey towards re-release and encourage co-operation generally with professionals (Fitzalan Howard et al., 2018). Collaborative working in general has been found to be effective in challenging and potentially emotionally charged criminal justice tasks (Shingler, Sonnenberg & Needs, 2018), and recall clearly fits this description.

Whilst collaboration in re-release planning is important, it is also important to acknowledge that the process of planning for re-release is often beset by delays and bureaucratic hurdles. These can be demotivating and distressing for people who can feel forgotten and stuck in a system without hope. It can take many months for Parole Board hearings to be organised. In some cases, prison teams will not begin to put in place support until a release date is known. It is essential to maintain contact with recalled people throughout this process so they continue to feel that they matter (see Chapter 10), and that there is a familiar person to whom they can turn to for support. For example, Nick recognised that his recall was partly attributable to Class A drug use, which in turn was partly attributable to his experience of unbearable emotional distress. He believed that in order to be more successful at his next release, he needed to be stabilised on an opiate blocker. However, prison prescribers were reluctant to introduce an opiate blocker without a definitive release date. As an indeterminate sentenced prisoner awaiting a parole board hearing date, this was impossible, and put him in a double jeopardy situation: the Parole Board might be reluctant to re-release him if he were not stabilised on a medication, as this was part of the picture of his recall. Yet the prison would not begin a course of opiate blockers without a release date. Our role in this situation was to work together as a team to communicate to prison colleagues the importance of stability for Nick, and support his self-assessment of his needs. The ongoing involvement of community practitioners can keep the prospect of re-release in the forefront of the minds of prison colleagues, and ensure that working towards the goal of community stability is prioritised even from prison. Our role also involved just listening to his frustrations and enabling him to build the skill of seeking support which will also serve him well on re-release.

Relatedly, Edgar et al. (2020) reported a view that prison-based interventions tended to be over-prescribed for recalled people, because, in the words of a professional interviewed by Edgar et al: "You've got the automatic assumption that because you've been recalled any of the work you've done to reduce your risk doesn't count for anything...and that leads on to the questionable area of over-treatment" (p. 51). There is a view that there are significant disparities between the skills and progress needed to reduce the effects of offence-related risk factors (and consequently prove risk is reduced), and the skills and abilities needed for successful community resettlement (Farrall, 2004; Martin, 2018). If recall was attributable to offence-related factors then more prison-based intervention could be warranted. However, the research suggests that most recalls are compliance and resettlement related, suggesting that attention would better be spent post-recall on planning for desistance-related needs rather than risk-related needs (Farrall, 2004). Therefore, prioritising skills that will enable emotional and practical stability, developing a sense of agency, and building community links would seem to be more effective than imposing further risk-reducing treatment in many cases.

In addition to identifying what triggered recall, it is also crucial to discuss and analyse successes in the community, and what skills and strengths people used, developed and maintained. Recall undermines pre-recall achievements (Fitzalan Howard, 2019) and can leave people forgetting about their successes. Therefore, taking a strengths-based approach, in which achievements in the community are explicitly discussed, remembered and brought to the forefront, can help to challenge the feelings of despair and hopelessness associated with recall and build confidence for re-release. To support this, we sometimes encourage people to write down their good memories of being in the community, their achievements and what they did well. This has provided the foundation for discussions about preparing for re-release, and can provide a positive framework for people to build on. Even if things went badly wrong, it is unlikely that a period in the community has been without any positives, high points or achievements, and it is important to recognise and remember these.

As already discussed, professional relationships are central to effective re-release preparation. Building and strengthening community relationships whilst in prison can enable people to feel more ready to face the challenges of the community. It can maintain the connection, help people feel remembered and important (see Chapter 10), and can provide a sense of confidence that there is support that can be drawn on if things get tough again. Wayne explains that what he most needs to prepare for re-release is:

> The continuity of support from people I have formed trusting relationships with. I will need this support whilst I work out how damaged the relation-ships [are] I have in the community, if they are repairable and if so how I can do this. I know I need support with managing and where possibly repairing these relationships. I need support to help me access services like the GP, dentist and mental health support. I will need help with accommodation in the future. I want to start afresh, I don't want any reminders of the past me I don't want any clothing or possessions that I had prior to my recall and want to start a new life. I know I will do best when I have structure to my days and do things with my time, I will need help with this, and I need psychological support to help me manage my thoughts which can be extremely distressing.

Wayne's comments suggest that having trusting relationships with community professionals has enabled him to identify the emotional and practical support he needs, and give him a sense of confidence that he can "start a new life". He has hope for the future, and is thinking about building a new identity, and leaving behind the person who was "a mess, mentally and physically" at the point of recall.

Finally, it is important to acknowledge the sense of vulnerability that many people experience following recall, but especially those who are serving inde-terminate sentences. We have heard numerous accounts of people feeling more unsettled in the community than in prison, of prison being a safe place, of the community presenting significant and daunting challenges, and feeling under scrutiny and at the mercy of one's probation officer. Edgar et al. (2020) reported on the inability of IPPs to live a normal life in the community, as a result of the ever-present fear of recall. This fear is persistent: John has been living successfully in the community for almost three years yet still reports fear of recall affecting how he manages situations at work and how he engages with people in the community, reflecting, "what if someone takes a dislike to me and reports me for doing something I haven't done?" There is little we can do to change this, but we can listen, validate and acknowledge that fear.

Conclusions

Recall is generally experienced as painful and damaging. The majority of people seem to feel that their recall was unfair and unnecessary. Even people who feel they were rightly recalled struggle with the emotional and practical aftermath. Therefore, it seems sensible that recall is only used as a last resort, a position with which most recalled people and criminal justice professionals would seem to agree (Edgar et al., 2020). It also seems, from the literature and from the reports of people who have experienced recall that maintaining contact post-recall is the single most effective thing professionals can do. Maintaining contact seems to offer a sense of being valued, being visible and remembered, as well as enabling feelings of hope for recovery from recall.

Notes

1 The Offender Rehabilitation Act (2014) resulted in prisoners serving sentences of less than 12 months having to undergo a period of probation supervision. When the licence period is less than 12 months, people are subject to "PSS" (post-sentence supervision). Under PSS recall works differently – people can only be returned to prison for 14 days following a hearing at a magistrate's court.
2 Technically, people serving IPP sentences can apply for the sentence to be removed ten years after their first release. Extensive searches have not revealed how many IPP sentences have actually been removed. In response to a tweet about the subject in December 2021, one comment was "It is far more likely to have met someone who has walked on the moon". Another response indicated that at that time, no-one had applied and had their licence terminated.

References

Canton, R. (2022). After-care, resettlement and social inclusion: The role of probation. *Probation Journal*, 69(3) 373–390.

Croft, J. & Winder, B. (2018). "License conditions … don't stop you committing offences and they don't protect the public, they're just there to make you feel worse": A qualitative analysis of the experiences of individuals who have served prison sentences for a sexual offence and been recalled to prison. Unpublished research paper.

Digard, L. (2010). When legitimacy is denied: Offender perceptions of the prison recall system. *Probation Journal*, 57(1), 43–61.

Edgar, K., Harris, M., & Webster, R. (2020). *No life, no freedom, no future: The experiences of prisoners recalled under the sentence of imprisonment under public protection*. London, UK: Prison Reform Trust.

Farrall, S. (2004). Social capital and offender reintegration: making probation desistance focused. In S. Maruna & R. Immarigeon (Eds). *After crime and punishment: Pathways to offender reintegration* (pp 57–82). Cullumpton, Devon: Willan Publishing.

Fitzalan Howard, F. (2019). The experience of prison recall in England and Wales. *The Howard Journal of Crime and Justice*, 58(2), 180–201.

Fitzalan Howard, F., Travers, R., Wakeling, H., Webster, C., & Mann, R. (2018). Understanding the Process and Experience of Recall to Prison. Ministry of Justice Analytical Summary. Retrieved from https://assets.publishing.service.gov.uk/government/uploads/system/uploads/attachment_data/file/723265/Understanding_the_process_and_experience_of_recall_to_prison.pdf.

Her Majesty's Inspectorate of Probation (HMIP) (2020). A thematic review of probation recall culture and practice. Retrieved from https://www.justiceinspectorates.gov.uk/hmiprobation/wp-content/uploads/sites/5/2020/11/Recall-thematic.pdf.

Jacobson, J., & Hough, M. (2010). *Unjust Deserts: Imprisonment for Public Protection*. London: Prison Reform Trust.

Jarvis, D., Shaw, J., & Lovell, T. (2022). Service user experiences of a psychologically enhanced resettlement service [PERS] in an English open prison. *The Journal of Forensic Practice* (ahead-of-print).

Jewkes, Y. (2005). Loss, liminality and the life sentence: Managing identity through a disrupted lifecourse. In A. Liebling & S. Maruna (Eds.) *Effects of imprisonment* (pp. 366–388). Uffculme, Devon: Willan Publishing.

Martin, S. (2018). Does preparing for parole help prepare for life? *Prison Service Journal*, 237, 46–49.

Maruna, S. (2001). *Making good: How ex-convicts reform and rebuild their lives.* Washington: America Psychological Association.

Ministry of Justice (April 2019, re-issued February 2020). Recall, Review and Re-release of Recalled Prisoners Policy Framework. Retrieved from https://www.gov.uk/government/publications/recall-review-and-re-release-of-recalled-prisoners.

Ministry of Justice (2022). Offender Management Statistics Bulletin, England and Wales. Quarterly: January to March 2000. Retrieved from https://assets.publishing.service.gov.uk/government/uploads/system/uploads/attachment_data/file/1094703/OMSQ-Q1-2022.pdf.

Nugent, B. & Schinkel, M. (2016). The pains of desistance. *Criminology & Criminal Justice*, 16(5), 568–584.

Padfield, N. (2013). Understanding recall 2011. *University of Cambridge Faculty of Law Research Paper* (2).

Padfield, N., & Maruna, S. (2006). The revolving door at the prison gate: Exploring the dramatic increase in recalls to prison. *Criminology & Criminal Justice*, 6(3), 329–352.

Parole Board. (2018). Licence conditions and how the Parole Board use them. Retrieved from https://www.gov.uk/government/news/licence-conditions-and-how-the-parole-board-use-them.

Parsons, K. (2019). *Listening to the subject experts: an exploration of the views of residents in Approved Premises and of Probation Officers to recall decision making.* Unpublished manuscript. Cambridge, UK: Institute of Criminology, University of Cambridge.

Phillips, L. A., & Lindsay, M. (2011). Prison to society: A mixed methods analysis of coping with reentry. *International Journal of Offender Therapy and Comparative Criminology*, 55(1), 136–154.

Prison Reform Trust (2018). Broken trust: The rising numbers of women recalled to prison. Retrieved from https://prisonreformtrust.org.uk/publication/broken-trust-the-rising-number-of-women-recalled-to-prison/

Rennie, A., and Crewe, B. (2022) 'Tightness', autonomy and release: The anticipated pains of release and life licencing. *The British Journal of Criminology*.

Shingler, J., Sonnenberg, S. J., & Needs, A. (2018). Risk assessment interviews: Exploring the perspectives of psychologists and indeterminate sentenced prisoners in the United Kingdom. *International Journal of Offender Therapy and Comparative Criminology*, 62(10), 3201–3224.

Shingler, J., Sonnenberg, S. J., & Needs, A. (2020). Psychologists as 'the quiet ones with the power': Understanding indeterminate sentenced prisoners' experiences of psychological risk assessment in the United Kingdom. *Psychology, Crime & Law*, 26(6), 571–592.

Tyler, T. R. (1990). *Why people obey the law: Procedural justice, legitimacy, and compliance.* New Haven, CT: Yale University Press.

Weaver, B., Tata, C., Munro, M., & Barry, M. (2012). The failure of recall to prison: Early release, front-door and back-door sentencing and the revolving prison door in Scotland. *European Journal of Probation*, 4(1), 85–98.

Young, J. E., Klosko, J. S., & Weishaar, M. E. (2006). *Schema therapy: A practitioner's guide.* New York: Guilford Press.

Part II

Specific issues in the transition journey

4 Trauma and release from prison

Understanding and navigating trauma responses in the community

Charlotte Purvis and Jenny Devine

Introduction

This chapter will explore the prevalence of trauma amongst men in the Criminal Justice System (CJS); the importance of understanding and formulating the impact of complex trauma on biological and relational systems; and from this, understanding emotional and behavioural responses. We highlight the layers of trauma that the men we work with have experienced across the lifespan and during their journey through the CJS. From this, we discuss common reactions to release; how complex trauma may underpin these reactions, and how professionals can best understand these reactions as learned coping strategies. This chapter is aimed at a wide CJS audience with the purpose of highlighting the value of trauma-informed thinking and approaches to working with men in the CJS as they transition from prison to the community.

Experience of trauma amongst imprisoned men

For the purpose of this chapter, we adopt the term "complex trauma", defined by Cook, Blaustein, Spinazzola and van der Kolk (2003) as "the simultaneous or sequential occurrences of child maltreatment - including emotional abuse and neglect, sexual abuse, physical abuse, and witnessing domestic violence - that are chronic and begin in early childhood" (p. 5). These experiences are then exacerbated or compounded by insecure and unsafe attachment relationships, disruption during key developmental transitions and further trauma throughout the lifespan, resulting in significant psychological and relational difficulties. Despite this, and the prevalence of Post-Traumatic Stress Disorder (PTSD) and Complex Post-Traumatic Stress Disorder (C-PTSD) in prisoner populations (Facer-Irwin et al., 2019; Facer-Irwin, Karatzias, Bird, Blackwood & MacManus, 2022), most of the men we work with do not have a formal diagnosis of a trauma disorder. It is possible that this is a consequence of the priority given to offending and risk over mental health conditions once people enter custody. As such, we steer away from framing trauma purely within categorical and formal diagnostic labels. In our view, it is more helpful to focus on themes of trauma experiences, the impact on development and how individuals survive and adapt to these. Often adaptations or coping strategies align

DOI: 10.4324/9781003308171-6

with symptoms within trauma diagnostic criteria, and we believe formulating in this way is more helpful than focusing on a specific label, given response to trauma is heterogeneous.

The majority of individuals serving prison sentences have experienced some form of childhood trauma (Wolff & Shi, 2012), but their experiences differ from those in the general population, both in terms of prevalence and variety. Those who are imprisoned have tended to experience a wider variety of traumatic events, which have often occurred at an early age, as well as persisting over a longer period of time (Bowen, Jarrett, Stahl, Forrester & Valmaggia, 2018; Facer-Irwin et al., 2019). There is a marked pervasiveness of Adverse Childhood Experiences (ACEs) within male prisoner populations (Ford et al., 2019) and in turn, ACEs are associated with harmful behaviours such as drug use, interpersonal violence, and entry into the criminal justice system (McCartan, 2020). Exposure to childhood trauma is also associated with increased levels of violent behaviour in youths and adults within the CJS (Cantürk, Faraji & Tezcan, 2021; Ford et al., 2019; Honorato, Caltabiano & Clough, 2016); increased prevalence of diagnoses or symptoms of mental disorder (Liu, Li, Liang & Hou, 2021); emotional and practical coping deficits; and significant disruptions to relational ties (Vaughn-Coaxum, Wang, Kiely, Weisz, & Dunn, 2018). The relationship between the child and caregiver is particularly important for healthy development (Cook et al., 2005), and therefore interpersonal trauma from caregivers can be one of the most psychologically destructive for children (Scheeringa, Zeanah, Drell & Larrieu, 1995; Spinazzola, Van der Kolk, & Ford, 2018). Complex trauma disrupts child development (Perry & Pollard, 1998; Van der Kolk, 2005), especially in the absence of protective factors. It can impact on attachment relationships in childhood and adulthood, and if unresolved can lead to transgenerational trauma-related behaviours (Zarse et al., 2019). It is also noteworthy that many research studies with imprisoned people have focused on direct experiences of abuse and neglect and have excluded indirect trauma experiences, such as witnessing intimate partner violence, parental imprisonment and substance misuse within the family home. Consequently, the level of childhood trauma within prisoner populations is likely to be vastly underestimated.

Prolonged trauma in early life has biological consequences. Brain development in the first few years of a child's life is critical to multiple functions (Bowlby, 1969) and early trauma can have a lasting structural and functional effect on the brain (Bremner, 2006). Effects include decreased volume of the pre-frontal cortex, which controls executive functions including cognitive flexibility, emotion regulation, inhibitory control and working memory (National Scientific Council on the Developing Child, 2011). When these "mental braking systems" are impacted by childhood trauma, it is perhaps not surprising that individuals experience significant difficulties in navigating change, novel or challenging situations. Individuals' brains have become hard wired for survival, rather than higher level cognitive order tasks, which impacts on their ability to regulate emotional states and moderate behaviour.

Prolonged trauma, without the buffer of attuned adult support, can also alter the functioning of neurochemical systems, for example, levels of cortisol and norepinephrine (Bremner, 2006). This in turn can lead to "toxic stress" (National Scientific Council on the Developing Child, 2003). Toxic stress is the result of "prolonged activation of the stress response, with a failure of the body to recover fully. It differs from a normal stress response in that there is a lack of caregiver support, reassurance, or emotional attachments" (Franke, 2014, p.392). Examples of toxic stress include abuse, neglect, extreme poverty, violence, household dysfunction, and food scarcity.

Finally, Porges' polyvagal theory (1995) centres on the premise that our Autonomic Nervous System (ANS) has evolved to navigate complex human relationships by attending to cues of danger and modulating behaviour to ensure safety. The ANS comprises the sympathetic nervous system (SNS, mobilising system, preparing the body for fight or flight in the face of threat) and parasympathetic nervous system (PNS) of which there are two branches. The dorsal vagal branch is the immobilising system (rest and digest, freeze / shut down); the ventral vagal branch supports "social engagement". The ANS relays information between the brain and body, communicating internal and external experiences that assist in assessing threat and safety, a process called "neuroception" (Porges, 2004). Porges highlights the importance of the social engagement system in navigating potential threat through attuned social interactions for example: seeking out social support, asking for help, signalling distress to others via social behaviour and facial expressions. However, individuals who have experienced complex trauma and poor attachment relationships have stronger primitive brain pathways (sympathetic and parasympathetic-dorsal) as a result of toxic stress. These individuals learned it was not safe to seek safety via social connection and relationships, resulting in their ventral vagus pathway being underused and underdeveloped, impacting on effective social engagement.

In summary, early life trauma can have significant biological and relational consequences. Repeated trauma experiences bring debilitating difficulties across the lifespan impacting on many facets of an individual's life including emotional management, social engagement, self-care, self-esteem, identity, relationships, employment and independent living skills. Consequently, many men moving from prison to the community have a range of additional, trauma-related needs with which they need support, and which professionals need to hold in mind when understanding emotional and behavioural responses on release. Through understanding the role the ANS plays in navigating human relationships, we can understand why many people in prison who have experienced complex trauma find it so hard to make use of social and professional support to navigate the prison-community transition.

Layers of trauma

As highlighted above, the men we work with have rarely experienced single trauma events, rather complex and cumulative layers of trauma across their lifespan including physical, sexual, emotional and structural victimization, before, during and after their imprisonment (Sloan Rainbow, 2018). Figure 4.1

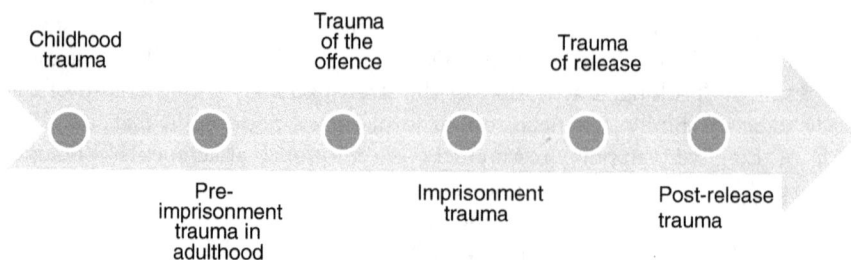

Figure 4.1 Layers of trauma in imprisoned men
Adapted from Liu et al. (2021)

highlights how trauma experiences can be accumulated and compounded across the lifespan, and at key transition points in the criminal justice pathway. We will now go on to discuss these layers of trauma in turn (childhood trauma has been summarised above).

Pre-imprisonment trauma in adulthood

Many individuals arrive in prison with their own unique trauma experiences. In order to manage symptoms of complex trauma, individuals can engage in increased risk-taking behaviours, including violence, substance misuse and thrill-seeking. Gilligan (1997) identifies that violent men "desperately want to feel that they are big, tough, independent, self-assertive, self-reliant men, so as not to feel needy, helpless, frightened, inadequate, unskilled, incompetent" (p.127). This illustrates how violence can become a trauma coping response, which in turn increases the risk of contact with the criminal justice system as well as exposure to more traumatic experiences (see also Billingham & Irwin Rogers, 2021). Thrill-seeking has also been found to be strongly correlated with PTSD symptoms, particularly negative mood and affect and hyperarousal (Contractor, Weiss, Dranger, Ruggero & Armour, 2017), suggesting it may also be used as strategy to counter the effects of trauma.

Trauma of the offence

The act of committing the offence and the subsequent conviction process can be traumatising events. It is often acknowledged that individuals who have offended may be victims of past trauma, but less consideration is given to the potential psychological injury to the offender of the crime they themselves have perpetrated (Mohamed, 2015). It can be an uncomfortable truth to accept that perpetrators of crime can experience symptoms of trauma as a result of their own actions. Over half of individuals convicted of murder have been found to report trauma associated with their offence (Papanastassiou, Waldron, Boyle & Chesterman, 2004), with a high prevalence of diagnosed trauma symptoms (Pham & Willocq, 2013). The experience of offence-related trauma has also been found to be significantly associated with higher levels of guilt in individuals who have committed violent or sexual offences, both in prison and mental health settings (Crisford, Dare & Evangeli, 2008; Papanastassiou et al., 2004). There are complexities in understanding how prior experiences of trauma impact upon post-offence-related symptoms, though it has been suggested that exposure to earlier trauma may sensitise individuals to the development of trauma symptoms as a consequence of their offending (Payne, Watt, Rogers & McMurran, 2008).

Imprisonment trauma

The experience of imprisonment can exponentially expose individuals to further trauma and increase the risk of developing or exacerbating trauma related symptoms or difficulties (Rennie & Crewe, 2023; Liem & Kunst, 2013). Research and examples of lived experiences have posited that the experience of being held in custody can be traumatic in itself (DeVeaux, 2013; Andersen et al., 2015), impacting on aspects of psychological and physical functioning. When considering the basic physical structure of the environment, various aural and aesthetic cues such as bars on the windows, long corridors and metal staircases can lead to the triggering of symptoms associated with anxiety or PTSD (Jewkes, Jordan, Wright & Bendelow, 2019). Levels of self-control and attentional performance have also been shown to be negatively impacted after only three months of imprisonment (Meijers, Harte, Meynen, Cuijpers & Scherder, 2018). Feeling trapped, feelings of loss, changes in identity and dehumanisation, characteristic of incarceration, have been further identified as adversely impacting on prisoners' well-being (Kelman, Gribble, Harvey, Palmer & MacManus, 2022). The traumatic experience of imprisonment can result in some people using maladaptive strategies to cope; evidenced in the high rates of violence, suicide and self-harm in custody (Ministry of Justice, 2022).

In addition to imprisonment being traumatic in itself, it is useful to acknowledge the re-traumatising effect of imprisonment on those who have experienced early life trauma. Prisoners' experiences of procedural justice, in particular how consistently rules are applied and the legitimacy of decisions, can affect the levels of tension and stress within the environment (McGuire, 2018). Uncertainty around policy and procedure and perceptions of unfair practice (Kelman et al., 2022) can further impact this. This can be re-traumatising, and can mirror actual, or perceived injustice from early childhood trauma. Childhood trauma-related deficits, such as limited emotional regulation, reduced impulse control and problem-solving skills are likely to lower an individual's ability to acclimatise to elements of the prison environment (Skarupski, Parisi, Thorpe, Tanner & Gross, 2016), including strict regimes, loss of control and privacy, disconnection from others and relational instability and unrest (Ford, Bellis, Hughes, Barton & Newbury, 2020), and potentially trigger re-traumatisation (Crisanti & Frueh, 2011; Krammer, Eisenbarth, Hügli, Liebrenz & Kuwert, 2018). Re-traumatisation can also develop as a result of living with the perpetual threat of physical, sexual and psychological harm (direct or witnessing), through increased proximity to other traumatised individuals who present a high risk of serious harm to others.

Long term imprisonment can result in adaptation of attitudes, thoughts, feelings and behaviours such as emotional detachment and physical and relational isolation, to survive the micro-climate of prison (Hulley, Crewe & Wright, 2016). Liem & Kunst (2013) identified various adverse effects of imprisonment including hypervigilance, withdrawal, suppression of emotions and an overall sense of distrust of the world. Individuals can develop a sense of helplessness, with impairments demonstrated in their decision-making abilities (Schill & Marcus, 1998). These methods of coping are often adaptive within the hostile context of custody, essentially maintaining survival and adapting to institutional life, but can be damaging for successful reintegration into the community, particularly after long-term imprisonment (Grounds, 2005; Haney, 2003).

Trauma of release

Release from prison into the community involves (1), re-entry, the act of leaving one place for another but also (2) reintegration into the community, a longer process which can take months or years to achieve (Munn, 2011). Individuals can experience a range of difficulties that can make the transition from prison to the community a potentially traumatising, and/or re-traumatising experience. This is particularly relevant when the realities of prison life are in stark contrast to the norms of community life. For example, those who have been imprisoned for a lengthy period re-enter a world where their skills have been lost, or are obsolete due to society's evolution. Consequently, they lack the ability or confidence to navigate everyday living tasks. Secondly, they face the challenges of life in the community with a conviction for a serious offence, not only practically in terms of accessing housing and employment, but emotionally and socially, in initiating, building and managing social relationships and acceptance by the community. Thirdly, acclimatisation to prison life can result in sensory overload when faced with the hustle and bustle of community life. There is often the assumption that release from prison is a good experience, however given the difficulties above, it is no wonder that some individuals experience getting out as equally painful to being in (Warr, 2016).

Post-release trauma

Whilst there is a risk of assuming that repeated imprisonment and release would acclimatise individuals to the release process, each release is likely to be a new experience (Bliss, 2015). Whilst Approved Premises (APs[1]) can provide a useful halfway stage between prison and independent living, they can also perpetuate the challenges of resettling, with social reintegration immobilised (Maier, 2021). Additionally, there are anecdotal themes around APs replicating prison life, or replicating childhood experiences of being housed in institutions. More broadly, the men we work with have experienced numerous additional traumas on release including physical and sexual assaults, discrimination and bullying in a range of community settings. Finally, living in the community under an indeterminate sentence (life sentences[2] and Indeterminate sentences for Public Protection, or IPPs[3]), can feel burdensome and without hope (Edgar, Harris & Webster, 2020; Shingler, Sonnenberg & Needs, 2020). Tom felt that, no matter whether he complied or not with his licence, being on an IPP sentence meant he would "never be allowed to move forward". People serving indeterminate sentences can be subject to supervision by the probation service for the rest of their lives, and consequently, are vulnerable to recall for the rest of their lives (see Chapter 3). This can create feelings of powerlessness, uncertainty and an absence of safety and security, mirroring childhood trauma experiences. Adam described being on an IPP licence in the community as "like having a noose around my neck". He felt as if his freedom was at risk anytime he was near anyone, so he isolated himself, physically and relationally in order to keep himself safe.

Problematic coping responses on release

As summarised above, the transition from prison to community can be challenging and potentially re-traumatising. In this section we discuss some common problematic ways in which people respond to the prison-community transition. We highlight the importance of viewing these responses through a trauma lens, in order to formulate the functions of the behaviour. We also discuss how conversations can be framed and navigated in order to validate the origins and maintenance of these responses across the lifespan. Without considering the functions of the responses through a trauma-lens, there is a risk of perpetuating cycles of shame and therefore reducing open dialogue. This in turn can lead to further withdrawal from services, resistance to professional input and consequently ineffective risk management plans.

Prison strips individuals of choice, autonomy and as a result, a sense of competence (Haggerty & Bucerius, 2020; Warr 2020). It often inadvertently removes individuals' sense of responsibility to help themselves, to manage their own lives and to develop purpose and meaning. However, prison is conflicting: whilst often traumatising, over time it can become a familiar container, particularly to people who have historically led chaotic and unstable lives. This may be because the regime provides a predictable and consistent structure to life. It also removes the individual from the outside world and the responsibilities that come with being an adult (including taking care of yourself, managing finances, navigating relationships and being dependable and supporting others). When released into the community, this containment immediately disappears. Individuals are faced with the prospect of navigating a new system. Whilst on some level appealing having been restricted for so long, the lack of containment that prison provides both physically and relationally (in the sense of clear roles rather than more nuanced relationships) is overwhelming. The men we work with often have longstanding and embedded unhelpful coping strategies for managing distress. Therefore, it is unsurprising they turn to old familiar methods to cope with the significant change and trepidation that accompanies release.

Substance misuse

There is a well-established link between childhood trauma and vulnerability to developing substance misuse difficulties (Moustafa et al., 2018; Maté, 2012). The draw to substances is particularly heightened during the early days of release from prison, when individuals can feel overwhelmed by both the sudden change in the physical environment and the complex interplay of emotions including excitement, fear and responsibility that come with having a level of increased freedom and choice within the limits of the licence conditions. The men we work with can be quick to seek comfort and familiarity in substances to relieve or escape negative emotional states triggered by release, and the expectations and challenges that come with it (see Chapter 6). This pattern can trigger hopelessness in both individuals and professionals, a sense of "here we go again". This narrative about relapse can interfere with exploration of the functions, and cost benefits of taking substances for that individual at that point in time. That is, there needs to be a greater understanding of substance misuse as a mechanism for managing thoughts and feelings, trauma triggers and subsequent emotional pain rather than a desire to get high. Tom recently told us exactly this: "I don't like doing drugs...I don't like who I become when I do them". He reported hating how it became more and more obvious he was an "addict" (e.g., his gaunt and "spaced-out" appearance) and how every day was exhausting trying to mask his addiction to professionals and hold in mind conversations in order to present as stable. Peter described drinking not to get drunk but to cope with the feelings of being "completely unskilled in [community] life". This progressed to alcohol dependency which then resulted in him drinking to manage the overt side effects of alcohol withdrawal which he saw as stigmatising him further as someone who could not cope with life.

Judgment and hopelessness from professionals about men returning to substances in the community often increases if people have been drug-free in prison, or stabilised on prescribed synthetic opioids. In situations such as this it is essential to understand the vast difference between these two settings, and the increased triggers, expectations and responsibilities that come with release. During his last recall to prison, Leo explained that although he felt positive about being released, as soon as he was in the community, his body "still felt inside [prison]". He felt anxious, restless, confused and disconnected. He had been released and recalled several times on an indeterminate sentence, and each recall was linked to a rapid relapse into illicit drug use, which in turn was directly related to his risk of causing serious harm. He spoke of being overwhelmed by appointments but felt infantilised by professionals' offers of support. He felt ashamed when he was unable to manage everyday tasks (e.g.

applying for benefits). Heroin and crack cocaine gave him an escape from feeling physically and mentally overloaded in the present day, but also dampened flashbacks from significant childhood and adulthood trauma.

Self-harm

Research suggests individuals can engage in self-harm for multiple reasons, including to reduce negative affect; to counter numbness or dissociation; to self-punish; or to communicate emotional distress (Gratz, 2003; Horne & Csipke 2009; Klonsky, 2007; Klonsky & Glenn, 2009). It is unsurprising, then, that men within the CJS, a population who more often than not have experienced significant ACEs, are at increased risk of self-harm. Ford et al. (2020) found that male prisoners who had experienced four or more ACEs were 15 times more likely to report lifetime self-harm. Prisoners serving indeterminate sentences have been shown to have increased anxiety and self-harm behaviours (Howard League for Penal Reform, 2007, 2013). Whilst data suggests women engage more frequently in self-harm, self-harm in men tends to result in greater severity of injuries and carry greater risk of lethal consequences (Ministry of Justice, 2022), even more so in IPP sentenced prisoners who have been recalled or who remain in custody post-tariff (House of Commons Justice Committee, 2019).

We have worked with men who have used self-harm to cope with activation of past trauma memories and present triggers. Al described how small things (a comment, a look, a sound) would trigger memories of abuse he experienced as a child. This felt unbearable and from a young age, Al turned to self-harm in order to feel in control; to distract him from his traumatic memories; and to provide a release from emotional pain. Anecdotally, we have seen how self-harm can increase during periods of stress and transition points within the criminal justice pathway (e.g., leading up to parole hearings; following a successful parole hearing but awaiting release; on release from prison; integrating into an AP; being recalled; see Padfield, 2013).

For men who use both substances and self-harm as a means of coping with distress, we have found the CJS can inadvertently create a dynamic where individuals favour self-harming due to the perception of fewer harmful consequences. Tom described how cutting himself felt like the "safer option out of the two": using substances would breach a licence condition, but self-harming would not. To Tom, it created an unspoken narrative that professionals were ok with him self-harming but not with him using substances, perpetuating his sense of being unworthy/defective and of professionals not caring about his welfare. Tom reported self-harming from nine years old and self-harm was the first thing he turned to when he experienced any difficulty. He described being trapped in a cycle when things became too overwhelming for him: "either because [self-harm] worked straight away and helped block things out, or it didn't and so then I would keep trying until it did". Additionally, he reported professionals tended to be warmer and more understanding about the functions of self-harm when compared to his substance misuse. Consequently, the system appeared to inadvertently reinforce self-harm as a coping strategy.

Deception

Hughes and Golding (2012) coined "the shield of shame" to highlight four methods in which children with trauma histories attempt to protect themselves from connecting with feelings of shame: (1) lying/deception, "I didn't do it"; (2) blaming others, "It was him"; (3) minimising, "It wasn't that bad"; and (4) rage "You always blame me". These protection strategies develop as a result of a child experiencing toxic stress and shame. When caregivers lack attunement and fail to repair ruptures in the adult–child relationship, the child is left with strong negative feelings without a narrative, leading to the internalisation of a global sense of inadequacy or being fundamentally bad. If this happens regularly, the child's sense of shame strengthens, as do strategies to avoid feeling it. The strategies above work to fight against shame. Deflecting attention away gives the child a sense of control over the situation, which counters and creates a barrier, to connecting with painful thoughts and feelings of being bad. Without therapeutic thinking and support, children who develop these strategies in early life take them in into adulthood.

Deception can elicit frustration in professionals and a feeling of personal attack. As professionals, we do not like to be deceived, particularly by people in whom we have invested time and connection. There can be a tendency to assume that deception is done with malicious intent, however it can serve multiple functions. It is easy to get caught up in an emotional response to being deceived. For example, if we are consumed by a sense of betrayal, or if we feel foolish for believing a person, we can fail to pay sufficient attention to the function of the deception. Exploring what need the individual was meeting by engaging in deception is key, not only to support the individual to open up about it and think about other ways they can achieve this need, but also for effective risk management through detailed analysis.

One topic often at the centre of deception is that of disclosing intimate or peer relationships. It is human nature to want to connect with others, as social bonds play an important role in our biological survival (Porges, 2015) and in mediating psychological and physical wellbeing (Uchino, 2004). Porges and Furman (2011) highlight how isolation and disconnection from others, actual or perceived, significantly impacts the nervous system. As such, it is unsurprising that after years of imprisonment and a lack of family ties, some men are intent on connecting to others, either through developing friendships or seeking romantic relationships.

Peter had many labels attributed to him over the years, including "psychopath", "pathological liar", and "predator". After working closely with Peter, it came to light he had some cognitive deficits and he had become good at masking his limited understanding of situations by giving closed answers, using stock phrases (such as "that's a good question") that gave a response but avoided answering, and deflecting through random tangents. Sometimes he would inadvertently lie as a consequence of not understanding questions. Other times the lie would be more deliberate, aimed at telling professionals what he thought they wanted to hear, to avoid conflict or punishment. Peter's childhood consisted of experiencing and witnessing severe physical, sexual and emotional abuse within the family home; hiding the truth and telling his parents what they wanted to hear was necessary for survival. As an adult, Peter wanted to connect with other people and make friends, often choosing people who were already vulnerable by virtue of their own needs and experiences and who were often ostracised from society. He would attempt to connect with such people quickly after release from prison. Peter had a historical serious violent offence, which increased anxiety amongst professionals about who he was associating with and the extent to which he presented a risk to them. Following release from prison, Peter was repeatedly told not to interact with adults who were classed as vulnerable, yet these were the individuals he felt most comfortable around. This led to Peter deceiving professionals about his whereabouts, even though he was subject to GPS monitoring[4] and his movements could be reviewed. When challenged about the deception, he would admit interacting with these individuals without any defensiveness. When asked why he had not been honest, he did not have an answer, he appeared frozen. The label of pathological liar lacked an understanding of the functions of the deception for Peter. Specifically, these functions included not understanding everything that was required of him as a result of his cognitive deficits; being desperate to feel connected to people with whom he felt comfortable; being terrified of ruptures in professional relationships (being reprimanded and having professionals be angry or disappointed with him); and being recalled back to prison. Consequently, Peter utilised a longstanding coping strategy of telling people what they wanted to hear, even if it did not make sense or led to more problems longer term.

O'Connell (2018) highlights trust and power as central factors influencing decisions to deceive in individuals who are traumatised: Can I trust you? Will you judge me? Can you hurt me? Will you use this information against me? These fears are entirely legitimate for the men we work with. In our roles as CJS professionals, we hold the power, so it is a legitimate concern for men to consider whether sharing information with us will have negative consequences for them. Individuals may also have experienced severe negative consequences throughout their lives just for being themselves, as children, adults and throughout the CJS. This in itself can drive the desire to deceive, as it creates an illusion of safety, even if just temporary, which is then reinforced. O'Connell (2018) reflects that individuals with a strong tendency to deceive are often aware they are lying; that it is not an effective strategy in the long run; and that it causes harm to themselves and other people. Tom recently spoke about how deception "feels like a poison eating away at you … especially when you are doing it to someone you care about, or someone you know cares about you". The person can hold these factors in mind, but still deceive when under threat.

Dismissiveness and disconnection

Many of the men we work with have a radar for threat, and are constantly assessing the physical and relational environment in order to maintain a sense of safety and control. They rely on keeping everyone at arm's length in order to feel safe, and as such their social engagement system (Porges, 1995, and see above) is chronically offline. This is a particularly valid and necessary coping response to survive prison. Warr (2016) describes the intensity of everyday life in prison: "every interaction, conversation, bodily movement, glance, laugh, smile, and even yawn must be monitored by the individual to ensure it is not causing offence, being taken out of context or rendering the prisoner vulnerable in the eyes of peers" (p. 590). This recognises the hostility of prison and the need to remain guarded and wary (see Shingler et al., 2020). In addition, there are consequences to being viewed in a negative light by prison staff, and this can add to a sense of scrutiny and threat. Prison is not an environment that easily allows for testing out safety in working professional relationships. Therefore, it is unrealistic to expect this survival strategy to disappear on release from prison.

Some of the men we work with enact keeping people at arm's length through a dismissive, critical or belittling manner, aimed at peers and professionals. Some individuals can be quick to blame professionals when they encounter inevitable barriers in resettlement or make understandable and common mistakes rather than considering their role in the dynamic. Like deception, blaming or dismissing other people is a coping response for managing chronic shame (Hughes & Golding, 2012), and from experience is a strategy that tends to appear when people are directly or indirectly challenged or asked to account for their behaviour. This tends to be a frequent dynamic during the initial prison-community release when the individual technically has more freedom, but alongside it, more overt scrutiny from professionals and more explicit conditions to abide by. On release, Adam frequently behaved in a dismissive and critical way towards residential support staff in the AP when they asked him to comply with hostel rules such as paying rent. He tolerated the same requests from his key worker and the AP manager, but voiced to professionals outside of the hostel that he felt "got at" every time he returned to the hostel. This was understandably difficult to navigate as professionals; it felt personal, rude and hostile. However, it was important to consider the function of this behaviour. As a child, Adam always felt different to his siblings, and ostracised by his father. He was viewed as the problem child within his family and received constant criticism and punishment and little nurture. This left him with the internalised view of himself as unlovable and defective, resulting in chronic feelings of shame. He became acutely sensitive to any perceived disrespect or criticism directed towards him, and found relief and power in criticising or dismissing others. Whilst on the surface Adam appeared to think very highly of himself and look down on others, the reality was the exact opposite; he disliked himself immensely. He struggled to understand why he interacted in this manner and wanted to build positive working relationships with professionals, but did not know how.

Trauma–informed formulation of resettlement difficulties

Working successfully with traumatised men in the CJS requires recognising the layers of trauma individuals have experienced across their lifespan, and formulating problematic and risk-related behaviours as coping strategies. This approach does not diminish the detrimental effects of these behaviours on others, or minimise the risk, but it does validate the function of these behaviours as attempts to meet core human needs (e.g. seeking safety, connection, support). Validation (acknowledging, see Linehan, 1993) can often serve as the first step to disarming shame. As discussed above, shame can trigger forms of defensiveness and exacerbate unhelpful coping strategies, hindering effective working relationships and progress. Validating behaviours as coping strategies can invite men to explore and understand, rather than avoid and minimise. Some men want to focus on understanding current patterns and triggers that keep them reliant on the coping strategy. Other men want to understand the current patterns and track these to the origins for a more in-depth understanding. Both are about exploring the functions of the strategy and looking at it through a trauma-informed lens. Next, we go on to discuss approaches that can be taken to validate, explore and help people to understand the origins and functions of their problematic coping strategies in order to begin to think about how to get their needs met in prosocial and healthy ways. As highlighted at the start, this chapter is written for a wide audience and therefore the following approaches are relevant to all CJS professionals, regardless of professional orientation or role, and can be utilised to formulate and engage individuals in a trauma-informed way in order to effectively manage risk of serious harm.

Explore current and historical use of the unhelpful strategy

First, consider inviting discussion about current situations in which the individual has used the coping strategy. Keep a neutral and curious stance, as offering judgment or correction is unlikely to create a dialogue of exploration. The aim is to try and develop awareness of the coping strategy as just that: a pattern of responding to specific situations. The aim is also to begin to identify key triggers (internal or external) that drive the coping strategy.

When trying to establish the function of the strategy, let go of assumptions or previous theories and explore it together with the individual. If the individual is open to it, explore the origins of the strategy. Take a curious stance and utilise questions such as: When did this coping strategy first appear in your life? Who was around, what was happening? Was it something you learned from adults? What happened when you used the strategy (e.g. what were the relational, emotional, and physical consequences?) This can help to develop understanding that at its origin, the strategy had value, that it served a purpose and acted to keep a person safe or reduce emotional distress. This can help people to develop self-compassion and understanding that as vulnerable children they did what they had to do to survive.

Explore costs and benefits of the unhelpful strategy

Exploring the costs and benefits of the coping strategy in the here and now can help to uncover the current consequences. What does the person gain from using the strategy? What would they lose if they gave it up? As criminal justice professionals, we are often so focused on the costs of problematic behaviour that we fail to see what the person gains from it. We have found this approach to be validating and enlightening for people, to have the benefits of problematic behaviour discussed openly and with support. Often this naturally allows the individual to move on to the costs to themselves and others, likely because they feel understood and therefore do not feel that they have to defend their continued use of the strategy. It can open discussions about choice and change. Jake used to find substances took him to a place of oblivion; it allowed him to disconnect from the constant fear and anxiety of being around people. We spoke about how this was an understandable method of trying to cope with the trauma he experienced, but did not understand, as a child. However, after waking up from a stress-related lapse into drug and alcohol use, he concluded: "this isn't working for me anymore". For the first time in his life, the negatives outweighed the positives, in that continued substance misuse would likely lead to the loss of his voluntary work, which gave him a strong sense of purpose and social connectedness.

Consider the wider context

It is important to recognise and discuss the systemic and legal context impacting the decision to use the coping strategy. For example, an individual may keep using drugs because they feel stuck and hopeless about being on an IPP sentence. Try and look at any problematic behaviour within the individual's own historical, custodial and interpersonal context. Avoid the fundamental attribution error (Jones & Nisbett, 1971) of locating all the deviance within the individual and their psychology. Look at their developmental and criminal justice experiences and see what they can tell you about the function, purpose and development of the strategy. As noted above, this is not to minimise personal accountability for a potentially harmful behaviour, but to understand that any human behaviour has a valid function, and this is about uncovering that.

Normalise the challenges of change

Individuals can talk rationally about the unhelpfulness of a coping strategy and know that it no longer serves them in the way it used to and yet still be emotionally drawn to using it during times of stress and uncertainty. It is imperative to normalise this; to communicate that everyone at some stage returns to old familiar patterns and habits when under emotional stress. Understanding this, and naming it is key, as both the individual and professionals can get stuck in a cycle of frustration in the early days of release from prison, where the individual talks convincingly about wanting to change the way they cope and then appears to do the absolute opposite. This process is normal: it highlights the stages between recognising something as a problem, setting an intention and then being able to take and maintain a different action (e.g., Prochaska, Norcross & DiClimente, 2013). At times like this, when the unhelpfulness of a behaviour has been recognised, but its pull remains strong, people can need a "cheerleader" (Linehan, 1993) to hold hope for them, to encourage them to draw on their inner strength, utilise safe coping skills and to reinforce the elements of the desisting identity that may be emerging.

Promote self-compassion

Promoting self-compassion (Neff, 2003; Gilbert & Procter, 2006) about an individual's own experience of trauma is important, but often overlooked in criminal justice settings for fear of being seen as an apologist for offending behaviour. There can seem to be a dichotomy between "victim" and "perpetrator", in which once someone has committed a serious offence (especially one that has physically or emotionally harmed others) they are no longer entitled to be a "victim" themselves. This is quite obviously nonsensical. As noted above, many people in prison have experienced significant childhood and later-life trauma that has played a pivotal role in their perpetration of serious harm towards others. Neff (2003) describes self-compassion as having three components; self-kindness, common humanity, and mindfulness. It may have a role to play in reducing crime and violent behaviour, through increased mindful awareness and self-regulation, which helps with emotional recognition and management and reducing impulsivity (Morley, 2015; Morley, Jantz & Fulton, 2019). Similarly, Woldgabreal, Day and Ward (2014) highlight the value in promoting positive psychology concepts, such as psychological flexibility, self-efficacy and self-compassion in probation supervision to increase engagement, compliance and prosocial choices. Therefore, our aim is to enable people to develop a trauma-informed dialogue towards themselves. People need to understand their unhelpful coping approaches are learned behaviours that developed in order to enable them to survive in the midst of chronic and enduring trauma. Enabling self-compassion for the traumatised child within can help to reduce shame and consequently reduce reliance on unhelpful and risky coping strategies which can lead to offending behaviours. It can help to contextualise the individual's past, present, and future: recognising who they are is not set in stone; they can evolve, develop new coping strategies and build a life worth living. Self-compassion also invites a kinder dialogue when individuals inevitably gravitate towards old coping strategies during times of stress, which can make it easier to acknowledge and step out of, than harsh criticism which creates a perpetual cycle of shame.

Promote opportunities for social engagement

Finally, it is important for CJS professionals to hold in mind that countering reliance on unhelpful coping strategies such as those discussed above, requires not only a focus on developing awareness (understanding origins and triggers) and skillset (positive emotional coping, assertiveness, everyday living) but also opportunities for positive and healthy social engagement leading to connection, purpose and meaning. This is essential given trauma leads to disempowerment and disconnection (Herman, 1992). Research highlights that social connectedness can have a direct impact on reducing serious sexual and violent offending (Stuart & Taylor, 2021). Hari (2019) similarly notes that "the opposite of addiction is connection" (p. 299). However, relationships and connectedness are often directly linked to someone's risk of harm (for example, when people have offended within the context of an intimate relationship). Treading the balance, between facilitating and supporting social and relational connections and managing risk of harm, is very challenging for professionals. Reflective supervision and discussion with colleagues can be pivotal in supporting us as professionals to manage this balance, recognising the benefits of connectedness alongside managing risk of harm to others.

Conclusion

This chapter highlights the prevalence of chronic trauma amongst men being released from prison. Whilst recognised in the literature, the complexity and endurance of trauma across the lifespan is often underestimated. This chapter briefly touches on the importance of recognising the biological and relational consequences of early and repeated trauma. That is, the men we work with have often developed strong primitive coping responses (e.g. fight, flight, freeze) in order to survive, rather than more neurologically advanced coping responses (e.g. safety through connection and engagement). Consequently, they have lacked the opportunities and the safety to develop and practice higher order cognitive processes and coping. This results in difficulties in safely understanding and managing emotions, relating to self and others and tempering impulsivity and other problematic behaviours. This chapter emphasises the importance of recognising the layers of trauma men in the CJS have experienced, and how each subsequent trauma compounds the former resulting in significant and enduring problematic patterns of coping. From this we highlight the importance of viewing common problematic responses during the prison-community transition through a trauma lens, with a focus on substance use, self-harm, deception, disconnection and dismissiveness. Formulating the functions and longstanding and reinforcing nature of these responses in a psychological way is key to creating a dialogue that encourages people to reflect on and recognise the origins of these responses. It also enables people to understand that these understandable but risky attempts to cope create another barrier to successful resettlement. Stepping away from old coping responses is a difficult and non-linear process. Adjustment to a new environment, such as during the prison-community release is likely to be emotionally, psychologically and practically overwhelming and therefore it is to be expected that men may gravitate to old and familiar coping responses to try and regain a sense of equilibrium. This is not to say professionals need to be accepting or lenient of these responses if they directly link to risk, but rather to be realistic and open to having conversations about the function and validity of these responses, even if problematic, in order to motivate and support a different path.

Notes

1 An Approved Premises or "AP" is a multi-occupancy hostel, run by the probation service.
2 https://www.sentencingcouncil.org.uk/sentencing-and-the-council/types-of-sentence/ life-sentences/
3 https://www.gov.uk/government/publications/police-crime-sentencing-and-courts-bill-2021-factsheets/police-crime-sentencing-and-courts-act-2022-imprisonment-for-public-protection-factsheet
4 See https://www.justiceinspectorates.gov.uk/hmiprobation/wp-content/uploads/ sites/5/2022/01/Electronic-monitoring-thematic-inspection.pdf for details of how GPS tagging is used in probation supervision.

References

Andersen, H. S., Sestoft, D., Lillebæk, T., Gabrielsen, G., Hemmingsen, R., & Kramp, P. (2000). A longitudinal study of prisoners on remand: psychiatric prevalence, incidence and psychopathology in solitary vs. non-solitary confinement. *Acta Psychiatrica Scandinavica*, 102(1), 19–25.

Billingham, L., & Irwin-Rogers, K. (2021). The terrifying abyss of insignificance: Marginalisation, mattering and violence between young people. *Oñati Socio-Legal Series*, 11(5), 1222–1249.

Bliss, J. (2015). Prison, re-entry, reintegration and the 'Star Gate': The experience of prison release. *Journal of Prisoners on Prisons*, 24(2), 23–34.

Bowlby, J. (1969). Attachment and loss: Volume I: Attachment, vol. 79. *The International Psycho-Analytical Library*, 1–401.

Bowen, K., Jarrett, M., Stahl, D., Forrester, A., & Valmaggia, L. (2018). The relationship between exposure to adverse life events in childhood and adolescent years and subsequent adult psychopathology in 49,163 adult prisoners: A systematic review. *Personality and Individual Differences*, 131, 74–92.

Bremner, J. D. (2006). The relationship between cognitive and brain changes in post-traumatic stress disorder. *Annals of the New York Academy of Sciences*, 1071(1), 80–86.

Cantürk, M., Faraji, H., & Tezcan, A. E. (2021). The relationship between childhood traumas and crime in male prisoners. *Alpha Psychiatry*, 22(1).

Contractor, A. A., Weiss, N. H., Dranger, P., Ruggero, C., & Armour, C. (2017). PTSD's risky behavior criterion: Relation with DSM-5 PTSD symptom clusters and psychopathology. *Psychiatry Research*, 252, 215–222.

Cook, A., Blaustein, M., Spinazzola, J., & van der Kolk, B. (2003). Complex trauma in children and adolescents: White paper from the national child traumatic stress network complex trauma task force. *Los Angeles: National Center for Child Traumatic Stress*, 35(5), 1–41.

Cook, A., Spinazzola, J., Ford, J., Lanktree, C., Blaustein, M., Cloitre, M., & Van der Kolk, B. (2005). Complex trauma. *Psychiatric Annals*, 35(5), 390–398.

Crisanti, A. S., & Frueh, B. C. (2011). Risk of trauma exposure among persons with mental illness in jails and prisons: what do we really know? *Current Opinion in Psychiatry*, 24(5), 431–435.

Crisford, H., Dare, H., & Evangeli, M. (2008). Offence-related posttraumatic stress disorder (PTSD) symptomatology and guilt in mentally disordered violent and sexual offenders. *The Journal of Forensic Psychiatry & Psychology*, 19(1), 86–107.

DeVeaux, M. (2013). The trauma of the incarceration experience. *Harvard Rights-Civil Liberties Law Review*, 48, 257–277.

Edgar, K., Harris, M., & Webster, R. (2020). *No life, no freedom, no future: The experiences of prisoners recalled under the sentence of imprisonment under public protection*. London: Prison Reform Trust.

Facer-Irwin, E., Blackwood, N. J., Bird, A., Dickson, H., McGlade, D., Alves-Costa, F., & MacManus, D. (2019). PTSD in prison settings: A systematic review and meta-analysis of comorbid mental disorders and problematic behaviours. *PLoS one*, 14(9). Retrieved from Retrieved from https://journals.plos.org/plosone/article?id=10.1371/journal.pone.0222407.

Facer-Irwin, E., Karatzias, T., Bird, A., Blackwood, N., & MacManus, D. (2022). PTSD and complex PTSD in sentenced male prisoners in the UK: Prevalence, trauma antecedents, and psychiatric comorbidities. *Psychological Medicine*, 52(13), 2794–2804.

Ford, K., Barton, E., Newbury, A., Hughes, K., Bezeczky, Z., Roderick, J., & Bellis, M. (2019). *Understanding the prevalence of adverse childhood experiences (ACEs) in a male offender population in Wales: The Prisoner ACE Survey*. Public Health Wales; Bangor University.

Ford, K., Bellis, M. A., Hughes, K., Barton, E. R., & Newbury, A. (2020). Adverse childhood experiences: a retrospective study to understand their associations with lifetime mental health diagnosis, self-harm or suicide attempt, and current low mental wellbeing in a male Welsh prison population. *Health & Justice*, 8(1), 1–13.

Franke, H. A. (2014). Toxic stress: effects, prevention and treatment. *Children*, 1(3), 390–402.

Gilbert, P., & Procter, S. (2006). Compassionate mind training for people with high shame and self-criticism: Overview and pilot study of a group therapy approach. *Clinical Psychology & Psychotherapy: An International Journal of Theory & Practice*, 13(6), 353–379.

Gilligan, J. (1997). *Violence, reflections on a national epidemic. 191.* New York: Vintage-Random House.

Gratz, K. L. (2003). Risk factors for and functions of deliberate self-harm: An empirical and conceptual review. *Clinical Psychology: Science and Practice*, 10(2), 192.

Grounds, A. T. (2005). Understanding the effects of wrongful imprisonment. *Crime and Justice*, 32, 1–58.

Haggerty, K. D., & Bucerius, S. (2020). The proliferating pains of imprisonment. *Incarceration*, 1(1).

Haney, C. (2003). *The psychological impact of incarceration: Implications for post-prison adjustment*. Paper presented at the US Department of Health and Human Services Conference, "From home to prison The effect of incarceration and reentry on children, families and communities". Bethesda, MD.

Hari, J. (2019). *Chasing the scream: The search for the truth about addiction.* London: Bloomsbury.

Herman, J. L. (1992). *Trauma and recovery.* New York: Basic Books.

Honorato, B., Caltabiano, N., & Clough, A. R. (2016). From trauma to incarceration: Exploring the trajectory in a qualitative study in male prison inmates from north Queensland, Australia. *Health & Justice,* 4(1), 1–10.

Horne, O., & Csipke, E. (2009). From feeling too little and too much, to feeling more and less? A nonparadoxical theory of the functions of self-harm. *Qualitative Health Research,* 19(5), 655–667.

House of Commons Justice Committee (2019). Prison population 2022: planning for the future (Sixteenth Report of Session 2017–2019). Retrieved from https://publica tions.parliament.uk/pa/cm201719/cmselect/cmjust/483/483.pdf.

Howard League for Penal Reform (2007). Indeterminate Sentences for Public Protection: Prison Information Bulletin 3. Retrieved from https://howardleague.org/wp content/uploads/2016/05/IPP-report.pdf.

Howard League for Penal Reform (2013). The Never Ending Story: Indeterminate Sentencing and the Prison Regime. Research Briefing. Retrieved from https://howa rdleague.org/wp-content/uploads/2016/05/never-ending-story-IPP.pdf.

Hughes, D., & Golding, K. S. (2012). *Creating loving attachments: Parenting with PACE to nurture confidence and security in the troubled child.* London: Jessica Kingsley Publishers.

Hulley, S., Crewe, B., & Wright, S. (2016). Re-examining the problems of long-term imprisonment. *British Journal of Criminology,* 56(4), 769–792.

Jewkes, Y., Jordan, M., Wright, S., & Bendelow, G. (2019). Designing 'healthy' prisons for women: Incorporating trauma-informed care and practice (TICP) into prison planning and design. *International Journal of Environmental Research and Public Health,* 16(20), 3818.

Jones, E. E., & Nisbett, R. E. (1971). *The actor and the observer: Divergent perceptions of the causes of behavior.* Morristown, N.J.: General Learning Press.

Kelman, J., Gribble, R., Harvey, J., Palmer, L., & MacManus, D. (2022). How does a history of trauma affect the experience of imprisonment for individuals in women's prisons: A qualitative exploration. *Women & Criminal Justice,* 1–21.

Klonsky, E. D. (2007). The functions of deliberate self-injury: A review of the evidence. *Clinical Psychology Review,* 27(2), 226–239.

Klonsky, E. D., & Glenn, C. R. (2009). Assessing the functions of non-suicidal self-injury: Psychometric properties of the Inventory of Statements About Self-injury (ISAS). *Journal of Psychopathology and Behavioral Assessment,* 31(3), 215–219.

Krammer, S., Eisenbarth, H., Hügli, D., Liebrenz, M., & Kuwert, P. (2018). The relationship between childhood traumatic events, social support, and mental health problems in prisoners. *The Journal of Forensic Psychiatry & Psychology,* 29(1), 72–85.

Linehan, M. M. (1993). *Cognitive-behavioural treatment of borderline personality disorder.* New York: The Guilford Press.

Liem, M., & Kunst, M. (2013). Is there a recognizable post-incarceration syndrome among released "lifers"? *International Journal of Law and Psychiatry,* 36(3–4),333–337.

Liu, H., Li, T. W., Liang, L., & Hou, W. K. (2021). Trauma exposure and mental health of prisoners and ex-prisoners: A systematic review and meta-analysis. *Clinical Psychology Review,* 89, 102069.

Maier, K. (2021). 'Mobilizing' prisoner reentry research: Halfway houses and the spatial-temporal dynamics of prison release. *Theoretical Criminology,* 25(4), 601–618.

Maté, G. (2012). Addiction: Childhood trauma, stress and the biology of addiction. *Journal of Restorative Medicine,* 1(1), 56–63.

McCartan, K. F. (2020). *Trauma-informed practice* (Academic Insights 2020/05). London: HM Inspectorate of Probation.

Meijers, J., Harte, J. M., Meynen, G., Cuijpers, P., & Scherder, E. J. (2018). Reduced self-control after 3 months of imprisonment; a pilot study. *Frontiers in Psychology*, 9, 69. Retrieved from https://www.frontiersin.org/articles/10.3389/fpsyg.2018.00069/full.

McGuire, J. (2018). *Understanding prison violence: A rapid evidence assessment.* Analytic Summary 2018. London: HM Prison and Probation Service.

Ministry of Justice, National Statistics (2022). *Safety in custody statistics, England and Wales: Deaths in prison custody to September 2022, assaults and self-harm to June 2022.* Retrieved from Safety in Custody Statistics, England and Wales: Deaths in Prison Custody to September 2022 Assaults and Self-harm to June 2022 - GOV.UK (www.gov.uk).

Mohamed, S. (2015). Of monsters and men: Perpetrator trauma and mass atrocity. *Columbia Law Review*, 115(5), 1157–1216.

Morley, R. H. (2015). Violent criminality and self-compassion. *Aggression and Violent Behavior*, 24, 226–240.

Morley, R. H., Jantz, P. B. & Fulton, C. L. (2019). The intersection of violence, brain net- works, and mindfulness practices. *Aggression and Violent Behavior*, 46, 165–173.

Moustafa, A. A., Parkes, D., Fitzgerald, L., Underhill, D., Garami, J., Levy-Gigi, E…, & Misiak, B. (2021). The relationship between childhood trauma, early-life stress, and alcohol and drug use, abuse, and addiction: An integrative review. *Current Psychology*, 40(2), 579–584.

Munn, M. (2011). Living in the aftermath: The impact of lengthy incarceration on post-carceral success. *The Howard Journal of Criminal Justice*, 50(3), 233–246.

National Scientific Council on the Developing Child (2011). Building the brain's "Air Traffic Control" system: How early experiences shape the development of executive function: Working paper no. 11. Retrieved from https://developingchild.harvard.edu/wp-content/uploads/2011/05/How-Early-Experiences-Shape-the-Development-of-Executive-Function.pdf.

National Scientific Council on the Developing Child (2014). Excessive stress disrupts the architecture of the developing brain: Working Paper No. 3. Retrieved from https://developingchild.harvard.edu/wp-content/uploads/2005/05/Stress_Disrupts_Architecture_Developing_Brain-1.pdf.

Neff, K. (2003). Self-compassion: An alternative conceptualization of a healthy attitude toward oneself. *Self and Identity*, 2(2), 85–101.

O'Connell, M. (2018, May 4). In Defense of Lying (Web log post). Retrieved from https://www.therefuge-ahealingplace.com/about/blog/defense-of-lying/.

Padfield, N. (2013). Understanding recall 2011. *University of Cambridge Faculty of Law Research Paper* (2).

Papanastassiou, M., Waldron, G., Boyle, J., & Chesterman, L. P. (2004). Post-traumatic stress disorder in mentally ill perpetrators of homicide. *Journal of Forensic Psychiatry & Psychology*, 15(1), 66–75.

Payne, E., Watt, A., Rogers, P., & McMurran, M. (2008). Offence characteristics, trauma histories and post-traumatic stress disorder symptoms in life sentenced prisoners. *The British Journal of Forensic Practice*, 10(1), 17–25.

Perry, B. D., & Pollard, R. (1998). Homeostasis, stress, trauma, and adaptation: A neurodevelopmental view of childhood trauma. *Child and Adolescent Psychiatric Clinics*, 7(1), 33–51.

Pham, T. H., & Willocq, L. (2013). Evaluation of traumatic stress in incarcerated homicide offenders. *Acta Psychiatrica Belgica*, 113(2), 39–46.

Porges, S. W. (1995). Orienting in a defensive world: Mammalian modifications of our evolutionary heritage. A polyvagal theory. *Psychophysiology*, 32(4), 301–318.

Porges, S. W. (2004). Neuroception: A subconscious system for detecting threats and safety. *Zero to Three (J)*, 24(5), 19–24.

Porges, S. W. (2015). Making the world safe for our children: Down-regulating defence and up-regulating social engagement to 'optimise' the human experience. *Children Australia*, 40(2), 114–123.

Porges, S. W., & Furman, S. A. (2011). The early development of the autonomic nervous system provides a neural platform for social behaviour: A polyvagal perspective. *Infant and Child Development*, 20(1), 106–118.

Prochaska, J. O., Norcross, J. C., & DiClemente, C. C. (2013). Applying the stages of change. *Psychotherapy in Australia*, 19(2), 10–15.

Rennie, A., & Crewe, B. (2023). 'Tightness', autonomy and release: The anticipated pains of release and life licencing. *The British Journal of Criminology*, 63(1), 184–200.

Scheeringa, M. S., Zeanah, C. H., Drell, M. J., & Larrieu, J. A. (1995). Two approaches to the diagnosis of posttraumatic stress disorder in infancy and early childhood. *Journal of the American Academy of Child & Adolescent Psychiatry*, 34(2), 191–200.

Schill, R. A., & Marcus, D. K. (1998). Incarceration and learned helplessness. *International Journal of Offender Therapy and Comparative Criminology*, 42(3), 224–232.

Shingler, J., Sonnenberg, S. J., & Needs, A. (2020). Psychologists as 'the quiet ones with the power': Understanding indeterminate sentenced prisoners' experiences of psychological risk assessment in the United Kingdom. *Psychology, Crime & Law*, 26(6), 571–592.

Skarupski, K. A., Parisi, J. M., Thorpe, R., Tanner, E., & Gross, D. (2016). The association of adverse childhood experiences with mid-life depressive symptoms and quality of life among incarcerated males: Exploring multiple mediation. *Aging & Mental Health*, 20(6), 655–666.

Sloan Rainbow, J.A. (2018) *'Male Prisoners' vulnerabilities and the ideal victim concept*, in M. Duggan, (Ed) *Revisiting the 'Ideal Victim': Developments in Critical Victimology* (pp.263–279). Bristol: Policy Press.

Spinazzola, J., Van der Kolk, B., & Ford, J. D. (2018). When nowhere is safe: Interpersonal trauma and attachment adversity as antecedents of posttraumatic stress disorder and developmental trauma disorder. *Journal of Traumatic Stress*, 31(5), 631–642.

Stuart, B. A., & Taylor, E. J. (2021). The effect of social connectedness on crime: Evidence from the great migration. *Review of Economics and Statistics*, 103(1), 18–33.

Uchino, B. N. (2004). *Social support and physical health: Understanding the health consequences of relationships*. New Haven, CT: Yale University Press.

van der Kolk, B. (2005). Developmental trauma disorder: Toward a rational diagnosis of children with complex trauma histories. *Psychiatric Annals*, 35(5), 401–408.

Vaughn-Coaxum, R. A., Wang, Y., Kiely, J., Weisz, J. R., & Dunn, E. C. (2018). Associations between trauma type, timing, and accumulation on current coping behaviors in adolescents: Results from a large, population-based sample. *Journal of Youth and Adolescence*, 47(4), 842–858.

Warr, J. (2016). The prisoner: Inside and out. In B. Crewe, Y. Jewkes & J. Bennett (Eds.) *Handbook on prisons* (pp. 586–604). Abingdon, Oxon: Routledge.

Warr, J. (2020). 'Always gotta be two mans': Lifers, risk, rehabilitation, and narrative labour. *Punishment & Society*, 22(1), 28–47.

Wolff, N., & Shi, J. (2012). Childhood and adult trauma experiences of incarcerated persons and their relationship to adult behavioral health problems and treatment. *International Journal of Environmental Research and Public Health*, 9(5), 1908–1926.

Woldgabreal, Y., Day, A., & Ward, T. (2014). The community-based supervision of offenders from a positive psychology perspective. *Aggression and Violent Behavior*, 19(1), 32–41.

Zarse, E. M., Neff, M. R., Yoder, R., Hulvershorn, L., Chambers, J. E., & Chambers, R. A. (2019). The adverse childhood experiences questionnaire: Two decades of research on childhood trauma as a primary cause of adult mental illness, addiction, and medical diseases. *Cogent Medicine*, 6(1), 1581447.

5 "180 prisoners and the noise ... it hits you, BANG!"

Sensory systems, incarceration and resettlement.

Jennifer Stickney, Christabel Budd and Mark

My journey to prison is still so clear to me. It starts from the court cells...

I sat in what felt like a square box with tiles everywhere all over the ceilings and walls. The smell was so musty, damp, cold and depressing. It was so quiet... left with my thoughts about what I had done and what had just happened to me.

I was quickly moved to the sweat box.[1] It's given the name sweat box for a reason. Six people crammed into a van. We were all in our own boxes [in the van], each box is one square meter small. Only enough room to sit and stand up ... nothing else ... no other movement possible, you can't stretch your legs out or up, nothing just sit or stand. The smell was awful, the smell of sweat, of someone being in the cells all weekend. It stunk. The bus was so noisy, the engine in the back was so loud and the other people in the bus were shouting all the time. All this made me feel so alert, too alert it went into fear.

When I arrived at prison, I was double cuffed. Both my hands handcuffed together and then cuffed to a prison officer. No one told me what was going on, it just happened. Prison is very big, when I arrived I felt very little. I felt unhuman, unworthy. Everything had suddenly been taken away from me, and then my clothing was too. This stripped me of my identity, and I didn't know why. ... Arriving in prison the noise was so loud and industrial, like the noise you hear of constant machines whirling. The smell was distinct, bleach, acid orange. The smell was clean, but you looked around and nothing was actually clean. The walls were dirty, dusty. Where I was sitting down, I looked around to find bogeys stuck to the walls, the smell was clean; the look was dirty, it didn't match. It was horrible.

As soon as I was taken onto the main wing the sound! 180 prisoners and the noise ... it hits you, BANG! Radios, music blasting, prisoners shouting, keys rattling, doors banging and crashing, officers running, alarms blaring.

I was taken to my cell, 6ft by 4ft room with a bunk bed and a toilet at one end. The smell of toilet was everywhere, you couldn't get rid of it.

DOI: 10.4324/9781003308171-7

The cell door was shut behind me! But the noise wasn't, there was no quiet. It was relentless. People shouting out the windows, people pressing alarms all night, people screaming in distress. It was mental. Night-time was quieter than the day, but it was still so noisy. It took a long time to get used to the noise.

The main things that really got to me, and still makes me feel on edge are the noise of keys. They were always jingling; some officers dragged the keys along the bars. It felt like a power trip to remind us that they have the keys, and we didn't.

Mark's account of arriving in prison provides an intensely rich sensory picture. It draws attention to the complexities of the sensory world and the significant impact of sensory experiences on feelings and behaviours. Mark's arrival in prison was traumatic and his overall experience of prison negative, but he found the process of release the hardest adjustment. He attributes this to the sensory experiences in prison having a direct impact on his ability to integrate back into the community, making him feel on edge, vulnerable and exposed in a way he had not experienced in prison.

The senses play a powerful role in the formation and retrieval of memories. They help us to anticipate events, prepare for situations, understand and navigate our environment and get ready to respond. Serres (2008) highlights we are sensory creatures. We sense first, then we feel, then we rationalise, then we understand and only from there can we communicate. We all have sensory needs to assist us in both navigating and feeling part of the world we live in. When there is disruption to the development of the sensory system (which can be caused by neurodevelopmental difficulties and/or traumatic life events), a person can have trouble using their senses to accurately interpret the world around them. Long term imprisonment can also affect the sensory system. When this is combined with childhood trauma and neurodevelopmental difficulties, both of which are overrepresented within the prisoner population (Bellis et al, 2016; Young et al, 2017) experiences can interact and have a severe impact on someone's ability to receive, process, understand and respond to sensory information in the world around them. This causes significant difficulties with engagement in everyday living.

This chapter will focus on the importance of understanding sensory experiences in order to support the pathway from prison to the community. It will particularly focus on those who have experienced childhood trauma followed by long-term imprisonment. We will start by explaining the nature of the sensory system and how it works to enable us to function effectively. We will progress to looking at sensory disruption and the challenges this can present for people on their journey from prison to the community. We will briefly look at how to identify sensory needs and why this is important and will finish with discussion on techniques and strategies that can be used to support people to manage their sensory needs as they resettle into the community. We will increase awareness and understanding not only of the importance of sensory experiences in the criminal justice system but also in our everyday lives; each person's sensory world is unique and understanding this enables a more nuanced and individual approach to services.

What is our sensory system and how does it work?

When describing the senses, the first to come to mind are typically sight, sound, touch, taste, and smell. However, there are three more hidden senses: vestibular, proprioception and interoception. The vestibular sense (which is situated in our inner ear) allows us to walk along a pavement without bumping into people or tripping over small holes. It is responsible for providing information to our brain about where our body is in space to help us balance and move smoothly. Proprioception uses receptors in our skin, muscles and joints to tell us when and with what force to use our muscles. Proprioception allows us, for example, to close a window with the right amount of force so it shuts but the glass does not break (Andersson, Sutton, Bejerholm, & Argentzell, 2021). Interoception allows us to notice the internal state or condition of our body, including sensations such as pain, hunger, thirst, heart rate, body temperature, sexual arousal and the need to urinate (Mahler, 2015). Box 5.1 below illustrates how our senses work together to enable us to engage effectively and efficiently in an everyday living activity.

Box 5.1 The Sensory Experience of Eating

Imagine eating your favourite food. You may initially think of the taste, but you may also be seeing the way it looks and noticing the smell. The environment in which you are eating will also affect your experience. You may be imagining eating your favourite food in a pleasant and comfortable setting. Once you move past the look, smell, and taste of the food you are introducing other senses. The feeling of texture in your mouth is the sense of touch. Proprioception helps you to know whether something is hard or soft by how much force you must apply with your teeth, jaw and tongue, and to be able to calibrate force to do this effectively and efficiently. To swallow you will need touch and proprioception to distinguish when the food has been chewed to an acceptable standard. Understanding how full your stomach is, requires interoception. Through the vestibular sense you know when your head is upright to ensure your body is in the right position for eating. During these stages you hear yourself processing the food, feel your mouth through touch and the force of weight. All of this is done whilst using all of your senses to perceive the environment in which you are eating, how you are sitting, the company you have, whether the room is hot, cold, loud, quiet, calm or busy. What seems like a simple act of eating is a complex sensory process, requiring all the senses to work together.

Box 5.1 demonstrates how our sensory experiences are a result of the inter-action and effect of multiple senses being stimulated at any one time (Geary, 2021). The brain receives sensory information, filters, organises and regulates it, in order to produce a behavioural response (Champagne, 2011a). This process is known as sensory modulation. Sensory modulation is essential to successful everyday functioning (Andersson et al., 2021) as it enables us to effectively prioritise which senses to attend to in the moment and enact an appropriate response. For example, when crossing a busy road, it is not a priority for the brain to notice and respond to the smell of the flowers. The priority is focusing on seeing the oncoming traffic, hearing potential cars coming around the corner, and knowing how to move the body across the road safely. In this moment the brain organises and regulates its responses to acknowledge the most important sensory cues and ignore irrelevant ones. Equally important is the ability to modulate the sensory input arising from our environment and our interactions with others. Sensory stimuli arising from social interactions must be noticed and processed to enable us to make sense of ourselves and others (Shuker, 2018). The senses work together to support effective social interaction (Gibson & vom Lehn, 2021) and it is through our senses working together: noticing smells, facial expressions, sounds, and how things feel and look, that we are able to make decisions about interactions with others (Grosjean, Matte & Nahon-Serfaty, 2021). Being able to rely on our sensory system to effec-tively anticipate what to expect from social interactions enables us to regulate our behavioural responses (Mahler, 2015) to help us to survive, protect our-selves, engage with others and interact with our environment.

Sensory modulation is of particular significance within this chapter as it is our brain's ability to filter and regulate sensory cues that informs our behavioural response to sensory stimuli. If we can regulate sensory information accurately, we are likely to react with an appropriate response. However, what happens when there has been disruption to the development of a person's sensory system? What happens to the ability to regulate sensory information and what can happen to behavioural responses?

The impact of trauma on the sensory brain

Our sensory experiences start before we are born. In utero, babies experience the beat of their mother's heart; as they develop, they hear sounds internally to the mother and externally in the world. These experiences start to prepare the baby for life outside of the uterus. After birth, the increased exposure to the sensory world supports the child to learn to survive and thrive. In early child-hood, "children depend on adults to provide for their sensory needs [in response to cues provided]. The sensory system develops through caretaking activities such as feeding, dressing, bathing, and play" (Bhreathnach, 2009, p.21). For example, the feeling of hunger through the sense of interoception causes a baby to communicate their need for food through rooting for milk or crying. A child who is wet and cold will experience these sensations through their sense of touch and may communicate their discomfort by crying, fussing or being unable to settle to sleep. If comforted and changed into warm dry clothes, the child can feel positive external sensations through senses such as touch, vision, and sound. There can also be positive internal (interoception) sensations arising from this interaction, such as feelings of calm, comfort and relaxation. Where the child is comforted and nurtured, internal and external receptors learn that positive sensations arise when a child feels safe and loved. This nurturing builds neurological pathways within the child's brain that over time enable them to learn that there is a relationship between their sensory experiences (feeling wet and cold), a behavioural communication of their sensory experiences (crying) and the outcome (being made physically and emotionally comfortable by a caring other). From this, we can see that positive sensory experiences in childhood enable both external and internal senses to integrate which supports a person in developing an understanding of how to positively navigate the world.

When a baby is born into an environment that does not provide positive sensory experiences, they start to understand the world in different ways. Without a nurturing foundation and positive sensory experiences at the very start of life, sensory systems can struggle to accurately interpret information, they can experience "impaired associative learning between internal states and external cues" (Murphy, Brewer, Catmur & Bird, 2017, p. 8). This can impact on a child's ability to feel safe and to understand and navigate the world around them accurately and effectively. For example, if a child's cries of hunger or discomfort are ignored or punished, they learn that communicating distress is ineffectual, which can affect their ability to trust their sensory experiences. A child who has grown up in an environment where they have not experienced internal sensations of what it feels like to be comforted and nurtured, may feel uncomfortable and even frightened when these sensations are experienced as they grow up. Murphy et al. (2017) suggest difficulties in being able to accurately predict internal sensory input, can result in a person experiencing challenges with understanding and controlling their emotional responses to situations, resulting in difficulties with emotional regulation.

Individuals who have experienced complex trauma[2] have commonly been exposed to repeated negative sensory experiences that can have pervasive effects on the development of mind and body (Champagne, 2011b; and see Chapter 4). Children who experience significant trauma quickly learn that they need to be alert to sensory cues in order to anticipate danger and therefore survive. Jeremy described how, as a child, he used to lie in bed waiting for his dad to come home. His ears were attuned to the different sounds that helped him anticipate his dad's behaviour: the sound of the front door closing, his voice and the feet on the stairs all indicated to Jeremy the mood his dad was in when he arrived home, and what behaviour to expect from him. For Jeremy, his auditory sense was of particular importance, an experience also reflected by Herrity (2020). Herrity highlights that the sense of hearing extends far "beyond the periphery of vision" (Herrity & Warr, in press, p.2) therefore is essential to assist in understanding situations, when vision is not possible. In Jeremy's case hearing was essential for survival.

Children, like Jeremy, who experience significant and prolonged trauma, learn that in order to survive they need to be alert to all sensory cues that will inform them of impending danger. For these individuals the limbic system, which is the part of the brain that receives sensory information, becomes overactive and triggers the release of adrenaline and cortisol to ensure that they are ready to respond. This means that the body can be in a permanent state of heightened alert and ready for fight or flight action (hyperarousal). Hyperarousal is characterised by a constant state of heightened physiological arousal, emotional overload and reactive functioning. Individuals who are hyperaroused commonly do not feel in control of themselves, therefore their behaviour can be seen in the context of them trying to gain some control. Many people who have experienced trauma live in a state of hyperarousal, which can manifest itself as hypervigilance, emotional tantrums, anxiety, preoccupation with relationships, and propensity for aggressive, destructive, self-harming or risk-taking behaviours (Kharsati & Bhola 2016; Kwon, Lee & Lee 2021; Kimble et al., 2014). With the limbic system dominating the reception of sensory information, other parts of the brain are not able to develop the mechanisms and connections to support it to effectively filter and organise sensory input. In turn this impairs the brains' ability to effectively modulate incoming sensory experiences.

For some the state of heightened alert becomes overwhelming and their physiological and sensory systems shut down resulting in a freeze like state (hypo-arousal). Hypo-arousal is characterised by a low state of physiological arousal, emotional numbing and restricted functioning (Raju, Corrigan, Davidson & Johnson 2012). It can manifest itself as flat affect, passive aggression, social withdrawal/disconnection from the world and disconnection between body and feelings. Individuals who are in a chronic state of hypo-arousal often engage in activities that activate their sensory system and enable respite from sensory numbness. The behaviours are commonly self-destructive, such as self-harm, eating disorders or substance misuse (Champagne, 2011b; Warner & Finn, 2020).

We can therefore understand how chronic childhood trauma can result in disruption to sensory modulation: the reception, processing, understanding and responding to sensory information is dominated by the search for cues of impending threat. Whilst this is important for survival, the attunement of the sensory system to perceived threat can be problematic when in reality there is none. This sensory disruption in turn impacts on a person being able to make an appropriate behavioural response, i.e., sensory modulation is interrupted. When sensory modulation difficulties go unnoticed and untreated, individuals are at increased risk of inappropriate behavioural responses to environmental cues (Ogden, Minton, & Pain, 2006; Harricharan, McKinnon & Lanius, 2021).

Herrity, Schmidt & Warr (2023) highlight the importance in differentiating between how something feels, and a feeling to help distinguish between a sensory experience and an emotion. This can be understood by Neil, who on release felt people around him were constantly watching him, noticing all his movements and behaviours. This evoked feelings of suspiciousness, paranoia and agitation towards others, resulting in him using substances to numb these unpleasant feelings. Whilst this familiar, but unhelpful, coping strategy reduced his feelings of suspiciousness and paranoia, it also stopped him engaging in everyday life, impacting significantly on his resettlement journey. Being able to differentiate between how something feels and a feeling enables us to develop a better understanding of how sensory input causes emotional responses in everyday situations and assists us in identifying how these can be managed. Both hyper and hypo-arousal states affect a person's ability to think effectively (Ogden & Fisher, 2015) and therefore respond effectively to the situation. This can increase risk to both themselves and others if a person is unable to regulate their emotional responses. Having strategies that enable individuals to modulate their sensory experiences to help manage both their emotional and behavioural responses to sensory experiences is instrumental in supporting people resettle into the community. Prior to discussing strategies of support, it is first important to understand the sensory experience of prison release.

The sensory experience of being released

The process of being released from prison can be an enormously challenging experience. From a sensory perspective, Herrity (2019) identifies that penal power does not just come from how prisons look, or how they are run but from their sound: jangling keys, slamming doors, alarms, bells, batons being run against the metal stairs, shouting during the day and at night. Each of these inescapable sounds communicates and reinforces to people their status and experience as "prisoners". However, whilst prisons by their nature are restrictive in all areas of life such as privacy, freedom, movement, access to activity, relationships and autonomy (Craswell, Dieleman & Ghanouni 2020; Sykes 1958), these restrictions can offer people with sensory difficulties some containment. Prison can be predictable, with familiar routines and rhythms. Sounds, smells and people become familiar; familiarity with prison routine can assist in noticing cues that enable engagement with the surroundings. For those being released following long sentences, the change from a predictable sensory environment to one that is unpredictable and unfamiliar can cause significant anxiety. As mentioned before, this state of anxiety can lead to hypervigilance. If not well managed, transitioning from custody to the community can become a negative experience. Sudden changes in sensory experiences can become overwhelming and lead to "sensory overload", when the brain takes in more sensory information than it can process, resulting in the body responding with the flight, fight or freeze mode. Sensory overload can impact on a person's ability to effectively understand the world around them, and thus affect good decision making, and the use of effective coping strategies.

Due to the stark difference in sensory experiences between prison and the community, once in the community, a person can be quickly transported emotionally back in time to memories of negative events. The account Mark gave at the start of this chapter is a reminder of the role our senses play in forming and recalling memories, and how difficult it can be to move on from our past when our senses can quickly remind us of where we have been. A smell may bring back traumatic memories from childhood, a visual cue may remind someone of their offence, the jangling of keys a reminder of prison, all of which can impact on a person's feelings, emotions, and behaviours and ultimately their resettlement experience. These cues cannot always be anticipated especially in the unpredictable community environment, making them harder to manage when they arise.

Understanding the impact of sensory experiences in prison, as well as those from childhood is important in supporting people to resettle back into the community. Mark observes that even after three years in the community the jangling of keys and locking of doors can transport his mind straight back to prison. This is unsettling and anxiety provoking, especially when the rest of his surroundings are incongruent with his sensory experience, for example, if he hears jangling keys when he is picking his children up from school, or in the supermarket. His sensory system has been triggered by a sensory memory of prison and his disrupted sensory system may begin to prepare him for fight or flight. Figure 5.1 below provides an overview of how each sense can react to sensory overload and identifies how this can impact on a person's resettlement experience.

Figure 5.1 helps us understand that when sensory modulation is unable to take place, our brains can easily become overloaded with sensory input. Sensory modulation difficulties can result in individuals being at a higher risk of engaging in unhelpful behaviours and riskier decision-making in response to their sensory experiences (Dunn et al., 2010; Sokol-Hessner, Hartley, Hamilton & Phelps, 2014). An example of this can be seen by Jake, following his release from prison. Jake arrived at the hostel having been exposed to many unfamiliar sensory experiences within a short period of time. As a result, he experienced difficulties in being able to modulate all of the incoming sensory input, causing sensory overload. Jake presented as hyper-aroused, agitated with poor concentration and difficulty in processing information. Whilst settling into the hostel, another resident unpredictably brushed passed him. Due to childhood trauma, neurodivergent difficulties and experiencing sensory overload Jake found the unexpected and unwelcome sensation of touch triggered him into becoming hostile and aggressive. Jake's experience demonstrates the impact sensory modulation difficulties can have on a person's ability to regulate their behavioural responses, especially when their body is in a hyper-aroused state.

Seeing: New and constantly changing environments are difficult to visually predict, making processing visual information confusing and disorientating. A busy shop on the way home from prison proved overwhelming for one man who had to wait for his family outside.

Hearing: Sounds are unpredictable; they vary in pitch and tone which can make conversations difficult to navigate. For Mark, the sound of the door to the probation office clicking shut behind him transported his memory back to being locked in and triggered memories of prison.

Taste: Food in prison can be bland, new or different tastes can feel overwhelming. One man on release ate the same food each day for many weeks. The familiarity and predictability of tastes helped him regulate his emotions.

Smell: Smells can quickly trigger memories of difficult times which can result in unexpected and unwanted emotional responses taking place when an old smell is triggered in a new environment. The acid orange cleaner and the smell of poor hygiene that Mark recalled were clear olfactory memories of prison life.

Touch: Individuals who have experienced significant trauma in childhood commonly find touch difficult to manage. Different types of touch can trigger uncomfortable feelings and negative emotional responses. Jakes experience of unpredictable touch when someone brushed passed him triggered him into becoming hostile and aggressive.

Proprioception: Our body needs feedback from our muscles, tendons, and joints to understand how to navigate the environment we are in. Feeling disconnected from our physical body can cause people to behave unpredictably and sometimes unsafely. This is commonly seen immediately on release when people rush around to complete many different tasks.

Vestibular: Difficulties with processing changing speeds of objects, people and spatial awareness may cause disorientation and impact the person's ability to effectively manage emotional responses. John spoke of the confusion he felt on release seeing the speed in which cars move in the community, which was very different from his experience of speed experienced in prison.

Interoception: Difficulty in understanding internal changes within the body can result in us not knowing how we feel which can cause us to misinterpret information and form incorrect conclusions. Darren attributed all uncomfortable internal sensations he felt to being physically unwell. Sensory support enabled him to better understand and interpret different internal sensations reducing hospital visits.

Figure 5.1 Why release can feel like a sensory explosion

Rob's experience below highlights the pleasures and the challenges that can be experienced shortly after release.

Box 5.2 Sensory overload after release: illustrated by Rob's experience

Following release from prison Rob describes how alien positive sensory experiences felt, and though enjoyable, how they took some getting used to. '[It] felt weird to sleep in a normal bed, springy. It took me ages to get to sleep. My sleep was staggered as getting used to a real mattress is really hard. The quilt and pillows holding me like I am being cuddled'. His view also brings to light some of the things we often take for granted in everyday life yet are a novelty on release, such as freedom when washing. 'Hot showers, I can have as many as I want a day. I can actually remove the head so I can get to those hard-to-reach areas.' In contrast to this Rob also described some of the difficulties he faced on a bus journey the day after he was released '... the whole noise and atmosphere is quite overwhelming... I lost it at a few people for being in my way,' and how 'screaming kids on the bus, crying babies, the ambulance siren, old people talking so loudly and the large crowds, ... I had to get off the bus, was all a bit too much'.

Rob's description of his positive sensory experiences following release provides a vivid picture of the impact of having items that provide the sensations of being physically nurtured and supported. His description also highlights the multi-sensorial challenges that people are exposed to on release, and the effect this can have on them both mentally and physically. Understanding how our sensory systems can become quickly overloaded, impacting on a person's ability to filter, organise and regulate sensory information is helpful when looking at the strategies we need to support people as they transition from prison to the community.

Champagne (2011b) highlights the link between the difficulties in sensory modulation and the effect this can have on a person's ability to engage in a wide variety of occupations. This was experienced by John during a period of Release on Temporary Licence (ROTL).[3] John described feeling unwell. He said his head felt heavy and foggy, and he could not process verbal information. He said his stomach felt strange, resulting in him choosing not to eat for fear that he would feel worse or be sick. He had not managed to sleep much, so during the day was keeping himself awake by drinking strong coffee. John described his heart racing, increasing his anxiety that he was unwell and not coping with his ROTL.

If we apply a sensory focus to John's experience, we could formulate a different interpretation. He was excited about ROTL. It was the middle of summer, and he was able to go to the beach, feel freedom for a few days and not feel contained by prison. Whilst there was inevitably some anxiety, the strange feeling he had in his stomach could be interpreted as excitement that he had not experienced for many years, rather than being unwell. By not eating, for fear of a stomach upset, his energy levels reduced, resulting in him feeling more tired and not as able to process information given to him. Drinking highly caffeinated drinks increased his heart rate contributing to his anxiety and reinforcing his interpretation that he was unwell and not able to cope on ROTL.

By using a sensory approach to understanding John's experience, we can look at strategies to help him manage his internal sensory system and in turn help him manage day-to-day living more effectively. This can assist John to understand that it was unlikely that he was unwell. Rather, due to his limited sensory experiences after many years in prison, and his experience of childhood trauma interrupting his ability to interpret interoception cues accurately, he did not have the reference points to process, understand, and reflect on what he was experiencing. He therefore was unable to engage in effective behavioural responses to manage his situation. The combination of sensory input, a person's life experiences and how a person's body physically responds to everyday stimulation is extremely complex. Anderson, Sutton, Bejerholm, and Argentzell (2021) highlight that whilst there may be commonalities, the way in which we experience sensory information is unique to each person and results in a unique emotional response.

How do we identify someone's sensory needs?

Whilst sensory assessment tools can be useful in identifying a person's specific sensory needs, these are not the only way to understand and formulate how a person is presenting. Our observational skills play a key role in being able to notice behaviours and consider whether it would help to formulate these within a sensory context. Dunn's Model of Sensory Processing (Dunn, 1997; Brown, Tollefson, Dunn, Cromwell, & Filion, 2001) identifies four patterns of sensory behaviour, which can help us in identifying sensory patterns and sensory needs (see Box 5.3):

Box 5.3 Patterns of Sensory Behaviours (Dunn, 1997)

Sensory Seeker: Enjoy intense sensory input, they might present as clumsy, loud and energetic. They can present as being unaware of personal space and boundaries and demonstrate a high pain threshold.

Sensory Avoider: Become easily overwhelmed and therefore tend to avoid sensory input that they perceive will make them feel uncomfortable. They tend to prefer to be alone and can become easily startled by unexpected sensations.

Sensory Sensitive: Notice sensory stimuli more readily. They can show tolerance of these up to a point but can quickly experience sensory overload and commonly respond irrationally to sensory stimuli rather than avoid this.

Low registration: Require a high level of sensory stimulation to register what is going on around them. They can present as lethargic, uninterested, self-absorbed or withdrawn; can appear unaware of what is going on around them.

Understanding sensory behaviours (as shown in Box 5.3) can assist us in knowing how to best engage with individuals and facilitate sessions. Knowing if a person has low registration to sensory information enables us to be creative in how we work with them to ensure they receive enough sensory input to hear information being given to them and enable them to react to this. This was seen when working with Frank who found receiving information when sitting down almost impossible, however when we introduced, into sessions, physical activity encouraging him to move around whilst listening and talking, he was able to hear and retain information more readily. For people who are sensory sensitive or avoidant it is important to ensure sensory stimulation is reduced to support engagement. We found when working with Mark that the sounds within the probation offices reminded him of being back in prison, which distracted him and impacted his ability to engage in sessions. By moving sessions to a quieter area, away from the probation offices, his engagement increased, making them more productive and meaningful to him. It is important to understand that one person can present with several of the above identified sensory patterns depending on the environment that they are in. Mark presented as sensory sensitive within the probation offices but when playing with his children showed sensory-seeking behaviours. By observing how people behave in different settings we can see sensory behavioural patterns within context. From this we can explore how best to support a person's sensory needs to enable them to engage and function to their optimal level with daily life.

Supporting sensory needs to facilitate resettlement

Within this chapter we have identified what the sensory system does and how it works, the impact of trauma on the sensory brain and how trauma affects sensory experience and behavioural responses. We have explored the sensory experience of those transitioning into the community and how we can identify people's sensory needs to support them in their daily lives. We will now move onto exploring strategies that can be used when working with individuals in their pathway from prison into the community. We recognise that there are many different ways of supporting people using sensory strategies. The ones presented below have been identified by the individuals we work with as useful in supporting them in managing their emotions and behaviours, particularly at times of change.

In-reaching into prison before release to understand sensory preferences

In-reach work enables community workers to have their first contact with the person in an environment in which they understand the rhythms, sounds and routine of life. This can reduce levels of arousal and assist in someone being able to focus on new conversations with new people. Within this environment we can start to understand a person's sensory behaviour patterns and how these might present in different community settings. This is helpful in release plan-ning in supporting community workers to understand and formulate different behaviours within a sensory context. On first meeting Jake in prison, he pre-sented as anxious and restless with difficulty in concentrating. As we got to know him, we could understand his behaviour in a sensory context where multiple sensory stimulations within a room including new people, new infor-mation and different sounds caused him to feel overloaded with sensory infor-mation and this was seen through his behaviour. By giving Jake an object in his hands (a pen) to focus on and fiddle with, enabled him to focus his attention on the object and our voices, reducing the sensory input experienced and enabling him to concentrate more easily. Understanding Jake's presentation in prison, regarding how he responded to sensory information enabled us to put in place plans on how he can be supported to hear and process information on release. Being able to formulate a person's sensory preferences whilst in prison enables community workers to understand how these might translate into in the community, which is helpful in release planning and preparation.

Personalised place of safety

For people to engage fully in their environment they need to feel safe (Champagne, 2011c). They also need an environment that invites engagement. Desolate environments can trigger unwanted memories and exacerbate sensory modulation difficulties (Hoover, 2018) resulting in unhelpful behaviours. For people to be able to engage meaningfully in successful resettlement, they need to feel safe and be in an environment that is conducive to supporting prosocial behaviour. Where possible, thinking about this prior to release can be the start of a positive release experience. Having access to items that make the envir-onment more sensorily positive can aid a person in managing their own sensory modulation. For example, in prison there is little control over room tempera-ture, lighting or noise levels. Blankets or fans can give people control of their room or body temperature; lamps can provide control of lighting; headphones or music systems can give control over noise levels. Kieran, who was living in a hostel, complained of stress and anxiety because of a persistent noise in his room, which was leading to tense and hostile encounters with hostel staff. His descriptions of himself and his life suggested that he was a "sensory avoider" and unfortunately, he had been given a room directly above the hostel kitchen. Engaging with hostel staff to understand Kieran's sensory profile enabled them to willingly support him to move into a different room which significantly reduced his exposure to unwanted and uncontrollable noise.

Where possible, we work closely with Approved Premise Hostels to look at the rooms allocated to the individual prior to release, to assist in supporting individuals with their specific sensory needs. The importance of this was high-lighted by Craig, who was noticed to have moved his mattress onto the floor and partly under his bed. On further exploration, he reported feeling exposed and uncontained in the unfamiliar environment of the new hostel room. The different sensory experiences he was exposed to including the sound of traffic and emergency vehicles outside his room, the noise inside the hostel and people coming into his room to do safety checks at night made him feel unsafe. Craig tried to contain himself at night-time by wrapping himself up like a cocoon to feel physically safe and sleeping under the bed to feel invisible. These were familiar coping strategies he had learnt as a child, triggered by loud unfamiliar sounds making him feel vulnerable. With this information we were able to work with him and hostel staff to support them in rearranging the room and providing ear plugs to block out night-time sounds that assisted him in gaining some control to feel safe and contained. Where appropriate we meet with keyworkers prior to a person's release, to discuss any specific sensory needs they have to ensure that behaviour can be seen in the context of sensory difficulties rather than behaviour problems.

Supportive structure and routine

Prisons run on routine. Opportunities for self-care (e.g., showering, eating and fresh air), leisure (e.g., gym) and being productive (e.g., workshops and education) are largely planned and predictable. Structure and routine can feel containing, as people's sensory systems know what to expect and when. This supports people in feeling in control of their emotions and behaviours. Release into the community can feel like an empty void, where people who have been in prison for a long time have limited skills and knowledge in knowing how to use their time effectively and productively. The rules, routine and structure of prison can be emotionally containing, release can feel unpredictable to the sensory system. Many people describe not being able to eat and forgetting to drink on release, as they are so attuned to the prison routine that without this, they forget what to do and when to do it. The lack of routine on release can result in internal cues of thirst and hunger going unnoticed or being misinterpreted, which can then lead to emotional dysregulation and engaging in unhelpful behaviours.

We work with individuals as they approach release and when they resettle to develop a timetable of activities. This provides a focus of how to use time, and supports them in planning how they will engage in the community. Timetables can act as reminders to help individuals engage in essential daily activities such as eating, drinking and showering, and developing a routine of activities that wakes the body up in the morning and winding down activities towards the end of the day. Champagne (2011a) highlights that "activities used to wake up and prepare for the day typically differ from those of night-time rituals used to prepare for going to sleep at night" (p.98). Engaging in familiar meaningful activities can create positive internal sensations as well as support emotional regulation.

We also assist people in preparing for events such as appointments in different environment that might cause challenges to the sensory system. An example of this is attending a meeting that involves walking past a pub: the visual and olfactory sensations could trigger unhelpful emotions and behaviours to someone who has had an alcohol problem. A timetable can help remind the person before the appointment of different routes to take or remind them of strategies that help them manage these sensory experiences. Timetables that support developing structure and routine need to be carefully managed to ensure they have a balance of activities to support a person to function and not induce sensory overload.

Sensorimotor activities

Sensorimotor activities can enable a person to understand the world they are in through co-ordinating multiple sensory experiences, e.g., combining seeing and hearing with proprioception. Different activities can be used to increase alertness for people who are hypo-aroused and decrease alertness in people who are hyper-aroused. These activities can support individuals in developing techniques that enable them to self-regulate their emotions to engage successfully in everyday activities.

Re, McConnell, Reidinger, Schweit, & Hendron (2014) identify that sensory enhanced Yoga can be effective for adults and adolescents to support self-awareness and emotional regulation. Spence (2021) identifies that yoga uses the senses of proprioception and interoception to engage in physical activities that increase self-awareness.

We have supported individuals to engage in activities such as sensory circuits, cycling, yoga swimming and gym-based activities to both improve their physical health and support them in being able to modulate their sensory input through rhythmic sensory based physical activities. Yoga cue cards that provide visual prompts can be helpful for people who respond to visual reminders of how to engage in an activity that can slow the mind and body down, to assist with emotional regulation.

Sensory toolkits

A sensory toolkit is a personalised box of items created by the individual who intends to use it. The purpose of it is to support managing sensory patterns of behaviour to assist in improving concentration and emotional regulation. Sensory toolkits can be used to support reducing arousal levels (for those who are hyper-aroused). Using items in the toolkit that involve deep muscle work such as resistance bands, putty to pull against or the repetitive bouncing of a ball engages the proprioception and vestibular senses, which can support the body and mind in slowing down, enabling a person to better concentrate. Smells that support relaxation such as lavender can be added to these toolkits or food that is calming such as chocolate. They can contain larger items like a blanket that a person can wrap around them and pull in tight, offering deep muscle pressure that supports relaxation and emulates the feeling of being hugged. Sensory toolkits can also be used to increase arousal levels (for those who are hypo-aroused) by using items that increase alertness. A fast game of catch, bouncing a moonball that recoils in an unpredictable way, a routine of physical activities that change quickly in line with someone's physical abilities can all increase someone level of alertness. These sensory actions can enable a person to be more focused and feel in control of their body and behaviour. Using an alerting smell such as lemon or grapefruit or eating alerting food such as, limes, chillies or sour sweets are all items that can be added to someone's sensory toolkit to increase alertness levels supporting improvement in engagement in daily life.

Within the service we work in, we support identified individuals in making and collecting items that enable them to develop their own sensory toolkits that are personalised for their own identified needs. Musil (2007) suggests that sensory toolkits should be affordable, easily accessible and small enough to be discrete. They should contain items that are permissible within the context of the environment a person is living in, and provide the sensory input required to meet the individual's needs. Sensory toolkits give individuals the autonomy of being able to manage their own sensory systems through a toolbox of activities known to support their needs, that assist them in either calming or alerting themselves and subsequently being able to engage more effectively in everyday life.

Conclusion

Our senses enable us to understand and respond to the world around us and our sensory experiences give meaning to an encounter (Geary 2021). This chapter highlights that a person's sensory experiences and behaviours need to be understood within the context of who they are and the environment that they are in. Increasing awareness within this area enables us to ensure that sensory difficulties are not automatically translated into criminogenic risk, but identified, acknowledged and understood. With this understanding, effective strategies can be developed and put in place to support individuals to successfully manage their sensory experiences independently as they move from prison to the community. As Mark reflected

> It has taken me longer to get used to living in the community than it did to cope with living in prison. I had to quickly get used to prison life, I had no choice. Prison is less about living more about surviving; the community is less about surviving more about living.

Notes

1 Sweat box – *prison transport bus.*
2 Complex trauma can be defined as an "experience of multiple, chronic and prolonged, developmentally adverse traumatic events, most often of an interpersonal nature and early-life onset" (van der Kolk, 2005 p. 402).
3 ROTL – Release on Temporary Licence allows people in prison to temporary access the community for short periods of time to support their resettlement and rehabilitation.

References

Anderson, H., Sutton, D., Bejerholm, U. & Argentzell, E. (2021). Experiences of sensory input in daily occupations for people with serious mental illness. *Scandinavian Journal of Occupational Therapy*, 28(6), 446–456.

Bellis, M. A., Ashton, K., Hughes, K., Ford, K., Bishop, J. &Paranjothy, S. (2016). *Adverse childhood experiences and their impact on health-harming behaviours in the Welsh population*. Cardiff: Public Health Wales NHS Trust.

Bhreathnach, É. (2009). Sensory attachment integration. *Adoption Today*, October, 20–21.

Brown, C., Tollefson, N., Dunn, W., Cromwell, R. & Filion, D. (2001). The adult sensory profile: measuring patterns of sensory processing. *American Journal of Occupational Therapy*, 55(1), 75–82.

Champagne, T. (2011a). *Sensory modulation and environment: Essential elements of occupation*. Australia: Pearson.

Champagne, T. (2011b). Attachment, trauma and occupational therapy practice. *Occupational Therapy Practice*, 16(5), 1–8.

Champagne, T. (2011c). The influence of posttraumatic stress disorder, depression, and sensory processing patterns on occupational engagement: a case study. *Work*, 38(1), 67–75.

Craswell, G., Dieleman, C., & Ghanouni, P. (2020). An integrative review of sensory approaches in adult inpatient mental health: Implication for occupational therapy in prison based mental health services. *Occupational Therapy in Mental Health*, 37(2), 130–157.

Dunn, W. (1997). The impact of sensory processing abilities on the daily lives of young children and their families: A conceptual model. *Infants and Young Children*, 9, 23–35.

Dunn, B. D., Galton, H. C., Morgan, R., Evans, D., Oliver, C., Meyer, M., Cusack, R., Lawrence, A. D. & Dalgleish, T. (2010). Listening to your heart. How interoception shapes emotion experience and intuitive decision making. *Psychological Science*, 21(12), 1835–1844.

Geary, P. (2021) Dining in prison: Sensory framing and performative perception in Rideout's Past Times. *Journal of the Performing Arts*, 26(3), 66–73.

Gibson, W. & vom Lehn, D. (2021). Introduction: The senses in social interaction. *Symbolic Interaction*, 44(1), 3–9.

Grosjean, S. Matte, F. & Nahon-Serfaty, I. (2021). "Sensory ordering" in nurses' clinical decision-making: Making visible senses, sensing, and "sensory work" in the hospital. *Symbolic Interaction*, 44(1), 163–182.

Harricharan, S., McKinnon, M. C. & Lanius, R. A. (2021). How processing of sensory information from the internal and external worlds shape the perception and engagement with the world in the aftermath of trauma: Implications for PTSD. *Frontiers in Neuroscience*, 16(15), 1–20.

Herrity, K., Schmidt, B. & Warr, J. J. (2023). Sensory "heteroglossia" and social control: Sensory methodology and method. In M. Dodge & R. Faria (Eds). *Qualitative research in criminology*. Cham: Springer.

Herrity, K. & Warr, J. J. (in press). "This is my home": the prison cell as a site of domicile-through-displacement in P. Davies & M. Rowe, (Eds.) *A criminology of the domestic*. London: Routledge.

Herrity, K. (2020). Hearing behind the door: the cell as a portal to prison life. In J. Turner & V. Knight (Eds.) *The prison cell: embodied and everyday spaces of incarceration* (pp. 239–259). London: Palgrave Macmillan.

Herrity, K. (2019). *Rhythms and routines: Sounding order in a local men's prison through aural ethnography* (Doctoral dissertation). University of Leicester, Leicester, UK.

Hoover, K. C. (2018). Sensory disruption in modern living and the emergence of sensory inequities. *Yale Journal of Biology and Medicine*, 91(1), 53–62.

Kharsati, N. & Bhola, P. (2016). Self-injurious behavior, emotion regulation, and attachment styles among college students in India. *Industrial Psychiatry Journal*, 25(1). 23–28.

Kimble, M., Boxwala, M., Bean, W., Maletsky, K., Halper, J., Spollen, K. & Fleming, K. (2014). The impact of hypervigilance: Evidence for a forward feedback loop. *Journal of Anxiety Disorders*, 28(2), 241–245.

Kwon, A., Lee, H.S. & Lee, S.H. (2021) The mediation effect of hyperarousal symptoms on the relationship between childhood physical abuse and suicidal ideation of patients with PTSD. *Frontiers in Psychiatry*, 12, 1–10.

Mahler, K. (2015). *Interoception: The eighth sensory system*. Kansas: AAPC Publishing.

Murphy, J.. Brewer, R., Catmur, C. & Bird, G. (2017). Interoception and psychopathology: A developmental neuroscience perspective. *Developmental Cognitive Neuroscience* 23, 45–56.

Musil, T. (2007). *Providing a tool basket for self-regulation for students with autism* (Master's thesis). British Columbia, Canada: Simon Fraser University.

Ogden, P. & Fisher, J. (2015). *Sensorimotor psychotherapy: Interventions for trauma and attachment*. New York: W. W. Norton & Company.

Ogden, P., Minton, K. & Pain, C. (2006). *Trauma and the body: A sensorimotor approach to psychotherapy*. New York: Norton & Company.

Raju, R., Corrigan, F., Davidson, A. & Johnson, D. (2012). Assessing and managing mild to moderate emotion dysregulation. *Advances in Psychiatric Treatment*, 18(2), 82–93.

Re, P., McConnell, J., Reidinger, G., Schweit, R. & Hendron, A. (2014). Effects of yoga on patients in an adolescent mental health hospital and the relationship between those effects and the patients' sensory processing patterns. *Journal of Child and Adolescent Psychiatric Nursing*, 27(4), 175–182.

Serres, M. (2008). *The five senses: A philosophy of mingled bodies*. London: Continuum International Publishing Group.

Shuker, R. (2018). Relationships, social context and personal change: the role of therapeutic communities. In G. Akerman, A. Needs & Bainbridge, C. (Eds.), *Transforming environments and rehabilitations. A guide for practitioners in forensic settings and criminal justice* (pp. 213–226). Abingdon, Oxon: Routledge.

Sokol-Hessner, P., Hartley, C. A., Hamilton, J. R. & Phelps, E. A. (2014). Interoceptive ability predicts aversion to losses. *Cognition and Emotion*, 29(4), 695–701.

Spence, J. (2021). *Trauma-informed yoga: A toolbox for therapists*. Eau Claire, WI: PESI Publishing.

Sykes, G.M. (1958). *The society of captives: A study of a maximum-security prison*. Princeton, NJ: Princeton University Press.

van der Kolk, B. A. (2005). Developmental trauma disorder: Toward a rational diagnosis for children with complex trauma histories. *Psychiatric Annals*, 35(5), 401–408.

Warner, E. & Finn, A. (2020). *Transforming trauma in children and adolescents: An embodied approach to somatic regulation, trauma processing and attachment building*. Berkeley, CA: North Atlantic Books.

Young, S., González, R. A., Mullens, H., Mutch, L., Malet-Lambert, I. & Gudjonsson, G. (2017). Neurodevelopmental disorders in prison inmates: comorbidity and combined associations with psychiatric symptoms and behavioural disturbance. *Psychiatry Research*, 261, 109–115.

6 Away from the chemical embrace

Navigating substance dependence from custody to community

Sue Ryan and Sam

This chapter will reflect a service user's and clinician's perspective on the transition from custody into the community whilst managing substance misuse difficulties. There are many practical and psychological barriers for people trying to return to society after a long custodial sentence (see Chapter 2), most of which are exacerbated when simultaneously trying to become or remain substance free. With so many transitions to adjust to, whilst also connecting to emotions that substances often masked, many individuals can experience release as an overwhelming and unmanageable challenge. Additionally, the criminalisation of substance misuse, either due to the illicit nature of substances or because addressing substance misuse can be a probation licence condition, brings an additional burden for individuals to carry on release into the community. This burden can become a barrier to being open and honest about the reality of the struggle faced.

Sam (a pseudonym), a user of services, agreed to write a contribution to this chapter, based upon his experience of serving various prison sentences over the past three decades and having been released ten years after he began his most recent sentence.

Sam's experience

I'm a released prisoner and drug addict, who has been to prison more times than is healthy for the average human's capacity to cope mentally and emotionally with captivity and the brutal regime prison provides. You'd think being released from prison would be a really happy time and full of relief and joy as a prisoner is reunited with family and friends. The reality is far more complicated, especially if you're a repeat offender, like me.

I was abused as a child in every way possible and with all the labels, mental, physical, emotional, sexual and this left me physically damaged. Like many addicts I've met, it drove me to seek comfort and escape and after trial and desperate searching, I found it in prison. This wasn't a course of therapy, in fact it wasn't anything that the regime provided, it was diamorphine, or to use it's more common name 'heroin'. The ultimate end of the road in drug journeys.

DOI: 10.4324/9781003308171-8

Smack, brown, gear, skag, nasty, dark, there are so many names for this little bag of powder. It looks harmless and everyone underestimates its effect, the damage it does to you, your family, your friends, your community, your future, health and wealth. You'll do it again and again because it works. It takes the pain away and cuddles and comforts you with a glow of 'fuck it', a haze of 'don't give a shit' and a chemical embrace that will replace food, sex, friendships, love, medication, sanity, trust and loyalty.

Day one of the many releases, £45 and now of no fixed abode. This reality occurred for me on several occasions and is a reality for many others, resulting in limited opportunities and dire consequences. If you're an addict of any sort, drugs, alcohol, gambling, the results will be the same, why try to stay 'clean' when you have nowhere to live. I was once released in winter wearing shorts and a t-shirt. I told myself that I 'needed' heroin to get through the cold nights. It broke me and left me depressed.

Day two of release brings cold, hunger, homelessness a path that was well trodden, this was the way my life had repeated. With little opportunity to find a stable base, a home to go to, it felt like I, and many others, were set up to fail. Due to these experiences, it led to me feeling that the prospect of release was something to be feared. A sense of hopelessness at how I may be able to turn my life around whilst having no fixed abode, no family or friends, no support. Getting off drugs, requires stability, hope, support of professionals and experience from like-minded people who have managed to get 'clean' and change their lives. The system needs to better invest in supporting individuals on release into the community otherwise the same results will occur; support stops at the custody gate.

So, on this release into the community, I had support, encouragement and a home and despite this IPP (Indeterminate Public Protection) sentence hanging over my head I feel like I'm winning. My past may still be haunting me but at last I'm getting help. I chose to stay in prison for two extra years in order to get a place at an Intensive Intervention & Risk Management Service and I'm so glad I did. I wish I'd had this support 20 years ago. I'm in the minority. I realise that and I still have problems to overcome, but I'm doing okay despite them. I'm so grateful for the help and support and I have trust from the people around me and I feel that they want me to succeed.

The first few months were a test of my commitment and patience. I was surrounded by staff at the hostel who were suspicious, hostile, who did not believe me and would accuse me of using drugs, expecting me to fail. I felt miserable. I stuck to attending the IIRMS. Prison is still only a 'mistake' away for me and that will always be there. Others on licence are in a similar position, a bad decision or series of them, one step away from prison and that is what the 'hang 'em and flog 'em brigade' don't get.

Reflections on Sam's narrative

Sam was released from custody after serving 10 years. He had developed a heroin addiction in his late 20s whilst in custody. This shaped his life thereafter where he became a user and seller of drugs for over 30 years. He has no family or friends from his past and there is a sadness regarding what he has lost. He experienced significant violence and this became normalised within his daily life. The level of brutality he was exposed to was toxic, some as a victim, other instances as the aggressor. His life has been limited and opportunities and relationships damaged. His physical and mental health has suffered as a result both of things over which he had no control and as a result of choices he made. He is easy to like, respect and feel compassion for. He elicits a motivational response from others to support him, was motivated to achieve a better future, and had services in place to support him.

Sam highlighted how the support on this release was different and how this initially enabled him to succeed. He was released with the support of an Intensive Intervention & Risk Management Service (IIRMS). IIRMS is the community aspect of the Offender Personality Disorder (OPD) Pathway (Department of Health/National Offender Management Service, 2011). The OPD Pathway aims to better meet the needs of a group of people within criminal justice settings who are assessed as presenting a high risk of harm to others and having personality difficulties impacting on their offending behaviour. This group have historically been misunderstood and marginalised by many standard health and criminal justice services. IIRMS provide a joint organisational approach between the National Health Service (NHS) and His Majesty's Prison and Probation Service (HMPPS), supporting individuals to adjust to community life through evidence-based interventions and providing opportunities to understand and develop life skills and self-awareness and access psychoeducation. Interventions are adapted to meet individual needs (Webster & Gardner, 2021) and are largely voluntary and not mandated. The OPD pathway provides a range of services within custody and the community for individuals with complex intra and interpersonal needs. Provision is targeted using a whole system, relational approach (Benefield & Haigh, 2020). This approach influences how the workforce consider and relate to those in their care/custody to help support understanding of the function of an individual's behaviour, their distress and their needs. This is done through formulation, consultation and training (Skett, Goode & Barton, 2017) and the development of specific intervention and therapeutic environments to aid change and enhance psychological thinking. As someone who has worked in forensic services for the past 25 years, the OPD pathway makes sense, it moves away from an unhelpful rhetoric about punishment and provides a more hopeful pathway with psychological understanding and partnership working at its core. It is still a drop in the ocean in terms of provision, but a welcome one.

Despite the availability of services, which Sam initially appreciated and found beneficial, his pathway away from substances was not straightforward. It felt difficult writing this chapter at a time when Sam appeared to be relapsing. He found it hard to be open and continued to deny his usage, despite falling asleep in sessions, looking dishevelled and losing weight. The team tried their best to work alongside him, to encourage him to feel safe to share what was going on, but he was unable to do so. Sam continued to attend the service, albeit less regularly and was less engaged when he did attend. He managed to exist in this way for a period of several months. His risk was being monitored and substance misuse was not linked to an increase in Sam's risk of violence, therefore, was not grounds on its own to initiate a recall back to prison. However, he was ultimately recalled for an allegation of an acquisitive offence, which led to the accommodation provider withdrawing his bed. Therefore, for Sam, his substance misuse was indirectly, but clearly, linked to his recall.

Prison is not a place where Sam could or would find any hope, but it could provide some containment, a route out of the circumstances in which he had become involved and perhaps enable him a period to press pause on his re-entry to the community. This could enable Sam to consider what he may need internally and from others in order to navigate the reality of community life once again and consider what got in the way of him making the transition on this occasion. Realistically, prison may also provide opportunities for him to continue misusing substances. There were mixed feelings amongst the team of professionals about Sam's recall: disappointment, frustration and sadness, but also a sense of relief as his health and wellbeing were deteriorating, and he appeared to be largely existing rather than living. There was also sadness at the experience of the support not being enough and the impact on Sam of having tried but being unable to cope without substances. However, the reality is that the route to abstinence and desistance is not straightforward (Shapland & Bottoms, 2011), otherwise Sam and many others would have managed this years ago. The team felt powerless to enable him to move through the challenges he was experiencing and efforts to support him to be more open and recognise the reality of his dependence felt fruitless. It seemed that Sam had lost any sense of hope or ability to find a way through, which impacted on his ability to successfully resettle in the community.

The systemic context: prison, release and society

Incarceration can be a traumatising experience and can strip individuals of connection, relational support and opportunities for growth and development. Similarly, release can be equally traumatising (see Chapter 4), as society can feel unwelcoming, rejecting, overwhelming and demanding, especially to those who have been in prison for many years. Although there is provision of some interventions in custody, targeted at offending behaviour and substance misuse, as well as opportunities for education and employment training, they take place within a restricted, unreal, and at times hostile environment that are not always conducive to providing a safe and stable place, essential for individuals to thrive. Prison was the environment where Sam began using heroin. Whilst he had used and misused illicit substances prior to his incarceration, prison was the place where he used a drug that he had previously consciously avoided. Perhaps prison led Sam to search for a disconnect, the "chemical embrace" to which he referred, that comforted him in the absence of any human connection within the prison environment.

Returning to the community is something that is often longed for by those in custody, but also feared (as Sam highlighted), due to the contrasting worlds, increased responsibility and exposure to multiple stressors. For many who have served long sentences, the outside world will have changed significantly, in particular when considering systemic and relational changes, technological and societal advances, and each person's unique position and narrative. All of these factors commonly contribute to individuals feeling that their expectations of release are at odds with the reality (see Chapter 2). This can result in individuals feeling overwhelmed and fearful about how to seek help, particularly if they were previously someone with a confident persona and/or a sense of notoriety. Re-emerging into the community can lead to a level of vulnerability that brings discomfort and uncertainty. One way to manage these feelings is to escape, to seek an alternative emotional state, a disconnect, in the familiar smell, taste and thrill of a drug. This experience and sensation are then sought repeatedly, in order to achieve the ultimate desired state, a settled feeling, oblivion, calmness, a sense of confidence and camaraderie. Yet the desired state can be disappointing, with a dissonance between hope and reality, perhaps symbolic of how release into the community can feel at times. This can be further compounded by the stigma associated with substance misuse that can leave individuals externally rejected and internalising the disconnection from society. The impact of this stigmatisation can contribute to individuals being reluctant to seek help (Radcliffe & Stevens, 2008; McCallum et. al., 2016; Mak et al., 2017) thus compounding the draw of substances.

Once someone becomes a user of illicit substances there is often a reaction from society to blame, judge and cease being compassionate, curious or creative in approaches to helping. Individuals are often perceived as less deserving of services and/or assistance due to their responsibility for ever having ingested a substance and therefore are commonly rejected by society (Jones, Simonson, & Singleton, 2010). There is a stigma towards those who misuse illicit substances, alongside stigma associated with their offending history, a "double distancing" of this group creating a distinction and separation from others in society. There appears to be a similar lack of curiosity, compassion and sensitivity in understanding the factors that have contributed to an individual becoming drug dependent in the first place. Perhaps there is a fear of contamination, hurt or harm by association. In general, society does not welcome ex-prisoners into the community and distances itself from understanding the systemic and individual factors that influence criminality. It holds a dominant narrative of solely locating blame and responsibility in the person who has offended, whereas the reality is more complex. As a society we need to be better at understanding the challenges faced by marginalised groups, by reaching into the communities to help shape the values, beliefs and trajectories that contribute to pathways into crime and/or drug dependence.

Working towards and maintaining desistance requires hope and optimism from the individual and those working alongside them (Farrall & Calvery, 2006; Le Bel et al., 2008) as well as opportunities to be part of society once again. This can only be achieved by whole communities working together to support the health and wellbeing of marginalised groups within society (Luchenski et al., 2018).

Relational dynamics: individuals, families, professionals

A common feature of the individuals that I have worked with on release from prison has been an enduring level of pain. The pain has been both psychological and physical and has resulted in individuals seeking ways to manage and moderate such feelings by reaching for substances to escape their reality, even if momentarily. This is seen in Sam's description of the role of substances in his life: "it takes the pain away, it comforts and cuddles you". What becomes problematic for individuals is not perhaps that they have used an illegal or legal substance, as this is commonplace within society, but the fact that substance misuse has become a way of life, a ritual, a habit, a dependence. Substance misuse issues have been prevalent for many individuals who are supported by IIRMS (Ryan, Eldridge, Duffy, Crawley, & O'Brien, 2022). Clinical experience over the past 15 years suggests that crack cocaine and heroin appear to be the most problematic in terms of taking an individual's whole focus. This results in lives no longer being full of ideas of growth, opportunity and pleasure, but instead preoccupied with money, superficial relationships with others with addiction issues and sourcing drugs. Individuals can reach a state where they lurch from one chemically induced state to the next, whilst hiding, averting the gaze, a disconnect as the shame of what is being consumed attempts to surface.

It is clear that the transition into community life is hard, perhaps harder than anticipated. The impact of substance misuse is physically and psychologically damaging to the individual. The impact on families and relationships can be equally catastrophic (Lander, Howsare, & Byrne, 2013) and lead to multiple ruptures and separation. This in turn can lead to increased isolation for those dependent on drugs, who become disconnected and uncertain about where they fit in society. Who are any of us without relationships? Yet relationships are often the roots of psychological distress, which drive the pathways into criminality and substance misuse in the first place (Hammersley, 2011). Therefore, relationships are imperative in healing those roots (Howe, 2005). Building relationships with workers (see Chapter 9) can be the starting point in learning how positive, supportive and trusting relationships can feel. From this, skills can be transferred into building social connections within the community, enabling a bridge to be scaffolded into a more hopeful future. If a person can feel safe and supported and they are within a window of change, then creating a containing space where the prospect of change feels possible may enable the person to move into the action phase of change (Prochaska & DiClemente, 1983). However, it is important to acknowledge that feeling and believing in hope for someone is not always easy and workers can become hardened, pessimistic and hopeless if not well supported in their roles. Supervision and teamwork are essential to discuss and recognise these dynamics in order to create and maintain healthy relationships that are hopeful about a person's future.

A relational approach to understanding substance misuse

Using a Cognitive Analytic Therapy approach (CAT; Ryle & Kerr, 2002) to guide psychological formulation and intervention can assist in understanding the relational dynamics that are commonplace when working with complexity. CAT is a relational approach that highlights how a person understands and responds to themselves and others, and also reciprocally, how they can elicit responses from others, often unconsciously. The beauty of CAT as an approach is that it moves away from pathologising and blaming people and highlights the normality of relational responding in both helpful and unhelpful ways. We all get caught in the dance (Potter, 2014) of relationships. By attending to how systems, workers and people we work with can all be drawn into relational dynamics, we can start to understand how people can get caught in repeating patterns of behaviour, which can leave individuals stuck and unhappy. Understanding this process can also enable us to see how systems and workers can get caught up in responding in unhelpful and at times harmful ways. CAT uses visual diagrammatic and narrative methods (see Figure 6.1 for an example) to help illustrate dynamics that can help an individual or team to be better aware of these processes. A common theme in the individuals that are managing substance misuse after release from custody has been mistrust. Individuals have often felt that others are *mistrusting* of them, leaving them feeling *mistrusted*.

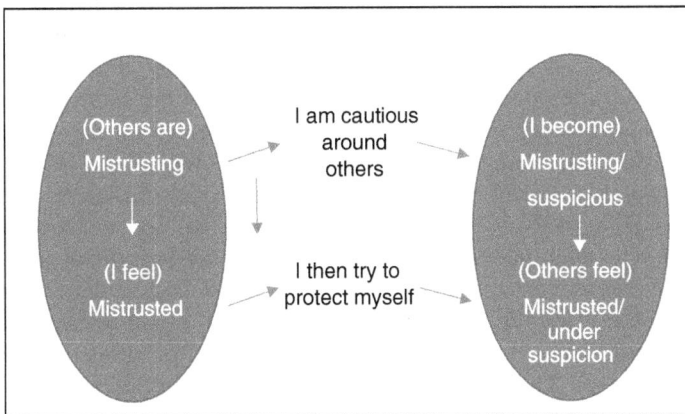

Figure 6.1 CAT illustration of reciprocal relational dynamics.

The person can then respond to this experience of feeling mistrusted by wanting to protect themselves through being cautious, feeling mistrusting and suspicious of others' motives, leaving the other feeling under suspicion. This reciprocal mistrust dynamic can be played out within relationships with family, friends or workers. It can permeate relationships impeding the ability to create a safe and supportive connection, which is crucial to building hope and trust.

A topic that often appears to feature in discussions within teams and with individuals who have misused substances is that of "truth and lies". Truth and lies are binary, black and white concepts with premature certainty (Stewart, Valentine, & Amundsen 1991) and conviction. Discussions over whether an individual has used substances, whether they are being dishonest and what this means regarding their overall intention and current state of mind and engagement can be challenging and feel blaming and pejorative. They can also reinforce the "mistrusting–mistrusted" dynamic illustrated above. Adhering to binary concepts when navigating complex issues results in a simplistic, reductionist narrative (Pycroft, 2014) of the multiple and changeable factors that impact upon decisions to use substances. The pull to know the truth and the impact on workers of having believed someone who has been dishonest about their usage can leave one either pulling towards an unhealthy scepticism for fear of getting it wrong again in the future, or at the opposite pole, to have faith and be perceived as being gullible, lacking credibility or professionalism. It can lead to the focus being centred on drug testing, on "finding out the truth", which can get in the way of fostering a trusting relationship. However, avoidance or reluctance to facilitate drug tests can be an avoidance or a rejection of worker responsibility and leave workers open to criticism from the system and colleagues. A contract of expectations, or a working agreement between individuals and workers regarding the focus of interventions and monitoring can be helpful to build a collaborative approach.

An individual may be masking or deceiving the worker (and/or themselves) about their substance use, their struggles and their reality, due to possible fear of sanctions, shame or fear of rejection or exclusion from services. They may have lost hope, but not be able to consciously connect to these issues, due to substances masking their emotions and thoughts. Working with dishonesty and deception (see Chapter 4) can be one of the most challenging aspects of working with individuals who are engaging with services but are still using substances. The dilemma of when and how to challenge individuals regarding what can be seen or what is suspected is difficult to balance with maintaining a therapeutic relationship and a sense of hope. This area is additionally complicated by the role of the probation supervision (for those released from prison on licence). There is often an expectation on the individual to address their substance misuse. Being open and honest about the (inevitable) challenges of becoming or remaining substance-free whilst also being subject to licence conditions that could technically punish any substance misuse by recall, is a tricky balance for the individual and worker to navigate. Mason's (1993) concept of "safe uncertainty" is useful to hold in mind. It refers to a collaborative understanding, where different possibilities regarding change and responsibility are considered, of which the individual and worker may have been previously unaware, a process that evolves where parallel ideas are considered.

Developing a collaborative formulation with an individual regarding their emotional responses and how they cope can help to increase insight into what is driving their substance misuse. Figure 6.2 below is a fictional example of a collaborative diagrammatic CAT formulation, with common features of the struggles that individuals have faced when re-entering community life with substance-misuse issues. Having simple pictures, tailored to the individual's core issues, to illustrate painful emotions, can enable thinking and talking together. It can also create a shared understanding and "short-hand" to notice and draw attention to barriers to effective working and connection between individual and worker. For example, a worker might ask "is the padlock on your door again?", to highlight, in an unthreatening way, when an individual appears to be distancing or withdrawing from a discussion. Figure 6.2 illustrates how the individual has internalised a sense of others judging them (from early relationships), which has then left them feeling judged: this role is likely to be featured within current relationships. The individual is also likely to become judging of others, so this dynamic is something experienced and also reciprocated (*judging to judged*). Similarly, the experience of others being mistrusting of them can link to feeling judged (*mistrusting to judged*), which can be reciprocated so the individual can be judging of others, leaving them mistrusted. Both emotional experiences leave the individual feeling the deep pain of injustice, anger, rejection, loneliness and hopelessness. Such pain is difficult to tolerate and therefore, this begins to make sense of why the individual has sought ways to dampen down these feelings via drug and alcohol misuse. Although drug misuse can serve as a valid function in the moment (that of reducing unbearable emotional pain), it can contribute to a sense of feeling overwhelmed, of lacking control, and feeling unable to cope. When the effects of the drugs wear off, the feelings return alongside the often anxious state of either the "beer fears"[1] and/or the lows associated with the physical and psychological withdrawal from the drug. The process of co-constructing the diagram together, "relationship mapping" (Potter, 2020) of externalising internalised feelings and thoughts onto paper, can help to build a collaborative understanding and can help an individual to feel more contained. The aim is then to help identify how else an individual might cope with painful feelings, perhaps incorporating skills training to improve emotion regulation or distress tolerance. Although emotional suppression via substances may still be a choice for them, they also have other strategies to try.

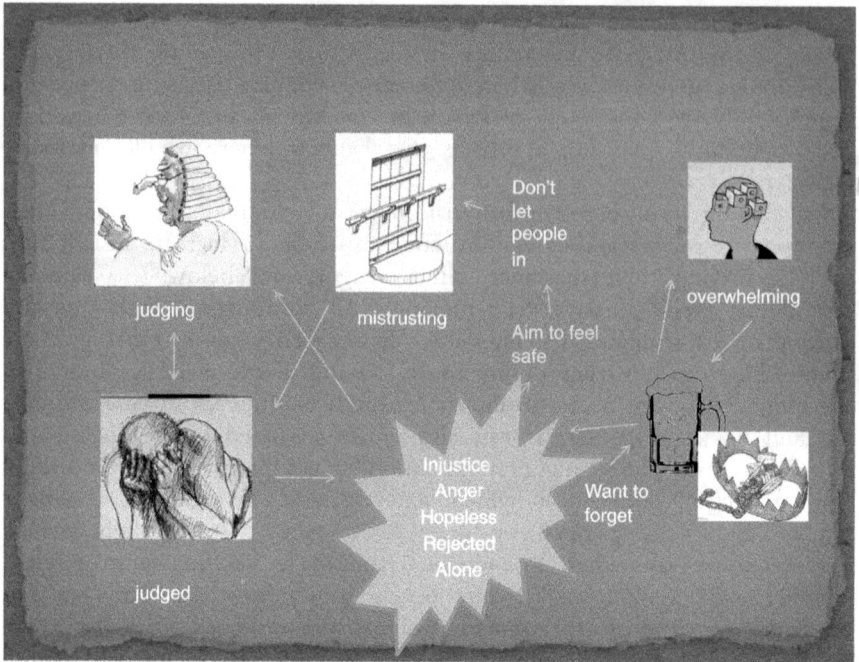

Figure 6.2 Example of a CAT formulation of substance misuse

It is also important to note that it is not just what an individual brings to the relationship that is important, but also what is brought by the worker and the organisational and systemic context. Thinking about issues within a CAT framework enables a more collaborative relationship to be created and enables space to consider what factors within the system, the worker and the person themselves may help or hinder a collaborative relationship. This reduces the tendency to locate responsibility for all issues *within* the person being supported. This can be a useful reminder to help individuals and teams consider what is impacting upon an individual and what service(s) and organisational response might be most effective.

Navigating the professional relationship

In order to enable meaningful engagement, professionals have to maintain hope and connection to the experience of the individual. We need to understand and validate the struggle, the slips, lapses and relapses, sense of embarrassment, fear of failure, of being found out, disowned and shamed. We need to find a way to be alongside people, to remain compassionate, curious and connected, whilst also hopeful even through fluctuations in motivation. We need to appreciate the reality, the level of rationalisation and denial and see these as part of the process of recovery and change rather than a deliberate attempt to deceive. We all carry our own biases, prejudices, tolerance and limits and if we are to work effectively with a marginalised group, it is essential that we are aware of them and are prepared to reflect on and discuss them in professional supervision and support sessions. Such issues will impact upon the therapeutic relationship and can impede an individual from making best use of the support and intervention that is available (Linn-Walton & Pardasani, 2014). The worker's connection with an individual can be understood as being on a continuum, as illustrated in Figure 6.3 below.

The connection can range from being *disconnected*, "*tuning out*" as workers themselves are mentally elsewhere, not listening to the person's words or reality. This can be for a number of reasons. The worker may feel that the individual is not being open about their issues, so there is a level of superficiality between what is being spoken and perceived reality. The worker can feel that they have reached an impasse, that the individual is somewhat unreachable, and/or perhaps has lost hope in their own ability to manage their substance misuse. This area is a risky place for the ongoing relationship and is a sign that the worker needs to reflect upon what is interfering in the relationship connection and consider how they can have an open discussion with the individual regarding what may be getting in the way of their alliance. It is imperative that a worker uses clinical supervision to reflect upon such issues and reflect upon the emotional processes that may be at play (Linn-Walton & Pardasani, 2014).

The worker can also reach a point, of being "over-involved", where they struggle to separate from the person they are working with and can take on too much responsibility. This can leave the person disempowered and dependent. Whilst this can come from a genuinely connected and compassionate place it may be an indication of the worker not reflecting upon their position (individually and in supervision), not being adequately self-aware, supported or supervised in their role and believing that they can "will" the individual into change. This area can lead to a blurring of boundaries, with the worker feeling personally responsible and accountable and the individual dependent and over-reliant upon the worker to assist.

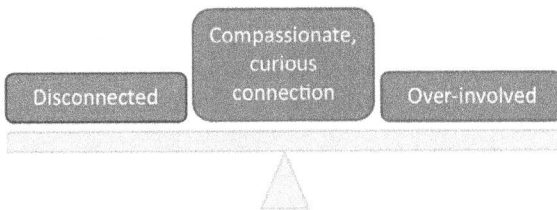

Figure 6.3 The continuum of connection (adapted from "The Boundary See-Saw Model", Hamilton, 2010).

The worker aims to be "compassionately, curiously connecting", which is the optimum position to enable a sense of understanding and development. This point of the therapeutic alliance enables the working relationship to foster realisation of the extent of the challenges and inner dialectical pulls between abstinence and using. Within this position, the worker remains curious and interested in the individual's situation and seeks connection and understanding to help aid their recovery. Being alongside the individual, providing sufficient support and guidance, whilst also being aware of the limitations of what the worker can do and offer, they should aim to be supporting in a non-judgemental way.

As mentioned earlier, working with individuals who misuse substances can be painful, leaving a worker feeling mistrustful and lacking faith in individuals to be able to change or recover. This can permeate outside of work and workers can be more pessimistic and lack faith in individuals generally. They may begin to feel ineffective, doubting of systems and practice. These experiences can lead to feelings of burnout (see Kurtz, 2005) and the disconnection referred to earlier, which can vicariously traumatise workers (McCann & Pearlmann, 1990). The work can feel overwhelming: connecting to the distress that individuals face and continue to experience, the challenges endured, the impact of multiple traumas, rejection and exclusion. It exposes the depths of suffering and the injustices of life. It illustrates the multiple experiences of individuals and the differentiation from those who have privilege, opportunity, choice and support. Support for workers to be consciously aware of such issues, reflect upon the impact on their wellbeing and practice and support to remain compassionately curious about an individual's experience are essential. This provision can easily be undermined if it is not part of a wider system that promotes such reflectiveness, openness within a wider trauma informed culture (see Harris & Fallot, 2001).

Conclusion

This chapter illustrates the complexity of navigating the transition from custody to community life for individuals with a history of substance misuse. It highlights how release into the community can be feared due to past experiences and the lack of provision and support. It brings attention to how services and workers may inadvertently undermine the hope within an individual and leave them feeling mistrusted and hopeless regarding their future. When workers reflect upon their position within supervision, supported by organisational systems that promote such practice, this can enable workers to consider what they bring to the relationship and how more can be achieved by being alongside and enabling a client to feel supported, empowered and enabled, to navigate the transitions into community life.

Despite what can be achieved, there are often lapses, and several attempts to recover, to abstain to navigate re-entry into community life and to find a connected and trusted relationship with professionals to help support and foster meaning and a sense of hope. Whilst we often do not know how we impact individuals with whom we work, we know at a relational level that how we are treated and left feeling by people matters and it is often what we remember. We need to get better at working collaboratively and relationally with individuals who have complex needs. We need to challenge the pull to offer simplistic solutions and instead create systems that are underpinned by a compassionate and caring approach, where staff are supported to express the impact of the work upon them. Then maybe we can help more people to settle into the community on release from prison, supporting the opportunities for them to feel welcomed and to develop increased ways to cope that enable them to understand themselves and better connect with who they are and what they can be.

Note

1 Beer fears: term used to describe feelings of anxiety in not remembering what happened, and sometimes feelings of regret after excessive alcohol/substance misuse.

References

Benefield, N., & Haigh, R. (2020). Personality disorder: breakdown in the relational field, in Ramsden, J., Prince, S. and Blazdell, J. (Eds), *Working Effectively with Personality Disorder: Contemporary and Critical Approaches to Clinical and Organisational Practice* (pp. 35–53). West Sussex: Pavilion.

Department of Health/National Offender Management Service. (2011) *Consultation on the Offender Personality Disorder Pathway Implementation Plan.* Leeds: DoH/Ministry of Justice.

Farrall, S., & Calverley, A. (2006) *Understanding desistance from crime*, Crime and Justice Series. London: Open University Press.

Hamilton, L. (2010). The boundary see-saw model: Good fences make for good neighbours. In A. Tennant & K. Howells (Eds.). *Using Time, not Doing Time: Practitioner Perspectives on Personality Disorder and Risk* (pp. 181–194). Hoboken, New Jersey: Wiley & Sons Ltd.

Harris, M., & Fallot, R. (2001). *Using trauma theory to design service systems. New directions for mental health services.* San Francisco, CA: Jossey-Bass.

Howe, D. (2005). *Child abuse and neglect: Attachment, development and intervention.* London: Palgrave Macmillan.

Hammersley, R. (2011). Pathways through drugs and crime: Desistance, trauma and resilience. *Journal of Criminal Justice*, 39(3), 268–272.

Jones, R., Simonson, P., & Singleton, N. (2010) *Experiences of stigma – everyday barriers for drug users and their families.* London: UK Drug Policy Commission.

Kurtz, A. (2005). The needs of staff who care for people with a diagnosis of personality disorder who are considered a risk to others. *Journal Of Forensic Psychiatry & Psychology*, 16(2), 399–422.

Lander, L., Howsare, J., & Byrne, M. (2013). The impact of substance use disorders on families and children: from theory to practice. *Social Work in Public Health*, 28(3–4), 194–205.

Le Bel, T. P., Burnett, R., Maruna, S., & Bushway, S. (2008). The 'chicken and egg' of subjective and social factors in desistance from crime. *European Journal of Criminology*, 5(2), 131–159.

Linn-Walton, R., & Pardasani, M. (2014). Dislikable clients or countertransference: A clinician's perspective. *The Clinical Supervisor*, 33(1), 100–121.

Luchenski, S., Maguire, N., Aldridge, R. W., Hayward, A., Story, A., Perri, P., Withers, J., Clint, S., Fitzpatrick, S., & Hewett, N. (2018). What works in inclusion health: overview of effective interventions for marginalised and excluded populations. *The Lancet*, 391(10117), 266–280.

Mak, W. W., Chan, R. C., Wong, S. Y., Lau, J. T., Tang, W. K., Tang, A. K., Chiang, T. P., Cheng, S. K., Chan, F., Cheung, F. M., Woo, J., & Lee, D. T. (2017). A cross-diagnostic investigation of the differential impact of discrimination on clinical and personal recovery. *Psychiatric Services*, 68(2), 159–166.

Mason, B. (1993). The human systems: Towards positions of safe uncertainty. *Journal of Systemic Consultation and Management*, 4, 189–200.

McCallum, S. L., Mikocka-Walus, A. A., Gaughwin, M. D., Andrews, J. M., & Turnbull, D. A. (2016). 'I'm a sick person, not a bad person': Patient experiences of treatments for alcohol use disorders. *Health Expectations: An International Journal of Public Participation in Health Care and Health Policy*, 19(4), 828–841.

McCann, I. L., & Pearlman, L. A. (1990). Vicarious traumatization: A framework for understanding the psychological effects of working with victims. *Journal of Traumatic Stress*, 3(1), 131–149.

Potter, S. (2014) Helper's Dance. In J. Lloyd, & P. Clayton (Ed). *Cognitive analytic therapy for people with intellectual disabilities and their carers*. London: Jessica Kingsley.

Potter, S. (2020). *Therapy with a map. A cognitive analytic approach to helping relationships.* West Sussex: Pavilion Publishing and Media Ltd.

Prochaska, J. O., & DiClemente, C. C. (1983). Stages and processes of self-change of smoking: Toward an integrative model of change. *Journal of Consulting and Clinical Psychology*, 51(3), 390–395.

Pycroft, A. (2014). Complexity theory: An overview. In A. Pycroft & C. Bartollas (Eds.), *Applying complexity theory: Whole systems approaches to criminal justice and social work* (pp 13–37). Bristol: Policy Press.

Radcliffe, P., & Stevens, A. (2008). Are drug treatment services only for 'thieving junkie scumbags'? *Drug users and the management of stigmatised identities. Social Science & Medicine*, 67(7), 1065–1073.

Ryan, S., Eldridge, A., Duffy, C., Crawley, E., & O'Brien, C. (2022). Resettle intensive intervention and risk management service (IIRMS): A pathway to desistance? *The Journal of Forensic Practice*, 24(4), 364–375.

Ryle, A., & Kerr, I. B. (2002). *Introducing cognitive analytic therapy: Principles and practice of a relational approach to mental health*. Chichester, West Sussex: John Wiley & Sons.

Shapland, J., & Bottoms, A. (2011). Reflections on social values, offending and desistance among young adult recidivists. *Punishment & Society*, 13(3), 256–282.

Skett, S., Goode, I. & Barton, S. (2017). A join NHS and NOMS offender personality disorder pathway strategy: A perspective from 5 years of operation. *Criminal Behaviour and Mental Health*, 27, 214–221.

Stewart, K., Valentine, L., & Amundsen, J. (1991). The battle for definition: The problem with (the problem). *Journal of Strategic and Systemic Therapies*, 10, 21–31.

Webster, N., & Gardner, S. (2021). Offender personality disorder pathway Intensive Intervention Risk Management Service (IIRMS): Barriers to engagement and a vision for the future. *Probation Journal*, 68(1), 47–63.

7 "How could I know what to do?"

Supporting people in building practical skills for resettlement and reintegration

Jennifer Stickney, Alan Hirons and Hannah Jenner

Introduction

Learning, developing, and applying skills that enable us to live independent productive lives as adults starts from a young age and continues throughout a person's life span (Feldman, 2011). Many people in prison, particularly those serving long sentences, have experienced layers of chronic trauma, occupational disruption,[1] occupational deprivation[2] and institutionalisation. These circumstances prevent or reduce the ability and opportunity to develop, often taken for granted, practical skills essential for successful community living.

Within this chapter we draw on our experience as Occupational Therapists working with people who are receiving services as part of the national Offender Personality Disorder Pathway (Skett, Goode, & Barton, 2017). A prime function of our work is facilitating individuals' development, application and maintenance of practical skills needed for everyday living as they move from prison into the community. For the purpose of this chapter, we have defined practical skills as *the combined mental and physical actions that enable people to adaptively and effectively engage with everyday life situations with a degree of predictable outcome*. Whilst we touch on the relational element within practical skills, we do not focus on this extensively as it is covered in more detail in Chapter 9.

Our experience leads us to propose that the range and quality of the practical skills that people have available in the context of their physical and social environments is a critical component in the success or otherwise of their return to community living and desistance. Our experience indicates that people's practical skills should not be 'taken for granted' or regarded as 'common-sense' and that their development and maintenance is a consequence of many developmental, relational, social and environmental factors. We assert that when people experience the consistent and ongoing feeling of 'competence' resulting from effective application of their practical skills, these experiences contribute to the formation of more adaptive identities and roles and the associated activities of these identities and roles. Critically, these experiences have the potential to provide evidence of the usefulness of engagement with other people to support "immediate survival, emotional regulation, and the development and maintenance of quality of life" (Hirons & Sutherland, 2020, p.159).

DOI: 10.4324/9781003308171-9

In this chapter we explore the repercussions of attachment disruption and chronic childhood trauma in limiting a person's ability to learn and develop practical skills from our perspectives and experiences as community practitioners. We explore the impact of prison on practical skills and the consequences of this on people's transition to the community. We then present a model that one of the authors has developed to contextualise and facilitate the work of developing people's practical skills. Finally, we highlight the key areas we focus on, as community practitioners, to support people on release from prison to learn and apply practical skills to support their everyday community living.

We have included the voices of a range of people with lived experience with whom we have worked, to provide increased insight into the obstacles they face and the impact these have on their resettlement experience.

The impact of attachment disruption and childhood trauma on learning practical skills

Learning how we look after ourselves and engage with our surroundings begins from birth. The learning and development of skills is impacted significantly by the quality and degree of attunement of care received within the first few years of a person's life. Within caring and nurturing environments children commonly learn and develop "good habits" (Giovagnoli, 2018, p.182) such as having a bath, cleaning teeth, eating regular meals, changing clothes when dirty and going to bed at a particular time. Habits can be defined as "acquired behaviour patterns regularly followed until they become almost involuntary" (Habit, 2019). Habits form the starting point that structure the actions (skills) of everyday living and facilitate internalised role development (Kielhofner, 2008). When children are bought up in uncaring environments, it is much more difficult for good habits to be learnt. As a result, children growing up in these environments are likely to not have the skills to know how to look after themselves or their surroundings effectively (Heckman, 2006). This is highlighted by Paul who reflected:

> As a boy, in 1948, I lived in a 2-bed cottage on a farm with no electricity with my granny, mother, auntie, and three uncles. The house was filthy, infested with fleas … I spent as much time as I could outside, nobody was really interested in me. I don't remember ever having a bath or brushing my teeth, my clothes were old with holes all over them, I never remember them being clean, I was never shown how to wash them.

Attachment theory (Bowlby, 1969) and the importance of having a secure attachment to a primary caregiver is well researched and can begin to help us to better understand why many of the people that we work with have difficulties with the knowledge and application of practical everyday living skills. Ainsworth, Blehar, Waters and Wall (1978) introduced the idea that secure attachment is essential for *exploration*. Feeling unconditionally loved by another person acts as the foundation for exploring environments, objects and ideas, enjoying learning and developing skills. In addition to this there is evidence to suggest that secure attachments form the foundations of epistemic trust (Fonagy, Luyten & Allison, 2015). Epistemic trust describes the willingness to accept new information from another person as trustworthy, generalisable, and relevant. It has been suggested that "attachment may mediate the reliable transmission of knowledge from one generation to the next" (Fonagy & Alison, 2014, p. 373). Those who have an insecure attachment to their caregiver feel less safe, are less able to trust and therefore are less able to learn from others and social experiences (Fonagy & Allison, 2014). Corriveau et al. (2009) found that children with insecure-disorganised histories displayed behaviour that evidenced chronic epistemic vigilance or epistemic hypervigilance. That is, they regarded all information sources with suspicion and showed little confidence in their own perception. If all information is perceived as suspicious it makes learning new information and skills challenging.

Childhood trauma contributes to disturbance in learning. When a child experiences significant and chronic trauma, their primary focus is on survival. This can result in them being stuck in a chronic state of *fight, flight*, or *freeze* (Kozlowska, Walker, McLean, & Carrive, 2015; see Chapters 4 and 5), whereby most of their energy is applied to self-preservation. In this state the connection between the brain's ability to process information, the body's internal drive and the child's ability to meaningfully engage in life is impaired. Consequently, the child has limited capacity and motivation for learning and developing skills, such as interactive play, problem solving with others, interpersonal communication, emotional regulation, and empathy (Seifert, 2016).

In addition to the trauma a child experiences from maltreatment, abuse, neglect and emotional abandonment, it is important to consider the impact that living in an unpredictable, inconsistent and dangerous environment can have on a child's development. Sampson and Laub (1990) bring attention to the established relationship between childhood environmental factors and adult criminality such as aggression and antisocial behaviour. One of the many consequences of uncaring and abusive environments is that a child is exposed to "bad habits, those that powerfully take control of our behaviour" (Giovagnoli, 2018, p.182). Abusive parents or other significant individuals commonly neglect to support a child in developing good habits; rather, they model antisocial or criminal behaviour (Prather & Golden, 2009). This can ultimately result in children following similar behaviour and activity patterns to their caregivers as they grow up, having learnt few good habits and associated roles that provide the baseline for developing practical skills, essential for lawful community living (Herrenkohl, Jung, Lee, & Kim, 2016). The combination of low epistemic trust, being stuck in a chronic state of *fight, flight*, or *freeze* and living in uncaring and abusive environments result in a child being unable to engage in and integrate positive social learning.

The impact of prison on the ability to learn, develop and apply practical skills

The Ministry of Justice Prison Strategy White Paper (2021) highlights that the purpose of prisons is to protect the public, punish the offender, and promote rehabilitation to reduce reoffending. However, with the length of custodial sentences on the rise (Prison Reform Trust, 2022a), overcrowding in prisons (Howard League for Penal Reform, 2019) and significant staff shortages (Prison Reform Trust, 2022b) there is an increased tension between being in custody and being rehabilitated where "'rehabilitation' as a goal of imprisonment arguably seems like a well-meaning but fruitless endeavour" (Jewkes & Gooch, 2019, p.115). The Prison Strategy White Paper (Ministry of Justice, 2021) acknowledges the challenges of prisons today and the need for a more personalised approach to supporting people's journey through prison, where individuals' skills and strengths are recognised as well as their needs and risks.

Within this section we highlight the impact of a number of key themes that, from our experience, negatively impact on the development and application of practical skills required for successful community resettlement. These include institutionalisation and associated themes of depersonalisation, loss of choice, reduced resources for self-care, and lack of access to information technology.

Institutionalisation

Prison for some people can feel safe, containing, familiar and comfortable in stark contrast to their experiences of the outside world as highlighted by Rob.

> Rob reflected that the three years he had spent at the same prison was the longest he had ever stayed in one place. He felt settled there, understood how life worked, had a place where he felt a sense of community and belonging.
>
> Rob's experience highlights that some of those who have spent many years in prison are familiar and skilled in navigating this environment and, whilst it is often not a place people enjoy being in, it can feel like home.

Haney (2003) describes the process of people adjusting to and managing prison life as "prisonization", which is a "unique set of psychological adaptations that involves the incorporation of the norms of prison life into one's habits of thinking, feeling and acting" (p. 5). The changes that are required to help people survive in prison, such as "social withdrawal", adapting to being "emotionally over-controlled" (Crewe, Hulley, & Wright, 2019, p. 7), and "dependence on institutional structure, hypervigilance, interpersonal distrust and suspicion" (Haney, 2003, p. 81) are likely to act as barriers in managing release and community resettlement.

Schinkel (2021) highlights that prison erodes people's sense of "belonging to life outside [which] presents a significant barrier to long-term desistance" (p. 14). On recall back to prison Neil stated:

> How could I know what to do, I am institutionalised. I have spent most of my teenage and adult life in jail, I don't have the skills any more to live on the outside.

This reflection represents the damage prison can do to both people's skills and to their belief in their ability to cope on release. Edgar, Jacobson and Biggar (2011) highlight concern that prison should not turn people into *good prisoners* but support the development of skills that assist with coping and managing living outside of the prison gates.

Some people approaching their release date become more consciously aware of their limited skills and lack of knowledge about how to successfully navigate community living. At these times individuals experience feelings of fear and anxiety about how they are going to survive in the community. For some, this anxiety and fear can be so strong that there is little incentive to be released, as captured by Sean:

> What has the outside got for me, I am OK in prison I've been here long enough, over 27 years. I know how to do prison. I don't know how to do anything on the outside; what is there for me out there.

And for others, once they are released, it is experienced as so challenging they feel unable to remain in the community, as reflected by Wayne:

> On release I felt I didn't belong in the world any more... I knew I had two choices either I go back to prison, or I take my life... so I walked out of the hostel, missed my curfew and got myself recalled.

Depersonalisation

As part of the process of institutionalisation and prisonisation, we identify that prisons have a tendency to mould individuals into generic prisoners, with a consequent loss of personal sense of identity. Individuality is not acknowledged, and prison regimes remove opportunities for freedom of choice, personal planning and problem solving. After the initial induction into prison life a person may be allocated programmes to attend to address their offending behaviour, or education to help them focus on developing work-related skills. They may be allocated a job to occupy them, which pays a token amount of money to motivate engagement, but not enough to help save for release. Commonly, prison work does not prepare people for the demands of employment in the community, as work within prison is rarely comparable to that in the outside world. There are few opportunities to develop or maintain more generalised practical skills, such as how to use a household washing machine, iron a shirt, budget or operate ever-changing technology. Rather than supporting and actively teaching practical skill development in preparation for release, prison life generally erodes skills and identity. It creates feelings of frustration and an inevitable dependency on others to resolve difficulties and plan for the future.

Loss of choice

Prison regimes limit people's ability to apply choice to their lives. Taking away choice jeopardises people's ability to retain skills, such as effective decision making, prioritising tasks and problem solving. It can therefore be an unexpected shock on release when people are required to make decisions for themselves, problem solve and prioritise what to do, when and in what order. This in turn can affect their view of themselves regarding their skills and competencies in managing community living.

Using the specific example of food,

> The majority of what prisoners eat in prison is determined for them. Unlike in the community, prisoners do not have the freedom to decide what or how much they want to eat, nor are they able to choose when they eat the majority of their meals.
>
> (HMIP, 2016, p. 3)

This lack of choice impacts on people in prison's understanding of what constitutes a healthy, balanced diet, how to plan and put together a balanced meal and how to manage portion sizes all of which are important skills in preparation for when a person moves into the community.

Reduced resources for self-care

Prison exacerbates difficulties in prioritising self-care as there is currently no set standard to ensure all those in prison have regular access to showering facilities. It is therefore easy for those who do not have the habits or skills in self-care to miss these opportunities and neglect themselves. Poor personal hygiene can become a perpetual cycle that creates barriers to social inclusion, which further impacts upon mental health, self-worth, routine and motivation (Stewart, Judd, & Wheeler, 2022).

Lack of access to information technology

Jewkes and Reisdorf (2016) identify that prisoners "constitute one of the most impoverished groups in the digital age" (p. 1). Lack of access to technology in preparation for re-entering society makes individuals feel more isolated, as they are unable to keep up with current media content. Prisons function in a timeless state, where there is little connection with community advancements. The increased use of technology in the community over the last 40 years in addition to the reduction in face-to-face contact, a legacy from the COVID-19 pandemic, is not emulated within the prison estate. As a result of this ever-changing world, the reality of living in the community can be very different from a person's memories of what life was like before prison, especially for those being released following long custodial sentences (Taxman, Young & Byrne, 2002).

Limited opportunities to graded transition from prison to the community

Open prisons are designed to offer a graded approach to release through gradual exposure to the community using ROTL (Release on Temporary Licence).[3] ROTL enables people to experience different environments, using both day and overnight release to support gaining understanding and skills in different areas of community living. However, ROTL is generally only available in open prisons, limiting who has access to a small minority of people. Therefore, for most people being released, there is a sudden change from being completely dependent on an institution to having to be instantaneously independent (Taxman et al., 2002).

Challenges with community re-entry and resettlement

The lived experience voice in this chapter highlights that many who have had attachment disruption, chronic childhood trauma and are released from prison following a long sentence lack knowledge in general life skills. Jones (2004) recognises the importance of people having the skills to meet their basic needs on release from prison, which in turn assists in reducing recidivism. He suggests that if people are not able to meet their basic needs, such as accessing food, water, suitable clothing and safe housing, they are unlikely to be able to focus on becoming law-abiding citizens.

In our experience, on release people often have lists of things they state they want to achieve, including getting a job, a flat, finding a partner, joining the gym, and going on holiday. However, release is often much harder than anticipated and whilst some people have felt able to navigate everyday life in prison, release is a harsh and stark reminder of how lacking they are in practical skills for adaptive community living. We identify three core themes, that of 'feeling overwhelmed', 'feeling unskilled' and 'needing secure housing' which describe the experience of the move from prison to the community.

Feeling overwhelmed

The reality of release can feel overwhelming and stressful; especially if compounded by unrealistic expectations and feeling deskilled. These feelings can have a detrimental effect on motivation, self-belief and ultimately health, which in turn can negatively affect community resettlement (Oettingen, 1996). It is not unusual for people to excitedly welcome release, but quickly find it unexpectedly stressful. Gary spoke of the effect prison had on him after 18 months of being inside:

> [Prison] made me institutionalised, dependent on others. I find thinking for myself..., doing anything for myself hard. It is much easier being back inside, you don't have to worry about where you are going to sleep, finding food, paying bills. My brain sort of shuts down [being outside] ... it's really hard, man... I sort of think why bother... I've lost all motivation.

As Gary identified, stress affects our cognitive abilities, impacting on rational decision making, effective problem solving and motivation (Social Exclusion Unit, 2002; see Chapter 2). Developing the skills in knowing how and what to prioritise is important when having to juggle many tasks that can feel impossible without support. Rob spoke of how difficult he found release:

> I had so many things to think about and do, each one made me feel overwhelmed. I really wanted to make things work, I didn't want people to know I was struggling, but the more I tried the harder things seemed. I was so focused on not messing up, I ended up really messing up.

Feeling unskilled

The lack of ability to carry out what many see as simple, taken for granted, practical everyday domestic tasks can be a fundamentally shameful experience on re-entering the community. Rob reflected:

> I had to have one of the lads [in the hostel] show me how to use a washing machine as nobody has ever shown me before.

Rob's experience demonstrates the combined impact of not having a significant caregiver to teach daily living skills as a child and living in an environment that did not encourage social learning. This combination resulted in Rob experiencing embarrassment on release about his limited domestic skills. He wanted to be seen as skilled and competent, but, like many others, found release highlighted the lack of skills he had in managing everyday living. This affected his self-esteem and self-belief, and his ability to make effective decisions. In order to gain some sense of control, he turned to familiar maladaptive coping strategies that increased his risk to others and resulted in recall back to prison.

Keith's reflection below exemplifies the shame, embarrassment, and frustration he felt on the realisation he did not have the money awareness he needed during a ROTL:

> The first time I went out on ROTL I was given an envelope at the [prison] gate and told that was my money for the day. I didn't think

anything of it until I got off the bus in town. I opened the envelope and inside was plastic money, looked like the sort you find in monopoly. I thought the officers had me for a mug, I felt really mad …they had a joke on me and had given me toy money. This was the first time I had been out in 30 odd years; I was spuing… Then I watched this lady. She went up to a coffee van and paid for the coffee with plastic money. I had no idea money had changed so much. No one told me, how was I supposed to know. I felt stupid. I wish I had been told.

Over a third of people in prison do not have a bank account (Bath & Edgar, 2010). Being able to open a bank account in prison is rare and opening a bank account in the community after serving a long sentence is challenging. Limited access to and awareness of money management can cause significant difficulties immediately on release and can affect a person's sense of self. Mark's statement below highlights the difficulties this can cause in resettlement.

I don't think they [society] want people like me to succeed. I have been trying for three years to open a bank account and keep giving up. Too many hurdles, the looks I am given in the bank… I hate it, it is too hard. I feel like I am always under the radar. That is where they want me, if they let me rise above the radar, they would have to do something to help me, and they don't want to. So here I am under the radar trying to live my life.

Once a person has a bank account set up, they are in a better position to successfully apply for benefits. However, without knowledge or support claiming benefits can be complex and challenging. McNeil and Whyte (2007) highlight that financial insecurity and debt problems are significant risk factors to re-offending. Money management and financial knowledge are skills that can be taught and developed (Koenig, 2007) and as Mark demonstrates, providing accurate support on release from prison can ameliorate difficulties experienced in this area.

Many of the older population on release struggle with how to use modern technology, more specifically the internet and smartphones; how to call from them, answer them, send and receive messages and voicemails. Those who are younger tend to adjust to technology more easily, but some have limited knowledge and understanding around online safety, and the implications of putting themselves in risky situations through using technology carelessly. The Centre for Social Justice (2021) identifies that "The lack of access to digital technology and the internet [in prison] presents serious obstacles to prisoners who are attempting to find employment or to access the welfare system [on release]" (p. 29).

Needing secure housing

Grimshaw and Fraser (2008) identify that access to the right housing is one of the most important aspects of resettlement. Stable accommodation increases individuals' opportunities to access employment and training (Harper & Chitty, 2005) and improves prosocial community connections that support desistance. Williams, Poyser and Hopkins (2012) highlight that 60% of prisoners believed that having a stable place to live was important in stopping them from reoffending. It is therefore imperative that when looking at practical skill development and application on release from prison, that this is seen within the context of where a person is living, and their accommodation needs. For people to be able to learn and develop new skills, they need to be in an environment where they feel safe-enough, supported and have opportunities to develop and test their epistemic trust in those around them, which in turn supports social learning.

The Model of Wellbeing in Health and Justice

In response to the Ministry of Justice Prison Strategy White Paper (2021), which acknowledged the need for a more personalised prison regime, His Majesty's Prison and Probation Service (HMPPS) Future Regime Design Team engaged two Occupational Therapists within the National Health Service (NHS) to review literature of what constitutes a healthy, balanced lifestyle and how this can be transferred to the new National Regime Model (as described within the Ministry of Justice Prison Strategy White Paper 2021) within the prison estate (and on release). This literature review led to the development of the Model of Wellbeing in Health and Justice, Diagram 1 (Gunderson, Holmes, & Stickney, 2023). This model provides a framework for developing and maintaining skills that support a healthy, balanced lifestyle for people within the criminal justice system. It draws attention to the value of developing a range of practical skills including *productive use of time* (activities that provide a sense of accomplishment, achievement and give someone a sense of validation and worth), *self-care* (activities that support physical, mental and emotional wellbeing), and *leisure* (activities that are done for enjoyment, pleasure, satisfaction and can support self-regulation). This model also incorporates the importance of *mattering* (Rosenberg & McCullough, 1981; activities that help people feel that they are important, significant and what they do matters). Mattering is of particular interest within criminal justice settings as specific links are made between individuals who have a low sense of mattering and those who engage in antisocial and offending behaviours (Marshall, 2004; Lewis, 2017; see Chapter 10). The Model of Wellbeing in Health and Justice encourages prison services to review regime delivery within the framework of a healthy, balanced lifestyle to support health and wellbeing throughout a person's journey within the criminal justice service. Maintaining and developing practical skills whilst in prison can be instrumental in supporting people to manage both prison life and enabling them to be better prepared for the skills needed on release.

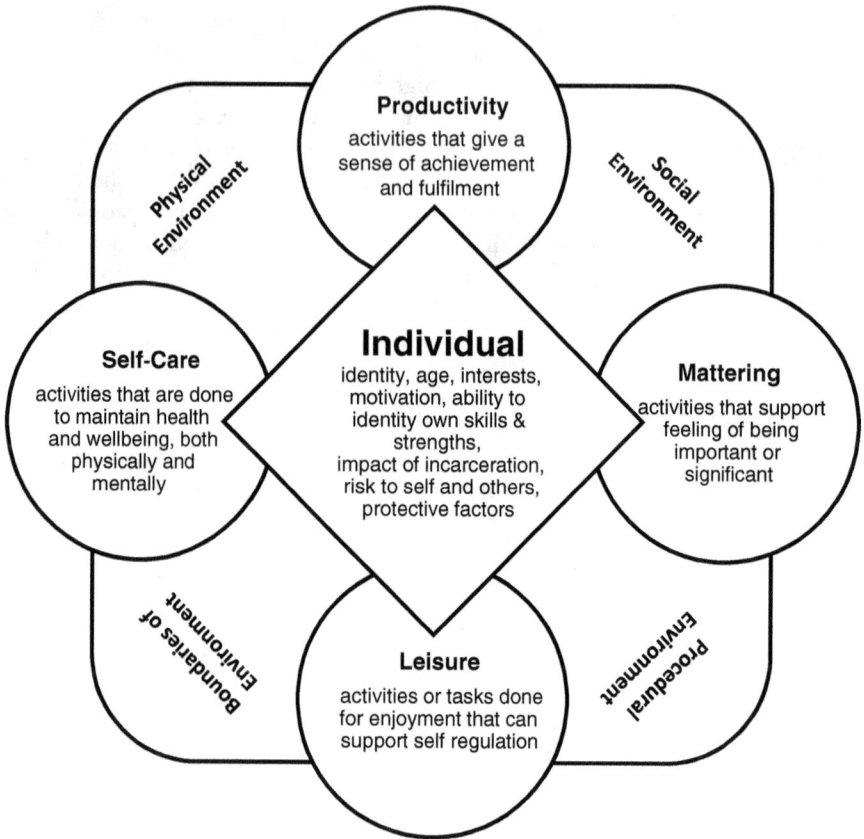

Figure 7.1 Model of Wellbeing in Health and Justice. Copyright © (2022) Holmes, E. & Stickney, J. Model of Wellbeing in Health and Justice, Future Regime Design (HMPPS). Reprinted with permission.

Key areas to assist in the development and application of practical skills

Within the final part of this chapter, we identify the key areas we focus on to support people moving from prison to the community in order to develop practical skills. We bring together the themes we have discussed in this chapter to facilitate a personalised approach for each individual being supported, which can be broadly seen through using the different components that form the Model of Wellbeing in Health and Justice.

Practical skills and good habits

The voices of people with lived experience throughout this chapter highlight the shame, embarrassment, and a real sense of hopelessness in not having the skills needed for community living on release from prison. They also highlight the impact that not having these skills has on self-worth and feeling accepted. These voices are reminders of the importance of having effective strategies and plans in place to support developing practical skills on release. Luther, Reichert, Holloway, Roth, and Aalsma (2011) acknowledge the importance of focusing on meeting individuals' basic needs on re-entry into the community to facilitate successful resettlement and reduce recidivism.

Good habits "reduce the complexity of daily life; they simply make our daily life easier and pleasant" (Giovagnolo, 2018, p. 181). They form the foundation in developing skills that support structure and routine, which in turn improves prospects for social inclusion and engagement in daily life. The formation of good habits can be supported through a number of behaviour-change techniques. These include, but are not limited to, action planning (planning when, where and how the behaviour is going to be performed); demonstration and teaching; rehearsal and repetition; prompts/cues; self-monitoring and social support (Lally & Gardner, 2013; Gardner & Rebar, 2019; Fritz, Hu, Gahman, Almacen & Ottolini, 2020).

Using different professional lenses can assist in formulating alternative explanations for behaviour, which interferes with practical skill development and social engagement. Understanding the root cause to practical skill difficulties (e.g., skill deficit, lack of motivation, poor memory, lack of access to personal values, impact of mental health problems, etc.) helps in tailoring interventions to address the presenting difficulties. Liaising with other professionals both in prison and within the community can support forming and implementing effective strategies to aid the development of good habits.

It is important that we consciously synthesise and utilise different professional perspectives; specifically, these are *occupation and health* (Occupational Therapy), *attachment, trauma, and epistemic trust* (Psychology) and *offender rehabilitation* (Probation). We are then more able to develop effective formulation and understanding of people's individual circumstances and their struggles to develop and enact practical skills.

Trusting and therapeutic relationships

"In the absence of trust, the capacity for change is absent" (Fonagy & Allison, 2014, p. 375). Therefore, the first step in supporting individuals in developing practical skills needed for community resettlement is to build a trusting relationship and, in turn, develop the potential for a reduction in epistemic vigilance, an increase in epistemic trust and consequently increased access to social learning. The subject of relationships is covered in Chapter 9, but is an important factor to note here due to the role professional relationships play in supporting practical skill development as a person re-enters the community. Welford, Milner and Morton (2021) highlight that building community focused relationships can support well-co-ordinated release plans and "reduce the risk of the prison leaver returning to people or places that might lead to missing appointments or reoffending" (p. 36).

People's expectations and values

Unrealistic aspirations about what life will be like on release causes significant difficulties when these aspirations are not realised. For people who find emotional regulation difficult and ruminate on perceived failure, the use of language when framing discussions around expectations for release preparation is important. Whilst it is not uncommon to set goals, and have goal planning meetings, the word 'goal' creates a platform to base success and failure. Jones, Papadakis, Orr and Strauman (2013) highlight that "failure to make progress toward personal goals can lead to negative affective states, such as depression and anxiety" and "rumination in response to goal failure may prolong and intensify those acute emotional responses" (p. 1). We therefore avoid using the words 'goals' and 'goal setting' and instead work with people to identify and understand their values (how they wish to 'be' and 'do' in their lives; LeJeune & Luoma, 2019). We explore how each person can enact their values in their lives, alongside understanding their agency of thought (why is this important and what motivates them; Van Ginneken, 2015). From this position we collaboratively develop plans that are more realisable and achievable within the context of each person's values. Within these plans, we use language that reflects support, hope and optimism to encourage persistence and perseverance in the face of adversity when working towards what is important (Van Ginneken, 2015). We regularly revisit plans to ensure that they reflect the changing values of each person as they move into the community and resettle.

Suitable housing

Suitable accommodation on release from prison is a person's first and most essential requirement (Edgar, Aresti, & Cornish, 2012). Without a permanent residence the chance of making any kind of progress in other spheres of life is compromised. Priority has to be given to securing appropriate accommodation where a person can feel safe in a stable home. Whilst access to the right housing is one of the most importance aspects of resettlement (Grimshaw & Fraser, 2008) due to a lack of housing in England and Wales this can be enormously challenging. We work closely with offender managers and housing officers to identify the type of accommodation each individual needs and, where supported accommodation is identified, we assist in the referral process for this.

Identity and meaning through practical skills

All of the key areas identified above individually and collectively contribute to the ultimate task of assisting people who have experienced multiple layers of adversity and lack of opportunity, to engage more consistently in the ongoing process of developing adaptive and pro-social identities. Our experience indicates that engagement in these key areas, provides an essential and effective foundation to facilitate thinking and participation in the development of practical skills, which ultimately enable more successful transition from prison to the community. Our deliberate emphasis in this chapter on practical skills goes beyond them just being needed for effective community living, but that the ongoing experience of doing them and the consequences of doing them, speaks directly to people's sense of identity in relationship to themselves and other people.

Conclusion

As community Occupational Therapists, our work is focused on assisting people to enact occupations: daily life activities and practical skills, which they need to, want to or are required to do. The Occupational Therapy profession identifies the immediate relationship between what people *do and do not do* in their daily lives and their experience of health, relationships and quality of life.

Our observations as community practitioners are that because the *doing* of daily life activities are obviously done by everybody in their daily lives, the notion of practical skills becomes 'taken for granted' and it is assumed they occur naturally and normally as part of human development. However, we know from the early life experiences of the people we work with, that the development of practical skills cannot be a 'taken for granted' process and needs to be understood in the context and consequence of attachment disruption, trauma and loss. Indeed, we do the people we work with a disservice when we hold either consciously or unconsciously this 'taken for granted' stance.

We assert to effectively engage with and be of service to people leaving prison and ultimately society, that the processes of developing and enacting practical skills, needs to be consciously and deliberately enacted.

Notes

1 Occupational disruption – "occurs when a person's normal pattern of occupational engagement is disrupted due to significant life events" (Whiteford, 2000, p. 201).
2 Occupational deprivation – "state in which a person or group of people are unable to do what is necessary and meaningful in their lives due to external restrictions" (Whiteford, 2000, p. 200).
3 ROTL – Release on Temporary Licence. This is part of the process for the resettlement and rehabilitation where individuals in prison can spend time in the community as a way of preparing for release.

References

Ainsworth, M. D. S., Blehar, M. C., Waters, E., & Wall, S. (1978). *Patterns of attachment: Assessed in the strange situation and at home*. Hillside, NJ: Lawrence Erlbaum.
Bath, C., & Edgar, K. (2010). *Time is money – Financial responsibility after prison*. London: Prison Reform Trust and UNLOCK.
Bowlby, J. (1969). *Attachment and Loss*. New York: Basic Books.
Collins Dictionary (2019) Habit retrieved from https://www.collinsdictionary.com/dictionary/english/habit.
Corriveau, K., Harris, P. L., Meins, E., Fernyhough, C., Arnott, B., Elliott, L., Liddle, B., Hearn, A., Vittorini, L., & De Rosnay, M. (2009). Young children's trust in their

mother's claims: longitudinal links with attachment security in infancy. *Child Development*, 80, 750–761.

Crewe, B., Hulley, S., & Wright, S. (2019). *Experiencing long term imprisonment from young adulthood: Identity, adaptation and penal legitimacy*. Ministry of Justice analytical series. London: HMPPS.

Edgar, K., Jacobson, J., & Biggar, K. (2011). *Time well spent: A practical guide to active citizenship and volunteering in prison*. London: Prison Reform Trust.

Edgar, K., Aresti, A., & Cornish, N. (2012). *Out for good: Taking responsibility for resettlement*. London: Prison Reform Trust.

Feldman, R. (2011). *Development across the life span* (6th ed). New Jersey: Pearson/ Prentice Hall.

Fonagy, P., & Allison, E. (2014) The role of mentalizing and epistemic trust in the therapeutic relationship. *Psychotherapy*, 51(3), 372–380.

Fonagy, P., Luyten, P., & Allison, E. (2015) Epistemic petrification and the restoration of epistemic trust: A new conceptualisation of borderline personality disorder and its psychosocial treatment. *Journal of Personality Disorders*, 29(5), 575–609.

Fritz, H., Hu, Y. L., Gahman, K., Almacen, C., & Ottolini, J. (2020). Intervention to modify habits: A scoping review. *Occupational Therapy Journal of Research: Occupation, Participation and Health*, 40(2), 99–112.

Gardner, B., & Rebar, A. (2019). Habit formation and behavior change. In: *Oxford research encyclopedia of psychology* (pp. 1–26). Oxford: Oxford University Press.

Giovagnoli, R. (2018) From habits to rituals: Rituals as social habits. *Open Information Science*, 2(1), 181–188.

Grimshaw, R., & Fraser, P. (2008). Prisoner resettlement and accommodation: Challenges for the new corrections. *Criminal Justice Matters*, 56, 18–43.

Gunderson, C., Holmes, E., & Stickney, J. (2023) *The National Regime Model: A partnership approach to transforming prison regimes; improving outcomes for staff and prisoners in England and Wales*. Manuscript submitted for publication.

Haney, C. (2003). *The psychological impact of incarceration: Implications for post-prison adjustment*. Paper presented at the US Department of Health and Human Services Conference, "From home to prison The effect of incarceration and reentry on children, families and communities". Bethesda, MD.

Harper, G., & Chitty, C. (2005). The impact of corrections on reoffending: a review of "what works". Home Office research study 291. London: Home Office.

Heckman, J. (2006). Skill formation and the economics of investing in disadvantaged children. *Science*, 312(5782), 1900–1902.

Her Majesty's Inspectorate of Prisons (HMIP) (2016). *Life in prison. Food.* London: HMIP.

Herrenkohl, T. I., Jung, H., Lee, J. O., & Kim, M-H. (2016). Effects of child maltreatment, cumulative victimization experiences and proximal life stress on adult crime and antisocial behavior. U.S. Department of Justice. Retrieved from: https:// www.ojp.gov/pdffiles1/nij/grants/250506.pdf.

Hirons, A., & Sutherland, R. (2020) Re-imagining interventions. In J. Ramsden, S. Prince & J. Blazdell, (Eds) *Working effectively with personality disorder: Contemporary and critical approaches to clinical and organisational practice* (pp. 155–167). London: Pavilion Publishing.

Howard League for Penal Reform (2019). *Revealed: The scale of prison overcrowding in England and Wales*. London: Howard League for Penal Reform.

Jewkes, Y., & Reisdorf, B.C. (2016). A brave new world: The problems and opportunities presented by new media technologies in prisons. *Criminology and Criminal Justice*, 16(5), 534.

Jewkes, Y., & Gooch, K. (2019). The rehabilitation prison: An oxymoron or an opportunity to radically reform imprisonment. In P. Ugwudike, H. Graham, F. McNeill, P. Raynor, F. S. Taxman, C., & Trotter (Eds). *The Routledge companion to rehabilitative work in criminal justice* (pp. 153–166). Abingdon, Oxon: Routledge.

Jones, M. (2004). Maslow's hierarchy of needs can lower recidivism. *Corrections Today*, 66(4), 18–21.

Jones, N. P., Papadakis, A. A., Orr, C. A., & Strauman, T. J. (2013). Cognitive processes in response to goal failure: A study of ruminative thought and its affective consequences. *Journal of Social and Clinical Psychology*, 32(5), 482–503.

Kielhofner, G. (2008). *Model of human occupation: Theory and application* (4th ed). Baltimore: Lippincott Williams & Wilkins.

Koenig, L. A. (2007). Financial literacy curriculum: The effect on offender money management skills. *Journal of Correctional Education*, 58(1), 43–56.

Kozlowska, K., Walker, P., McLean, L., & Carrive, P. (2015). Fear and the defense cascade: Clinical implications and management. *Harvard Review of Psychiatry*, 23(4), 263–287.

Lally, P., & Gardner, B. (2013). Promoting habit formation. *Health Psychology Review*, 7(1), 137–158.

LeJeune, J., & Luoma, J. B. (2019). *Values in therapy: A clinician's guide to helping clients explore values, increase psychological flexibility, and live a more meaningful life.* California: New Harbinger Publications.

Lewis, D. M. (2017) A matter for concern: Young offenders and the importance of mattering. *Deviant Behavior*, 38(11), 1318–1331.

Luther, J., Reichert, E., Holloway, E., Roth, A., & Aalsma, M.C. (2011). An exploration of community re-entry needs and services for prisoners: A focus on care to limit return to high-risk behavior. *AIDS Patient Care and STDs*, 25(8), 475–481.

McNeil, F., & Whyte, B. (2007). *Reducing reoffending*. Cullompton, Devon: Willan Publishing.

Marshall, S. K. (2004). Relative contributions of perceived mattering to parents and friends in predicting adolescents' psychological well-being. *Perceptual and Motor Skills*, 99(2), 591–601.

Ministry of Justice (2021). The prison strategy white paper. Retrieved from: https://assets.publishing.service.gov.uk/government/uploads/system/uploads/attachment_data/file/1038765/prisons-strategy-white-paper.pdf.

Oettingen, G. (1996). Positive fantasy and motivation. In P. M. Gollwitzer & J. A. Bargh (Eds.), *The psychology of action: Linking cognition and motivation to behaviour* (pp. 236–259). New York: Guilford Press.

Prather, W., & Golden, J. A. (2009). Learning and thinking: A behavioral treatise on abuse and antisocial behavior in young criminal offenders. *The International Journal of Behavioral Consultation and Therapy*, 5, 75–105.

Prison Reform Trust (2022a). Bromley briefings prison factfile (Winter 2022). Retrieved from: https://prisonreformtrust.org.uk/wp-content/uploads/2022/02/Winter-2022-Factfile.pdf.

Prison Reform Trust (2022b). Prison: The facts Bromley Briefings (Summer 2022). Retrieved from: https://prisonreformtrust.org.uk/wp-content/uploads/2022/07/Prison-the-facts-2022.pdf.

Rosenberg, M., & McCullough, B. C. (1981) Mattering: Inferred significance and mental health among adolescents. *Research in Community and Mental Health*, 2, 163–182.

Sampson, R. J., & Laub, J. H. (1990). Crime and deviance over the life course: The salience of adult social bonds. *American Sociological Review*, 55(5), 609–627.

Schinkel, M. (2021). Persistent short-term imprisonment: Belonging as a lens to understand its shifting meanings over the life course. *Incarceration*, 2(1), 1–20.

Seifert, K. M. (2016). Attachment and the development of relationship skills. *Journal of Psychology and Clinical Psychiatry*, 5(2), 1–9.

Skett, S., Goode, I., & Barton, S. (2017) A joint NHS and NOMS offender personality disorder pathway strategy: A perspective from 5 years of operation. *Criminal Behaviour and Mental Health*, 27, 214–221.

Social Exclusion Unit (2002). *Reducing re-offending by ex-prisoners.* London: Social Exclusion Unit.

Stewart, V., Judd, C., & Wheeler, A. J. (2022). Practitioners' experiences of deteriorating personal hygiene standards in people living with depression in Australia: A qualitative study. *Health and Social Care in the Community*, 30, 1589–1598.

Stickney, J., Holmes, E., & Gunderson, C. (2023). *Future regime design: A partnership approach to transforming prison regimes, improving outcomes for staff and prisoners in England and Wales.* Manuscript submitted for publication.

Taxman, F. S., Young, D., & Byrne, J. M. (2002). *Offender's views of re-entry: Implications for processes, programs and services.* Rockville, MD: Bureau of Governmental Research.

The Centre for Social Justice (2021). *Digital technology in prisons: Unlocking relationships, learning and skills in UK prisons.* London.

Van Ginneken, E. (2015). The role of hope in preparation for release from prison. *Prison Service Journal*, 220, 10–15.

Welford, J., Milner, C., & Morton, R. (2021). Improving service transitions for people experiencing multiple disadvantage: Prison release. *Fullfilling Lives.* Retrieved from: https://www.tnlcommunityfund.org.uk/media/insights/documents/Improving-service-transitions-for-people-experiencing-multiple-disadvantage-Prison-release-2021.pdf?mtime=20211214162243&focal=none.

Whiteford, G. (2000). Occupational deprivation: global challenge in a new millennium. *British Journal of Occupational Therapy*, 63, 200–204.

Williams, K., Poyser, J., & Hopkins, K. (2012). *Accommodation, homelessness and reoffending of prisoners: Results from the surveying prisoner crime reduction (SPCR) survey.* London: Ministry of Justice.

8 "I don't have relationships anymore…"

Navigating licence conditions and transition into the community for men with sexual convictions

Nicholas Blagden, Kellsey McCann and Samantha Macmillan

Introduction

Most men with a sexual conviction will be released back into the community on licence. The Licence Conditions and Policy Framework (HMPPS, 2021) states that the aims of a licence period are to be preventative, not punitive, ensure public protection, prevent re-offending and secure the successful reintegration of the offender into the community. Licence conditions are thus used within the UK to protect the public, to prevent re-offending and to secure the successful re-integration of the offenders into the community (National Offender Management Service (NOMS), 2015). For individuals with sexual convictions within the UK a set of general licence conditions are applied with additional conditions if deemed necessary. However, there has been very little empirical attention paid to how licence conditions are experienced, the impact they have on people's transition from prison to the community and the role they play in the daily lives of men with sexual convictions under supervision.

As of June 2021, there were 87,550 people in prison in the UK (Sturge, 2021). Of these, around 20% have been convicted for a sexual offence (Ministry of Justice (MoJ), 2020). Since 2010, sentence lengths for those with sexual convictions have increased by over 20%, with an average sentence of five years in prison (Williams & Bailey, 2019). The overwhelming majority (>99%) of these individuals are men and most will be released into the community. There are approximately 54,000 people living in the community who, as a result of the Sex Offences Act 1997, are required to register with the police because they have committed a sexual offence. It is also estimated that there may be over 50,000 people under investigation for a sexual offence at any one time.

There is ongoing debate as to whether the aims of licence conditions are achieved by the licence process and whether an increase in punitive approaches is actually effective. There is a growing body of literature which asserts that certain conditions may actually impede the reintegration process and instead act as a constant reminder of the punishment society believes is apt for certain

DOI: 10.4324/9781003308171-10

offender groups (McCarthy & Brunton-Smith, 2018). Owing to the nature of their crimes, individuals who have committed sexual offences typically face more extensive, additional and restrictive conditions than other offending groups, including curfews, monitored relationships, exclusion zones and "no association" rules that limit contact with other offenders. There are concerns that many of the areas where restrictions are most stringent (monitoring of employment, relationships and housing), provide some of the most important protective factors for such individuals (LeBel, Burnett, Maruna, & Bushway, 2008). Creating barriers that impede individuals' access to "social capital" has been shown to predict future offending behaviours (Tolson & Klein, 2015), and thus may act in a way that is contradictory to the original ethos of reducing recidivism rates.

Narratives of re-entry and sexual crime

Maruna and LeBel (2003) argue that there are broadly three narratives of community re-entry; control, support (needs-based) and strengths-based. Control narratives are an approach to risk management that favours intense community monitoring, supervision and threat of sanctions (e.g., recall/breaches) as a method of quelling criminality and keeping the public safe. Public safety and protecting the vulnerable from victimisation are inherently good things and we must protect the public from sexual harms. However, control narratives have largely failed in having any significant impact on recidivism and there is little evidence that they contribute to any meaningful behaviour change (Maruna & LeBel, 2003). Indeed, determining who is at risk, for how long and what the response should be are complicated issues, and any response to those with previous convictions needs to be proportionate and procedurally just. There is also a need to understand the context and trajectory of this group. For example, when aggregated across all risk levels, it has been found that the recidivism rate for those with sexual convictions is around 8% (Mews, Di Bella, & Purver, 2017). Low-risk offenders meet the desistance threshold at time of release, and within 10 to 15 years the vast majority of individuals with a history of sexual crime will be no more likely to commit a sexual crime than individuals who have been convicted of a nonsexual crime and who have no sex offence history. The risk of a further sexual offence declines the longer individuals remain sexual offence-free in the community. It is important then to help people lead offence-free lives. However, there is very little (if any) evidence that imprisonment or intense community supervision deters subsequent criminal behaviour (de Valk et al, 2015). Community notification and associated schemes, have been found to have a detrimental and disruptive impact on an individual's reintegration journey and further compound negative psychological consequences (Zevitz & Farkas, 2000; Lasher & McGrath, 2012).

There is a need then to go beyond "control" in order to keep people safe, as constant monitoring is not sufficient. Support or needs-based narratives suggest that those released from prison have multiple deficits and outstanding criminogenic needs (dynamic risk factors) that need intervention in order to reduce crime. These needs are well located within the "what works" literature and have a sound evidence-base (Maruna & LeBel, 2003; Mann, Hanson & Thornton, 2010). However, it has been argued that just focusing on deficits or reversing risk factors are not sufficient for lasting change (Ward, 2017). The strength-based narrative aims to redress this and provide a more positive and holistic narrative of re-entry. This narrative asks what people want from life and what contribution they want to make (Maruna & LeBel, 2003). The strengths-based narrative has parallels with promoting protective factors and the Good Lives Model (GLM; Ward, 2010). The GLM assumes that all humans fashion their lives around their core values and follow some sort of (often implicit) good life plan. The promotion of protective factors, which Ward (2017, p. 26) defines as "internal and external capacities and personal priorities that enhance individuals well-being and reduce the likelihood that they will harm others or themselves", are thus important for leading offence-free lives. It is therefore important that licence conditions do not unintentionally impede individuals as they seek to transition back into the community, while at the same time ensure that the public are safe.

Barriers to effective reintegration

The desistance literature suggests that punitive restrictions cause barriers to protective factors and hinder the transition from prison into the community (Brown, Spencer, & Deakin, 2007; Tolson and Klein, 2015). One key factor for "making good" is finding a place in society. Over 99% of people who serve custodial prison sentences for a sexual crime will leave prison and seek to integrate into the community. Waddell and Burton (2016) found that employment was central to people's identities and social status, as work is construed as a way of contributing and belonging to something. In research by Tovey, Winder and Blagden (2022) which focused on people with sexual convictions seeking employment, they found an acute sense of loss from the participants at being denied the opportunity to return to the workforce and there was a longing for relationships with peers. Social interactions with pro-social peers are a protective factor against recidivism and are of benefit to a person's general psychological well-being and social capital (Harris, 2020). While there are challenges for employers, the stigma of a sexual offence, fears around risk and what other workers may think/do, there is a general reluctance to hire people with sexual convictions (Tovey et al., 2022). Winder (2022) has delineated 13 factors relevant in reducing sexual recidivism and promoting community integration, two aims that are intertwined. Barriers include: the state of people as they exit prison (in terms of age and health, for example), and the restrictions and constraints upon people in the community. There are also gaps in provision for those transiting from prison to the community and challenges with reconnecting with family and friends. Some people will also be released into accommodation that is unfit for purpose (see Lomas, 2021). A further barrier is about self-identity: how people perceive themselves, and how others perceive and label them. What we call people has a significant impact on how people think about themselves, and how others think and behave towards them (Willis, 2018). These barriers to successful reintegration often lead to social isolation and prevent desistance from crime being achieved (Tewksbury & Mustaine, 2009).

The aim of this study was to gain an insight into the experiences of people with a sexual conviction as they return to the community, and to specifically explore their experiences of licence conditions, how they navigate such conditions and to understand the impact they have (positive and negative) for those transitioning back into the community.

Method

Participants and data collection

Data were collected through the use of a semi-structured interview, each lasting between 45 and 60 minutes. Interviews were conducted in a purpose-built interview room within a support centre or over secure video link. Participation was voluntary and all recruited participants ($n=$ 16) agreed to engage in the research process. The interview schedule was formed of five separate sections: (1) Rapport building; (2) Understanding their transition from prison into the community; (3) Understanding the impact of licence conditions and living conditions; (4) Post-release/reintegration; and (5) Hopes for the future. To facilitate discussion, all questions were kept open (Knight, Wykes, & Hayward, 2003). This style of interviewing also enables "rapport to be developed; allows participants to think, speak and be heard; and are well suited to in-depth and personal discussion" (Reid, Flowers, & Larkin, 2005, p. 22).

Data analytical procedure

Data were analysed using thematic analysis, a method for identifying, analysing, and reporting patterns and themes within a data set. Thematic analysis aims to capture rich detail and represent the range and diversity of experience within the data (Braun & Clarke, 2006), and has been described as a "contextualist method", sitting between the two poles of constructionism and realism. This position thus acknowledges the ways individuals make meaning of their experience, and, in turn, the ways in which the broader social context impinges on those meanings. As such, thematic analyses reflect "reality" (Braun & Clarke, 2006). The analysis adhered to the phases of qualitative thematic analysis as outlined by Braun and Clarke (2021), consisting of familiarisation and detailed readings of the data collected, progressing to initial and systematic coding of the data, and then generating initial themes from the coded data. The final phases included reviewing themes, ensuring that they were consistent with the coding and that they were grounded in the qualitative data (Braun &

Clarke, 2021). The final themes were representative of the sample. In this chapter data extracts are labelled "quotes", as this term was deemed more humanising than "extract". However, extracts/quotes are utilised in the analysis as outlined by Braun and Clarke (2013) and Braun, Clarke and Weate (2016) in which extracts are illustrative of a theme. In this chapter the quotes used revealed the complex meanings participants had on living with licence conditions (Oliver, Serovich & Mason, 2005).

Analysis and discussion

The superordinate theme and related subordinate themes presented in Table 8.1 are taken from a larger study on the transition from prison to the community for men with sexual convictions. The focus of this chapter is the role and impact of navigating and living with licence conditions as people return to the community.

When performing qualitative analysis, particularly in-depth analysis focusing on participant experiences, the task is to identify the underlying principles that organise the thinking of the participants, and thus the structures that influence perceptions, feelings, and behaviour (Skrapec, 2001). The experiences and structures relating to how participants perceived the impact of licence conditions are represented in the subordinate themes in Table 8.1. Each of those themes will be unpacked in the following analysis.

Subordinate theme 1: "I don't have relationships anymore..."

This theme highlights the relational challenges and impacts experienced by those who have a sexual offence conviction and who are on licence. The participants discussed how they perceived the relationships within their lives, and all spoke with hesitancy about establishing new relationships (romantic, friendship etc.) whilst on licence. The language used suggested there was a need to guard themselves from society's perceived punitive response, and that disclosure of offences would lead to rejection and stigma from the community with which they were trying to reintegrate. For good reason too, men with sexual convictions are stigmatised like almost no other group and face vociferous public indignation. Furthermore, such individuals do not live in hermetically

Table 8.1 Superordinate and subordinate themes

Superordinate Theme	Subordinate Themes
Impact of licence conditions and transition into the community	• "I don't have relationships anymore..." • Perceptions of (un)fairness • No Association

sealed vacuums and are fully aware of the public's views of them (Hudson, 2013).

Quote 1

Meeting new people is a lot more difficult, because obviously you have to be slightly more guarded. I don't want people to know my past necessarily. I think that's something that is – you have to be very confident it's a proper friendship before you disclose... I'm selective about who I become friendly with, I don't really want to go down the route of telling probation about this new friend and then social services being informed just so they can check.

Here, this quote/extract presents a duality that most participants shared. Firstly, disclosure opened up the possibility of stigma and rejection, while secondly, they were hesitant to find new relationships due to the processes that probation and social services would have to administer. Declaring relationships is a typical licence condition for individuals with sexual offences and this can provide a threat to social capital, the loss of which can lead to lowered expectations of rehabilitation and scepticism surrounding re-entry into the community (Tolson & Klein, 2015). The quote's description of having to be *slightly more guarded* and having to establish authenticity of a relationship before pursuing it is an often-shared sentiment for people in this position. This offers another example of the fear that surrounds embarking on new relationships when living within licence conditions. There is a sense of caution that overrides any optimism about forming new relationships, as having to experience the potential rejection after a new acquaintance is checked by authorities is deemed more painful than accepting solitude.

Quote 2

I have to report if I make friends or not and umm people are not quite open-minded once they get to know why you've been in prison ... and I just see it as ... while I'm on licence ... I should keep it as the way it is at the moment, just stay with the official contact with people, like probation, people that are here (centre), mental health, uhh sexual services, council workers ... and I uh, will say hello to people in the street and stuff like that, but I don't want to get too deep, if you know what I mean.

This quote continues the theme and here the participant describes not wanting to get *too deep* into relationships whilst he is on licence, suggesting that he perceives his current relationships as relatively superficial in comparison to others in society. Oftentimes, individuals with these offences experience very limited interactions with family or friends prior to their offences, such interactions are usually reported as shallow or superficial (Tewskbury & Lees, 2006).

Multiple rejections can lead to mirroring behaviours, where people limit interactions to protect themselves from the social harm of further ostracism. There is a sense of dependence upon supervisory support, as quote 2 highlights them as his only relationships. Official relationships were favourable compared to forming relationships with the wider community. This is a common theme shared across participants, that external, community relationships are perceived as risky, whereas supervisory relationships are seen as a necessity. This is some optimism from this participant, as he highlights that he will keep it this way "for the moment" until he is off licence, suggesting he feels that this pressure will be lifted when the conditions cease. Though, if those on licence are consciously waiting for conditions to end before pursuing a relational goal, it is possible that supervisory support will end at the time when they may need the most guidance (Digard, 2010).

Quote 3

> I don't have relationships anymore, I don't go through that kind of thing. The only thing I noticed is that when I first moved to *[city name]*, I was afraid of going downtown by myself, cause I thought I might have … sex offender on my forehead and was a bit nervous, and it was an inward, inward thing. But I spoke to the *[support organisation]* about that and they encouraged me to go downtown and meet them in the coffee shop, which we did and then …

Many desisters fear being "outed" as a *sex offender* to the wider community. Those with sexual offences report feeling more "known" to society, and this public labelling presents serious challenges for existing relationships, as well as for potential future relationships with others (Tewksbury & Lees, 2006). This quote describes this label as an *inward, inward thing*. The repetition of inward suggests that this fear is buried deep within him, thus it would be very difficult to uproot. As a result of this internalised label, the process of forming new relationships seems, at best, challenging. The statement "I don't have relationships anymore" is bleak and suggests that he may never pursue relationships again. Fatalistic phrases such as this are often shared by those labelled "higher risk" offenders, who face greater restrictions and tighter supervision (Kemshall, Dominey, & Hilder, 2012). The participant here offers little hope that they will achieve meaningful relationships within the foreseeable future, and this adds to the loneliness and social isolation experienced by this group. Licence conditions that focus on tight environmental controls and managerial approaches to supervision have been found to undermine the development of an intrinsically motivated non-offending identity (McAlinden, 2010). There is a shared experience of being *in* but not *of* society. Burrows (2016) describes men with sexual convictions as the "extreme other", with their negative self-concepts crafted from shame and reinforced by public misconceptions.

Quote 4

> I've left prison I've no friends ... er ... no relatives that I can actually talk
> to, that I have actually seen in ... fifteen years. The only people I know
> are the people like *(support centre manager)* and yourself, you know, profes-
> sional people. Apart from professionals I do not know any. I don't associ-
> ate with anyone, I do not talk to anyone...

Quote 5

> Yeah. I think... a lot of it is due to telling people what you've done. If you get
> to know someone and you get friendly with someone you've got to disclose
> what you've done and then they're just going to turn around and walk away
> from you or what have you. It's happened before and I don't like the feeling.

The loneliness of living under licence conditions is exemplified in the quotes 4
and 5, where the participant suggests that he has been socially isolated from
close relationships for at least 15 years. Often, family and kinship ties are irre-
parably broken by the nature of the sex offence committed, especially if victims
are part of the family itself (Farkas & Miller, 2007). There is again a sense of
hopelessness in the repairability of these relationships, as he construes himself as
having no friends or family. As families typically take the brunt of the burden
when aiding an individual to reintegrate, those without such ties to the community are left in a position of alienation, reliant upon professional services to
offer the first line of community support.

Subordinate theme 2: Perceptions of (un)fairness

Participants described how they felt that their conditions were not reflective of
the crime that they committed and acted as unnecessary barriers to various
factors such as friendships and employment. It was therefore seen that participants felt a desire for their conditions to be personalised, helping them to perceive the licence conditions as fair.

Quote 6

> I think a lot of conditions, especially for someone like myself who's on
> licence for life, I think they bung these conditions on generally. It's not
> much about the individual – it's not like 'he's done that so we'll add on
> that' I think they really need to look more at the individual because for me
> I've not acted in a group, the crime was only me ... so yeah I do find it
> quite restrictive that condition.

Quote 6 highlighted the lack of individualisation of the licence conditions for
the participant, he felt that this lack of individualisation made his life more

restrictive than he felt it needed to be. The participant expressed the need for his licence conditions to relate to the crimes he had committed, which implies the need for his treatment on licence to be fair and appropriate for his crime. This feeling of perceived fairness relates to procedural justice as those who believe licence conditions are fair are more likely to comply with restrictions and reduce reoffending (Gladfelter, Lantz & Ruback, 2018). It was an important theme within the data that licence conditions were tailored to the needs of the individual. Additionally, it seemed more important that the conditions were seen as fair than the amount of time that people had to abide by them. The participants seemed to emphasise the need to be viewed as individuals rather than all sex offenders being seen as one. Restrictive licence conditions tend to be overinclusive and exceed the non-punitive purpose of the conditions (Durling, 2006).

Quote 7

> "I just mentioned ... 'I'm going to stop in a village where my dad's buried and look at the grave' and she went 'no you won't, you will come straight here' and I said 'okay I'll do that' and she added a licence condition of banning me from going to the village ... You just don't need to do that. I told you what I was going to do, you said I couldn't and I said I wouldn't – you didn't need to add that.

Quote 7 highlights how participants felt that licence conditions were things that were done to them and that additional conditions were punitive and unfair. Procedurally just treatment is associated with higher outcome satisfaction ratings and decision acceptance, greater cooperation with, and confidence in, the Criminal Justice System, and more law-abiding behaviours (e.g., Casper, Tyler, & Fisher, 1988). There was a need for the monitoring process to be more collaborative and tailored to individuals, rather than prescriptive or reactive.

Participants shared that whilst they believed they were able to set goals within licence conditions, these goals were adapted to fit within their restricted post-release lifestyle. Some suggested that they felt goals were 'paused' until their time on conditions ended, whereas others suggested boundaries were helpful in guiding realistic goals.

Quote 8

> But most of the goals I've got, all of my goals, I do set within the perimeter of licence conditions being taken into account, there's no point, you know, to me, there is no point aiming for something knowing full well the licence conditions will prevent that. Unless, along with that I'm also fighting to get that condition either changed or removed, or whatever *[mhm]* not really, it's limited the goals I think ... would be the right wording for me.

Quote 8 describes having to set all goals within the perimeters of his conditions, perceiving them as a physical limiter to achieving his desired goals. Persistent barriers to goal achievement can propagate feelings of hopelessness with the individual feeling as though they are merely *existing*: this can result in apathy and affect motivation to continue efforts to reintegrate successfully into the community (Nugent & Schinkel, 2016). Throughout, the participants expressed a desire for goals to be linked to achieving a prosocial identity, including roles that assist with such identities, for example work or volunteer roles within the local council or church. Relational distance from the community is a significant pain that comes with desistance, with the most pain being felt by those who wish to engage in goals at the macro-level (Maruna & Farrall, 2004).

Subordinate theme 3: No Association

Every participant, and seemingly every person on licence for a sexual conviction, will have the additional condition of not to "associate with a known sex offender". The impact of this was discussed by all participants.

Quote 9

> it's mainly the ones [friends] that were sort of from the area and what have ya, the ones that I sort of spoke to quite a bit, and said ah here's me details, if you wanna keep in contact, but then obviously, yeah like as soon as I got out and they put the no association thing on there, it was like well there goes that idea of, 'cause obviously if you're out here then and they're getting ready for release and what have ya, and they're worried about something and you've obviously gone through it yourself then you can't even help 'em.

Quote 9 highlights the experience of not being able to associate with someone with whom a person had built up a relationship because they had a sexual offence conviction. The quote portrays a sense of hopelessness and feelings of uselessness as a result of not being able to put personal experiences and wisdom to use. The idea that "you can't even help 'em" highlights how a potentially important resource, i.e., other people with convictions, is not utilised and may make it difficult for some to transition into the community, especially those with a lack of support. This could potentially negatively affect the experience of reintegration because of a lack of social support, and how important this is to desistance and life satisfaction (Maruna & Toch, 2005; Bohmert, Duwe & Hipple, 2018).

Quote 10

> [the impact] on me, it's not being able to help as much as I want to because I think if, if I could only have just helped that person, he might've

not given up, he might've not reoffended, or he, I've, I've gave that person something so that I feel I've helped that person, that's helping me, give me the experience to help.

Linked to quote 9, the above quote highlights how the "no association" condition impedes the ability of the participants to help others reintegrate and desist from offending. Quote 10 highlights the participant's inability to fill the supportive role for others in similar situations to himself and it illustrates feelings of sadness and personal disappointment. Having such roles should not be underestimated. They are important in the "wounded healer" narrative and can be important in the desistance process. Reciprocity is a relational aspect of the desistance process and building on the capacity and opportunity to give back, to gain meaning from shared problems, to reciprocate, is an important consideration for criminal justice professionals, especially as it can help individuals enact "good selves" (see Perrin & Blagden, 2014). As LeBel, Richie, & Maruna (2015) conclude, helping others appears to have adaptive consequences for prisoners and ex-prisoners, and on these grounds, an argument can be made for increasing opportunities for reintegrating ex-offenders to engage in roles characterised by reciprocal helping.

Discussion

This study sought to understand the process of reintegration for people with sexual convictions, with a particular focus on navigating licence conditions. Developing relationships whilst on licence proved a significant theme. Attempting to establish new relationships whilst experiencing the fear of the "sex offender" label and the high likelihood of stigma and rejection was a potent challenge. These experiences of *otherness* and ostracisation are consistent with findings within this population (Burrows, 2016) and this study offers new insight into how the licencee perceives the conditions and how negotiating the label is a constant issue. The data presented here also points to an unintended consequence of licence conditions being a reinforcer of this label, due to it being a primary relational impediment in interactions with others. Some spoke favourably regarding their interactions with professionals, though there was a sense that many relied upon supervisory relationships to fill the void of social isolation from the community. Although empathic staff relationships can foster change within this group (Blagden, Winder & Hames, 2016), organic relationships that offer solidarity, reciprocity, subsidiarity, and a sense of "we-ness" are the most beneficial in fostering desistance in the community (Richards, 2022; Weaver, 2015; Weaver & McNeill, 2015). Such relationships provide deeper interaction than seen in the functional obligations of supervisory support, instead offering super-functional, entirely human interactions that are pivotal for true reintegration into society. Licence conditions appear to perpetuate a state of relational ambivalence, which can only cease when obligations to conditions end. Times of transition can be particularly destabilising for desisters (Digard, 2010), and thus it is concerning that many perceive this to be the only time they would feel able to pursue new relationships.

The participants explored perceptions of (un)fairness with licence conditions, which was experienced as a process done to the participant, rather than with them. There was a breakdown in communication between the participants and the professionals surrounding them and the feeling that licence conditions were generalised rather than specific. The generalised conditions created underlying feelings that the conditions were "stupid" and did not aid rehabilitation or reintegration. These experiences suggest a need to create more specific licence conditions for individuals in the system. This is supported by the literature that suggests the increased personalisation or co-production of licence conditions could increase the effectiveness (Weaver, 2015). Research has therefore suggested that a shift towards personalisation of licence conditions would encourage both fair treatment of individuals with convictions, whilst also effectively protecting the public from any risks (Weaver, 2015). The importance of communication and the relationship between the individual and their probation officer was also key for rehabilitation into the community. This relationship should therefore be stressed as important to the probation team, to ensure the individuals feel like they are being fairly treated as well as a way to build bonds to the community supporting desistance.

Licence conditions are currently delivered as a tool of risk monitoring and these findings challenge the legitimacy of such an approach. Future research should pay particular attention to what constitutes clear and individualised delivery of licence conditions. Also, exploring how conditions can be used to support the development of protective relationships and goals.

There are several limitations to consider within this study. The sample size was relatively small for research of this nature (Guest, Bunce & Johnson, 2006), and it is important to consider that these participants were recruited, and the interviews conducted through, a local support centre for people with sexual convictions. Firstly, this suggests that the participants may have more access to support in the community than many who experience licence conditions, thus findings may not be representative of all individuals' experiences of conditions. Secondly, the proximity to supervisory staff may have moderated some aspects of self-disclosure due to social desirability bias.

Implications for practice

One of the key implications of this research is to consider how licence conditions are operationalised and administered to individuals. There was general consensus within the data that licence conditions were not individualised and that conditions were things that were done to people rather than with them. There was a desire for people to have more say into the conditions that applied to them and the process should be more collaborative. This collaborative approach is likely to improve the perceptions of the conditions, improve compliance (both passively and actively), and enhance the working relationships between probation and the licence.

There is good evidence for collaborative approaches within the treatment and management of people for sexual offence convictions. Shingler and Mann (2006) argue that working collaboratively and showing a mutual commitment to the therapeutic process was vital to bolstering engagement in treatment for those with sexual convictions. Collaboration is also linked to legitimacy and procedural justice. Indeed, information gained through a joint, collaborative approach can be more relevant, comprehensive and accurate than that obtained through naïve objectivity or an adversarial approach dominated by suspicion (Daston, 1992). Procedural justice theory argues that experiencing fair and just procedures (*how* people make decisions and apply policies, rather than *what* the outcome is) leads people to view the law and authority figures as more legitimate and brings greater compliance with, and commitment to obey, the law (Mann et al., 2019). The theory states that the opposite is also true; where procedural justice is lacking there will be less compliance, both immediately and into the future (Murphy & Tyler, 2008). This is important when managing people in the community, as working collaboratively and allowing people a chance to "own" or invest in their own rehabilitation, is more aligned to desistance principles (Blagden & Wilson, 2020).

The contention here is that taking a more collaborative approach when setting licence conditions can be seen as an aspect of compassion-focused practice. Compassion has become a major focus for international research in prosocial behaviour in recent times, and the emergence of compassion-focused therapy is beginning to shape forensic practice (see Hocken & Taylor, 2021; Kolts & Gilbert, 2018). We would argue that when someone transitions from prison to the community, it is incumbent on those working with the individual to consider the strengths and human goods of that person and to focus on working compassionately with the individual (Blagden & Winder, in press). A turn towards compassion when setting collaborative licence conditions is important as it will assist not just in helping men lead meaningful offence-free lives, but also will allow an opportunity for growth and repair.

Conclusion

The findings reported in this chapter suggest that licence conditions are construed in a critical manner by those under their supervision. Many of the principles of risk monitoring and limiting conditions is in direct contrast to the factors that support desistance. Though some did report positive experiences regarding their interactions with professionals, this was in the void of feeling practically unable to access new personal relationships whilst under licence conditions. Implications from this study implore supervisory professionals to consider personalisation and compassion in the licence process, so that licencees understand the relevance to their reintegration journey, but also have a voice in their own rehabilitation.

References

Blagden, N., & Wilson, K. (2020). "We're all the same here": Investigating the rehabilitative climate of a re-rolled sexual offender prison: A qualitative longitudinal study. *Sexual Abuse*, 32(6), 727–750.

Blagden, N., & Winder, W. (in press) Understanding and rehabilitating men with sexual convictions: Theory, Intervention, and Compassion. In *The Oxford Handbook of Criminology*. Oxford: Oxford University Press.

Blagden, N., Winder, B., & Hames, C. (2016). "They treat us like human beings": Experiencing a therapeutic sex offenders' prison: Impact on prisoners and staff and implications for treatment. *International Journal of Offender Therapy and Comparative Criminology*, 60(4), 371–396.

Bohmert, M. N., Duwe, G., & Hipple, N. K. (2018). Evaluating restorative justice circles of support and accountability: Can social support overcome structural barriers? *International Journal of Offender Therapy and Comparative Criminology*, 62(3), 739–758.

Braun, V., & Clarke, V. (2021). Can I use TA? Should I use TA? Should I not use TA? Comparing reflexive thematic analysis and other pattern-based qualitative analytic approaches. *Counselling and Psychotherapy Research*, 21(1), 37–47.

Braun, V., & Clarke, V. (2013). *Successful qualitative research: A practical guide for beginners*. London: Sage.

Braun, V., Clarke, V. & Weate, P. (2016). Using thematic analysis in sport and exercise research. In B. Smith & A. C. Sparkes (Eds.), *Routledge Handbook of Qualitative Research in Sport and Exercise* (pp. 191–205). London: Routledge.

Braun, V., & Clarke, V. (2006). Using thematic analysis in psychology. *Qualitative Research in Psychology*, 3(2), 77–101.

Brown, K., Spencer, J., & Deakin, J. (2007). The reintegration of sex offenders: Barriers and opportunities for employment. *The Howard Journal of Criminal Justice*, 46(1), 32–42. https://doi.org/10. 1111/j.1468-2311.2007.00452.x.

Burrows, J. (2016). Fear and loathing in the community: Sexual offenders and desistance in a climate of risk and 'extreme othering'. In A. Robinson & P. Hamilton (Eds.) *Moving on from crime and substance use: Transforming Identities* (pp. 153–174). Bristol: Policy Press.

Casper, J. D., Tyler, T., & Fisher, B. (1988). Procedural justice in felony cases. *Law & Society Review*, 22, 483.

de Valk, S., van der Helm, G. P., Beld, M., Schaftenaar, P., Kuiper, C., & Stams, G. J. J. (2015). Does punishment in secure residential youth care work? An overview of the evidence. *Journal of Children's Services*, 10(1), 3–16.

Daston, L. (1992). Objectivity and the escape from perspective. *Social Studies of Science*, 22(4), 597–618.

Digard, L. (2010). When legitimacy is denied: Offender perceptions of the prison recall system. *Probation Journal*, 57(1), 43–61.

Durling, C. (2006). Never going home: Does it make us safer-does it make sense-sex offenders, residency restrictions, and reforming risk management law. *Journal of Criminal Law and Criminology*, 97, 317.

Farkas, M. A., & Miller, G. (2007). Reentry and reintegration: Challenges faced by the families of convicted sex offenders. *Federal Sentencing Reporter*, 20(1), 88–92.

Gladfelter, A. S., Lantz, B., & Ruback, R. B. (2018). Beyond ability to pay: procedural justice and offender compliance with restitution orders. *International Journal of Offender Therapy and Comparative Criminology*, 62(13), 4314–4331.

Guest, G., Bunce, A., & Johnson, L. (2006). How many interviews are enough? An experiment with data saturation and variability. *Field Methods*, 18(1), 59–82.

Harris, P. (2020). 'I think I had to move backwards before I could move forward again': a psychosocial case study exploring the interweaving of desistance from violent offending and professional youth worker identity formation. *Journal of Psychosocial Studies*, 13(2), 193–208.

Her Majesty's Prison and Probation Service (HMPPS). (2021). Licence conditions policy framework. Retrieved from: https://assets.publishing.service.gov.uk/governm ent/uploads/system/uploads/attachment_data/file/1010004/licence-conditions-policy-framework.pdf.

Hocken, K., & Taylor, J. (2021). Compassion-focused therapy as an intervention for sexual offending. In *Forensic Interventions for Therapy and Rehabilitation* (pp. 189–219). Routledge.

Hudson, K. (2013). *Offending identities*. Devon: Willan.

Kemshall, H., Dominey, J., & Hilder, S. (2012). Public disclosure: Sex offenders' perceptions of the pilot scheme in England. Compliance, legitimacy and living a "Good Life". *Journal of Sexual Aggression*, 18(3), 311–324.

Knight, M. T., Wykes, T., & Hayward, P. (2003). 'People don't understand': An investigation of stigma in schizophrenia using Interpretative Phenomenological Analysis (IPA). *Journal of Mental Health*, 12(3), 209–222.

Kolts, R., & Gilbert, P. (2018). Understanding and Using Compassion-Focused Therapy in Forensic Settings. In A. R. Beech, A. J. Carter, R. E. Mann & P. Rotshtein (Eds.). *The Wiley Blackwell Handbook of Forensic Neuroscience*, Volume 1 (pp. 725–754).

Lasher, M. P., & McGrath, R. J. (2012). The impact of community notification on sex offender reintegration: A quantitative review of the research literature. *International Journal of Offender Therapy and Comparative Criminology*, 56(1), 6–28.

LeBel, T. P., Burnett, R., Maruna, S., & Bushway, S. (2008). The 'Chicken and Egg' of Subjective and Social Factors in Desistance from Crime. *European Journal of Criminology*, 5(2), 131–159. DOI: https://doi.org/10.1177/1477370807087640.

LeBel, T. P., Richie, M., & Maruna, S. (2015). Helping others as a response to reconcile a criminal past: The role of the wounded healer in prisoner reentry programs. *Criminal Justice and Behavior*, 42(1), 108–120.

Lomas, J. R. (2021). *House, home, and hope: exploring the accommodation needs and experiences of people with sexual offence convictions* (Doctoral dissertation). Nottingham Trent University, Nottingham.

Mann, R. E., Hanson, R. K., & Thornton, D. (2010). Assessing risk for sexual recidivism: Some proposals on the nature of psychologically meaningful risk factors. *Sexual Abuse*, 22(2), 191–217.

Mann, R., Barnett, G., Box, G., Howard, F. F., O'Mara, O., Travers, R., & Wakeling, H. (2019). Rehabilitative culture in prisons for people convicted of sexual offending. In N. Blagden, B. Winder, K. Hocken, R. Lievesley, P. Banyard & H. Elliott (Eds), *Sexual crime and the experience of imprisonment* (pp. 1–33). Cham: Palgrave Macmillan.

Maruna, S., & LeBel, T. P. (2003). Welcome home? Examining the "Reentry Court" concept from a strengths-based perspective. *Western Criminology Review*, 4(2), 91–107.

Maruna, S., and Farrall, S. (2004) Desistance from crime: A theoretical reformulation. *Kolner Zeitschrift fur Soziologie und Sozialpsychologie* 43, 171–194.

Maruna, S., & Toch, H. (2005). The impact of prison on desistance. In J. Travis & C. Visher (Eds.), *Prisoner reentry and crime in America* (pp. 139–178). Cambridge, UK: Cambridge University Press.

McAlinden, A. M. (2010). The reintegration of sexual offenders. *Escape Routes: Contemporary Perspectives on Life after Punishment*, 158.

McCarthy, D., & Brunton-Smith, I. (2018). The effect of penal legitimacy on prisoners' postrelease desistance. *Crime & Delinquency*, 64(7), 917–938.

Mews, A., Di Bella, L., & Purver, M. (2017). *Impact evaluation of the prison-based core sex offender treatment programme*. London: Ministry of Justice.

Ministry of Justice (MoJ) (2020). *Offender management statistics, Probation (2020)*. London: Ministry of Justice.

Murphy, K., & Tyler, T. (2008). Procedural justice and compliance behaviour: The mediating role of emotions. *European Journal of Social Psychology*, 38(4), 652–668.

National Offender Management Service (NOMS) (2015). Licence Conditions, Licences and Licence and Supervision Notices. Ministry of Justice. Retrieved from: https://www.justice.gov.uk/downloads/offenders/psipso/psi-2015/psi-12-2015-licences-conditions-supervision.pdf.

Nugent, B., & Schinkel, M. (2016). The pains of desistance. *Criminology & Criminal Justice*, 16(5), 568–584.

Oliver, D. G., Serovich, J. M., & Mason, T. L. (2005). Constraints and opportunities with interview transcription: Towards reflection in qualitative research. *Social Forces*, 84(2), 1273–1289.

Perrin, C., & Blagden, N. (2014). Accumulating meaning, purpose and opportunities to change 'drip by drip': The impact of being a listener in prison. *Psychology, Crime & Law*, 20(9), 902–920.

Reid, K., Flowers, P., & Larkin, M. (2005). Exploring lived experience. *The Psychologist*. Leicester: British Psychological Society.

Richards, K. (2022). Circles of Support and Accountability: the role of social relations in core member desistance. *International Journal of Offender Therapy and Comparative Criminology*, 66(10–11), 1071–1092.

Shingler, J., & Mann, R. E. (2006). Collaboration in clinical work with sexual offenders: Treatment and risk assessment. In W. L. Marshall, Y. M. Fernandez, L. E Marshall & G. A. Serran (eds.) (pp. 225–239). *Sexual offender treatment: Controversial issues*. Chichester: John Wiley & Sons.

Skrapec, C. A. (2001). Phenomenology and serial murder: Asking different questions. *Homicide Studies*, 5(1), 46–63.

Sturge, G. (2021). *UK Prison Population Statistics*. House of Commons Library. Retrieved 16 September 2022, from https://commonslibrary.parliament.uk/research-briefings/sn04334/.

Tewksbury, R., & Lees, M. (2006). Perceptions of sex offender registration: Collateral consequences and community experiences. *Sociological Spectrum*, 26(3), 309–334.

Tewksbury, R., & Mustaine, E. E. (2009). Stress and collateral consequences for registered sex offenders. *Journal of Public Management & Social Policy*, 15(2).

Tolson, D., & Klein, J. (2015). Registration, residency restrictions, and community notification: A social capital perspective on the isolation of registered sex offenders in our communities. *Journal of Human Behavior in the Social Environment*, 25(5), 375–390.

Tovey, L., Winder, B., & Blagden, N. (2022). 'It's ok if you were in for robbery or murder, but sex offending, that'sa no': a qualitative analysis of the experiences of 12 men with sexual convictions seeking employment. *Psychology, Crime & Law*, 1–24.

Waddell, G., & Burton, A. (2016). *Is work good for your health and well-being? An independent review*. Department for Work and Pensions.

Ward, T. (2010). The good lives model of offender rehabilitation: Basic assumptions, etiological commitments, and practice implications. In F. McNeill, P. Raynor, & C. Trotter (Eds.), *Offender supervision: New directions in theory, research and practice.* Abingdon, Oxon: Willan Publishing.

Ward, T. (2017). Prediction and agency: The role of protective factors in correctional rehabilitation and desistance. *Aggression and Violent Behavior, 32,* 19–28.

Weaver, B. (2015). *Offending and desistance: The importance of social relations.* London: Routledge.

Weaver, B., & McNeill, F. (2015). Lifelines: Desistance, social relations, and reciprocity. *Criminal Justice and Behavior, 42*(1), 95–107.

Williams, F., & Bailey, J. (2019) *Working with people with sexual convictions in HMPPS* paper presented at Symposium on key issues in the imprisonment of people convicted of sex offences. University of Cambridge.

Willis, G. M. (2018). Why call someone by what we don't want them to be? The ethics of labeling in forensic/correctional psychology. *Psychology, Crime & Law, 24*(7), 727–743.

Winder, B. (2022). Reducing reoffending and increasing community (re)integration: effective practice when people have a sexual conviction. Clinks Evidence Library. https://www.clinks.org/publication/reducing-reoffending-and-increasing-community-reintegration-effective-practice-when-people-have-a-sexual-conviction.

Zevitz, R. G., & Farkas, M. A. (2000). Sex offender community notification: Managing high risk criminals or exacting further vengeance? *Behavioral Sciences & the Law, 18*(2–3), 375–391.

Part III

Professional approaches to resettlement

9 "It's not just words, it's something you can feel"

How therapeutic relationships can support prison-community transitions

Jo Shingler and Charlotte Purvis

> When first asked if I'd be willing to talk to them, my first thought? "More people with sticky beaks wanting to know my business". How wrong I was. These "people" care, want you to do well, succeed. It's not just words it's something you can feel. Most prisoners can see "real" and that's what these people are.

This quote from Nick illustrates the value of meaningful professional relationships. Relationships are important at all stages of someone's journey through the criminal justice system yet there is something particularly challenging about the step into the community, especially following a lengthy term of imprisonment, that brings the professional relationship into sharper focus. At a time of intense flux and consequent vulnerability, an experience of someone as empathic, responsive, warm and respectful, who is flexible but will also give guidance and direction (Marshall et al., 2005) could make the difference between someone asking for help or turning to old coping strategies as a way of seeking escape, comfort or reassurance.

The focus of this chapter is the value, meaning and nature of the therapeutic relationship as people transition between prison and the community. We will start with a brief review of the importance of the relationship in correctional work. We will then reflect specifically on the prison/community transition, and how and why the relationship is so crucial during this time. Finally, we will discuss how community practitioners can embody key values and principles in their professional relationships. At the same time, we will elucidate how those values and principles support the pathway to desistance. After much discussion and reflection, we have come to the conclusion that the question we should be asking ourselves is *not* "What should I *do* to build a therapeutic relationship?" but rather, "What sort of practitioner should I *be*?" (McNeill, 2006, p. 52). Whilst these things, of course, overlap, it is personal and professional values that drive behaviour. If we can develop and strengthen values that best support desistance, then the answers to questions about what we should *do* in a given situation will present themselves.

DOI: 10.4324/9781003308171-12

Why prioritise the relationship?

First and foremost, men navigating the prison-community transition value the presence of consistent and supportive relationships with professionals they trust. When Wayne was asked what was most helpful to him in navigating release, he said, "The continuity of support from people I have formed trusting relationships with". It is therefore not surprising that there is good evidence that the working relationship is central to a range of criminal justice outcomes (e.g., Lowenkamp, Holsinger, Robinson, & Alexander, 2014; Marshall et al., 2005; Shingler, Sonnenberg, & Needs, 2018; Willmot & Tetley, 2011), and that the relationship can be pivotal in ameliorating challenging and stressful encounters between people in prison and criminal justice professionals (Shingler, 2019).

Therapeutic style improves the outcome of correctional treatment programmes. Decades of research have indicated the superiority of cognitive behavioural approaches in correctional treatment (Andrews & Bonta, 2010; Hanson, Bourgon, Helmus, & Hodgson, 2009), but research repeatedly finds that client perception of the therapeutic relationship is more important than therapeutic modality or the application of various therapeutic techniques (Lambert & Barley, 2001; see also Burnett, 2004). Warm, empathic and directive group therapists achieve treatment gains that are not obtained by hostile therapists (Marshall et al., 2005). Correctional treatment programmes that use authority effectively (e.g., being firm but fair; being clear about rules and using positive reinforcement to encourage adherence to rules) and that prioritise openness, warmth, enthusiasm and development of mutual respect and liking do a better job of reducing recidivism than those that do not (Dowden & Andrews, 2004).

It is also clear that genuinely caring, supportive and hopeful relationships can make a difference to people as they navigate the transition from prison into the community (McNeill, 2006). Lowenkamp et al. (2014) found that people who were supervised by more motivational probation officers had better recidivism outcomes. Kenneally, Skeem, Manchak and Eno Louden (2012) found that a firm, fair yet caring approach by probation officers protected against re-arrest when compared with probation officers who focused primarily on care OR primarily on control. It is possible that firmness and clarity about rules and boundaries created a sense of safety and containment that was missing in purely caring relationships ("James" & Sainsbury, 2011). Further, Kenneally et al. (2012) found that the quality of the relationship protected against re-arrest even for high-risk offenders with problematic personality traits. Rex (1999) found that probation officers who showed concern for their supervisees as people were experienced as more valued and effective. Rennie and Crewe (2022) found that life-sentenced prisoners who felt their relationship with their probation officer was characterised by familiarity, rapport, and being treated as an individual, found it easier to accept the "tightness" of licence conditions. This group consequently felt more hopeful about their ability to succeed on release.

More generally, there is evidence that key elements of an effective working relationship, such as openness, transparency, collaboration and trustworthiness (Shingler et al., 2018) are related to acceptance of and compliance with criminal justice sanctions (Tyler & Huo, 2002) and continued engagement with services post-recall (Croft & Winder, 2018; Fitzalan Howard, 2019). Therefore, the building and maintaining of an effective working relationship is likely to be crucial to successful resettlement into the community.

What is it about the prison/community transition that makes the relationship so crucial?

The first few days and weeks of release can be lonely and dysregulating. There are considerable practical demands, coupled with the emotional stress of being in the community after many years in custody (as described in Chapters 2 and 7 of this volume). The prospect of life in the community can be frightening for people who have learned to adapt and cope in prison (Rennie & Crewe, 2022). It can feel emotionally and practically burdensome and overwhelming. Many people who have spent time in prison are inherently distrustful, as a consequence of trauma and poor early attachments; this can significantly impair the ability to form any sort of interpersonal relationship, including professional relationships (Ansbro, 2008). It is also evident that prison affects people's ability to relate to others. Firstly, imprisonment can result in experiences mirroring those of Post-Traumatic Stress Disorder (PTSD), including hyperarousal and hypersensitivity to threat; struggling to trust and connect with others; emotional numbing, detachment and coldness (Hulley, Crewe, & Wright, 2016; Liem & Kunst, 2013). Furthermore, the prison environment is often experienced as unpredictable and violent (di Viggiani, 2007; Needs, 2016, 2022; Sim, 1994), and surviving prison can mean inhibiting emotional expression and hiding vulnerability (di Viggiani, 2006; Shingler, 2019). This survival strategy is not conducive to the sort of emotional vulnerability that is the basis for trusting and supportive relationships (Butler, 2008; Jarvis, Shaw, & Lovell, 2022; Shingler, Sonnenberg, & Needs, 2020).

Secondly, prison disconnects people from social and emotional contacts. This can happen by a process of attrition, in which prisoners and their loved ones simply cannot sustain the effort it takes to maintain relationships, especially for people serving long or indeterminate sentences. It can also happen deliberately and intentionally, as either prisoners decide to cut off community ties in order to cope with long-term imprisonment (Schinkel, 2014), or as family members end relationships with those incarcerated. These challenges are exacerbated by the lack of access to people in prison. Although improved since Covid-19 (via increased use of videolinks and in-cell telephones), connecting with people in prison remains difficult.

In summary, people in prison are quite likely to approach release with their skills and orientation to relationships (professional or otherwise) significantly eroded, but also with fewer social contacts. This means that the process of building professional relationships with people as they transition from prison to the community is crucial. Professional relationships can take on a greater significance and play a greater role in supporting resettlement in the absence of non-statutory support; as Michael said to us "Without you I'd be lost". Therefore, the remainder of this chapter explores how to establish relationships that are experienced as genuinely positive and supportive, and that can facilitate hope, desistance and reintegration.

What sort of practitioner should I strive to be?

In this section, we intend to focus on therapeutic and interpersonal values, and how as practitioners we can embody these values in our practice. Although we are using values as our starting point, our behaviour communicates our values. So whilst we will, of course, talk about what we *do*, our emphasis here is on how to *be*.

Be connected

Nick wrote, "thank you for coming all this way when you didn't have to, I do appreciate it." and "Thank you for your email…it was good to read your words of support". John described how he valued face-to-face meetings when on Release on Temporary License (ROTL),[1] as he felt more able to talk and less inclined to hide and avoid problems. These examples reflect how much people appreciate efforts made to maintain contact with them whilst they are in prison. Visits, letters, phone calls and meetings on ROTL enable people to maintain a thread of connections with the community which can build hope that there is a life beyond prison. Wayne described how, "the continuity of support helped me feel connected to the community". There are structural and psychological barriers to forming connections with people in prison yet this group place a high value on connection with professionals ("James" & Sainsbury, 2011). Social and interpersonal connectedness is associated with healthy interpersonal functioning and resilience (Townsend & McWhirter, 2005), which is essential for successful transition from prison to community.

Relying solely on visits and meetings on ROTLs means opportunities to connect are infrequent or unavailable, especially for people in prison at a significant distance from services, or for people being released directly from closed conditions. Some prisons are still not able to offer videolink facilities for anything other than parole or court purposes. For some people, the barriers to communication in videolinks (time delays, difficulty judging non-verbal communication) render them counterproductive. Therefore, we have embraced written communication (via letters and emails using the "email a prisoner" service[2]) to build and strengthen connections with people in prison. Letters exist within the relationship between sender and recipient so they provide evidence to the recipient of care and concern (Moules, 2003). When a relationship already exists, a letter can feel familiar, in that it is written in the writer's "voice" (Moules, 2003). This can be particularly important post-recall, when people often feel abandoned and forgotten (see Chapter 3, and for Nick's comment on receiving a letter, "I can't tell you how much that meant, or how much I needed it at that moment"). A letter or email (which is usually printed out for people in prison) is also more permanent than a phone call, meaning that people can re-read letters, reflect on them, but also keep them as a reminder of a connection. Darren commented,

> I keep every letter, I file them in a paper wallet, each section is from a different person. I can then see who writes to me most, and look at the letters and remember what they are telling me... I can't always remember what people say to me so letters help me with that.

Letters can serve a number of functions. They can structure expectations about services, and communicate values. They can suggest, clarify or confirm agreed goals; they can summarise discussions that may have been had in person or by phone, in order to confirm and cement plans and intentions (Lown & Britton, 1991). In this way, letters can build trust, in that they can clearly lay out ideas and plans, to which professionals can be held to account (Graham, 2003). Letters can express hope, they can be future focused, positive and encouraging of agency (Alexander, Shilts, Liscio, & Rambo, 2008). Other elements of effective letters include praise, compliments and warmth; statements that predict or presuppose that things will get better; recognition of small changes; offering tasks or questions for the person to reflect on; recognition and validation of both suffering and strengths; and offering alternatives and encouraging thought and reflection (Alexander et al., 2008; Moules, 2002).

Letters can be used to make brief contact at times of stress, crisis or specific important life events. For example, we emailed a man to wish him luck at his parole hearing, and to keep alive a thread of connection to the community, ending the email with, "We hope to be meeting you in person in [the community] in the very near future". We recently emailed a man after he had been assaulted, to express sadness and concern for him. Feedback indicated that these letters were experienced as supportive and meaningful at a critical time to people who had few community contacts. As a team we send men and women in prison a birthday card – again, one man continued to thank us for this many months after his birthday. Sometimes this might be the only recognition people receive of their birthday: marking a significant life event in this way helps people to feel visible and valued. Using a letter to follow up videolink meetings and visits is also helpful. It both reinforces the content of the discussion (as discussed above), and can also maintain, develop and strengthen the connection. These things can be done at the beginning of a therapeutic relationship or when a relationship is established: it is about keeping in touch, demonstrating that the person matters, that you have kept them in mind, and that you are motivated to be connected.

There is, of course, opportunity for letters to be misunderstood and misinterpreted, however carefully they are written, especially if they are being sent to people who struggle with trust and can be prone to hostile attributions of others' behaviour (Moules, 2003). There will also be some practitioners who worry about blurring professional boundaries, especially when sending more personal written correspondence, such as birthday cards. It is therefore useful to discuss the aim and purpose of letter writing with colleagues and in professional supervision sessions. Colleagues can also be invited to proofread letters to ensure they remain professionally appropriate, and to reduce the chances of therapeutic ruptures. If an emotionally challenging letter is being sent, it is advisable to communicate with prison colleagues to offer support to the recipient to read, digest and understand the letter. Additionally, there are some people for whom written communication is inaccessible or burdensome, and we do not recommend its use in these circumstances. Forming a connection is an individualised approach, and we need to do what works for each person.

When working with people who are living in the community (and where possible for those in prison) we give them direct access to our professional mobile telephone numbers. We plan telephone or video calls with people (in place of a face-to-face session, or as an interim measure to offer additional support), but we also encourage people to telephone and text us, either in a moment of need or success, or to request additional input. Phone and text contact can be used for shaping up skills in asking for help; generalising skills or insights learned in therapeutic sessions; and building and/or repairing relationships (Linehan, 1993). It can be used to extend therapy, or for people to demonstrate action arising from therapeutic contact. People sometimes text to share a success, and we text to offer reinforcement, encouragement and support to help build hope and agency. Tyler left a voice message for his community psychologist describing how on the way home from an appointment, he had refused an opportunity to buy drugs, and decided to get something to eat instead. His message started with, "I've just done really well, yeah". This was responded to immediately by text: "Fantastic! I'm so pleased for you. Every step like this takes you closer to your goals. You are doing the best you can and the best you have ever done – keep reminding yourself of this. Well done!". Text messages have the additional benefit that they can be kept and re-read as reminders of praise, encouragement and success. We also believe that the act of giving someone a direct mobile number communicates a sense of trust (that they will use it appropriately) and motivation to engage with them: it is a clear message that "we want to hear from you".

As with letter-writing, the practice of sharing telephone numbers will be troublesome for some practitioners who will fear the breaching of professional boundaries. As in Linehan (1993) we set limits around telephone contact, including:

- We are not a crisis service and are not available 24 hours a day.
- Our help and support will usually be limited to what we can do on the phone – we are not about to drop everything and intervene physically.

- We provide clear information about our working days and hours, and that phones will be turned off outside of these times. When we are on extended periods of leave we change our voice greetings, so people know we are not accessible and how to access alternative support.
- We may not be able to answer unsolicited phone calls, as we have other people to see and other work to do. We encourage people to leave a voice message or send a text and we will respond as soon as possible.

Also consistent with Linehan (1993), practitioners will have different limits around how they want to manage telephone contact, just as there may be different limits and rules for different people, depending on how they have used telephone calls in the past. The central point is that each professional must "set his or her own limits, which in turn must be respected both by the [professional] and by the supervision/consultation team" (Linehan, 1993, p. 327). Here, Linehan emphasises the importance of professionals sticking with their own limits as well as these being respected by others. This is not to say this practice has been without periods of stress and anxiety. For example, colleagues recently picked up a number of voice messages after a weekend indicating that a person had made an attempt on their life. Another man left a doubtful sounding voice message from prison after a recall, saying "I think I'm strong enough not to do anything". We have safeguarding action plans in place for these circumstances (e.g., communicating with the person's probation officer; alerting police for welfare checks in the community; alerting safer custody teams in prison) and we discuss and debrief as a team to support each other. Even with these challenging situations, we believe that the benefits outweigh the risks.

To summarise, many people who have been embedded in crime and substance misuse for many years have deeply disrupted connections with others, and have often brought violence and abuse to their relationships. Their current and future relationships can be fraught with danger for them and for the people with whom they are in relationships. Enabling connections with professionals is a step towards making more pro-social and desistance-supporting connections with others and beginning to learn to navigate the complexities of relationships in a safe and contained way. In this way, being connected can support the pathway towards desistance.

Be human and humanising

This value refers to being our own human selves as practitioners alongside valuing each person for their own humanity. It involves breaking down barriers to connection by being a "human being in a situation with a human being" (Shingler, 2019, p. 83). It means showing ourselves to be essentially good people (Arcaya, 1978) and communicating that we believe the people we work with are essentially good people. It means creating opportunities for people to see themselves as fundamentally good people (who may have done bad things) and to deconstruct anti-social identities (Maruna, 2001). Being human is what our introductory quote refers to as being "real". People can feel stripped of humanity in prison (King & Crisp, 2021; Sykes, 1958) and within the criminal justice system (CJS) in general, as John commented, "in prison you are identified as a number not a person". A key therapeutic value, therefore, is to recognise people as human beings first and foremost. As Jude explained:

JS: What did you like about how you were treated?
JUDE: She treated me like a person.
JS: Can you describe what she did…?
JUDE: She was never cold and aloof with ya. You were an individual…it was like she cared, right? I don't know if she did or not but she came across as wanting to treat you more than a number.

Jude describes the value of being seen as an individual, as being treated with warmth and humanity. Finding and nurturing the good core self, believing in inherent decency and value is the centre of humanising. Maruna (2001) noted that belief in a "good core self" (p. 138) was an opening for desistance and recovery. Blagden, Winder and Hames (2016) found that feeling an absence of acceptance as a human inhibited people's ability to reflect on past behaviour. Tyler and Huo (2002) identified a sense of commonality and shared values and concerns (i.e., forming a human-to-human connection) as key elements of perceived trustworthiness in criminal justice professionals. Perhaps most importantly of all, Landy, Piazza and Goodwin (2016) found that the attributes required for rapport building, such as warmth and sociability, tended only to be viewed positively if they were accompanied by honesty and compassion. That is, if techniques for building relationships are used without a sense of humanity (i.e., regarded as purely strategic) they may be viewed with suspicion and consequently be counterproductive.

In order to fully comprehend the value of a human connection, Martin's (who was serving an indeterminate sentence) description of the opposite is illuminating:

They'd ask you a question and you'd have a conversation about the, the question or whatever. And then you'd ask them something like just as a normal conversation would go. And they'd be like "Oh, erm" and they'd be very guarded against what they said. And sometimes they might just say "oh we're not here to talk about me, der der der". But I think if you wanna get more out of people, treat them like normal human beings and like you're having a conversation. When I hear or see people act like that towards me it makes me clam up and I think well, that's suspicious to me I don't know why.

Anxiety about personal and professional boundaries can inhibit the sort of human connection that Martin wants, yet both psychologists and people in prison and on probation can see the value of this (Shingler et al., 2018). Martin also describes how a reluctance to talk human-to-human undermines trust. It is clear from the literature that trust is essential to effective professional relationships in criminal justice settings (Shingler et al., 2018, 2020). Some prisoners may be inherently distrustful and it is likely that prison exacerbates existing problems with trust, as discussed above. Therefore, a professional relationship that is based on humanity can be the springboard for developing trust. Building a trusting relationship with another can enable openness to alternative explanations and perspectives (see Gillespie, 2011). Trust is also central if people are to comply with criminal justice sanctions (Tyler & Huo, 2002), something that can be pivotal in successful community resettlement. Some approaches to communicating humanity and building trust include:

- Be clear that you are interested in the people you work with as *people* and in enabling them to build meaningful and fulfilling lives. For example, we are clear from the outset of contact that we want to support people to build a life free from crime, not just see them through their period of licence or probation order.
- Be consistent and reliable and persevere with people in order to create safety and build trust (Beckley, 2011; Sainsbury, 2011).
- Recognise and normalise fundamental human wants and needs, such as relationships, parenthood, even when there are risks. This is not to minimise risk, but to communicate that it is entirely normal to want an intimate relationship (for example) even when past behaviour has put others at risk.
- Relatedly, support people to address basic needs. Without food and a safe place to live people cannot make good decisions. Effective relationships in resettlement acknowledge the predicament people are in but also offer practical help and support (Canton, 2022). For example, we might support people to access food banks, debt relief, emergency benefit payments etc. We are not averse to buying someone a coffee or a sandwich if that seems to be what they need in the moment.
- Use language that communicates humanity. Get people's names right, use their pronunciations or contractions of their name and their own choice of pronouns. Use your own first name in introductions rather than professional titles and family names. Make sure people know to use your first name and gently correct people if they use titles and family names. As far as the CJS allows, use humanising language in written reports and correspondence. For example, avoid use of "caseload" or "case discussion" (these are people not cases), and instead refer to "list" or "professionals' meeting" or "consultation".
- Devise plans collaboratively (Shingler et al., 2018) to emphasise the human-to-human connection during the change process – we are two people working on a task together, both with unique expertise and a contribution to make – try to avoid the idea of the professional as the expert who has all the solutions.

- Using "limited self-disclosure" can be a way of supporting a more normal human relationship (Beckley, 2011). As Martin alludes to above, if people ask us normal questions about our lives, we tend to answer them, within our personal limits and limits of safety. We have found that intrusive questions (e.g., about where we live) are rare[3]. We share some personal information to communicate that we are human beings with lives and roles outside of work (Arcaya, 1978; "James" & Sainsbury, 2011). In contrast with Martin's experience, we encourage informal conversations about things unrelated to our professional roles. We are essentially the same person wherever we are in our lives: we are not playing a game to get people to comply (see Landy et al., 2016).
- Maximise transparency at all times, about goals and intentions; about the reasons for and outcomes of assessments; about therapeutic models of change; and about activities and exercises in therapy; about how information is used and shared. Explain why you are asking questions, how they contribute to the process of change, for example, "I am interested in who is in your life because I want to understand what your life is like, not because I want to check up on your movements".
- Using "here and now" disclosure in individual sessions can create safety and trust. This involves transparency about thinking and feeling in the moment, for example saying "I feel really sad for the 5-year-old boy who was left alone so much". Or, if someone makes an astute observation, or reads a situation correctly (e.g., "you seemed cross with me last week") it can be connecting and humanising to be honest about this, "you're right, I did feel frustrated". There is less room for hostile or paranoid interpretations if you are honest about what is going on for you. In the same vein, acknowledge and apologise for errors or mis-steps, and encourage discussions about behaviour that might have triggered schemas or emotional responses.

Be hopeful, promote agency

Prison, a "total institution" (Sykes, 1958) robs people of autonomy. The sense of being out of control, of lacking in agency, of being herded by the whims of a harsh and uncaring system is pervasive amongst prisoners, especially those serving indeterminate sentences (Jacobson & Hough, 2010; Jewkes, 2005; Warr, 2008). The "tightness" of power in prison (Crewe, 2011) emphasises prisoners' responsibility for wrongdoings but provides very little room for genuine choice and autonomy. Feeling powerless and seeing no options other than a life of crime is related to persisting with an offending pathway; feeling that you have a voice in your own life and future seems to be essential for successful desistance (Maruna, 2001). However, agency must be found or discovered by the individual: "desistance almost always seems to come from 'within'" (Maruna, 2001, p. 96), and for some, agency is well hidden amidst the hopelessness of incarceration. For these people, professionals can communicate hope and the possibility of an alternative identity and future when people cannot yet see it for themselves (Maruna, 2001; McNeill, 2006). This is the value we are referring to here: promoting and reinforcing agency for those who have found it, and encouraging the discovery of agency for those still looking. After all, most of the work towards change happens outside of professional contact and therefore requires personal agency (Maruna, Immarigeon, & LeBel, 2004). We need to promote agency in our contacts with people in order for them to be able to access it when they need it most. A conversation with a man in prison recently, went something like this:

P: I don't know why I always get drawn back to drugs, it's not like I am doing it to get high.

JS: so perhaps right now it is just what you do? When you are distressed, you turn to heroin because that is what you have always done?

P: yes that's right.

JS: So you know how you told me that you no longer wanted to be a violent person, you don't feel like a violent person, you don't see yourself as a violent person, I don't see you as a violent person, and you haven't been violent for many years?

P: Yes, I don't see myself as violent.

JS: How about if the next step for you is seeing yourself as someone who does not use heroin? Perhaps that might become something, like violence, that is just not you anymore? So right now, you go to heroin because that's what you do, that's what you have always done. But what if you didn't do that? What if your new identity was someone who doesn't use heroin? What would you do then, when you get distressed?

This is not to say that the shift away from class A drug use is easy or instantaneous. This conversation was attempting to sow the seeds of *hope* that things could be different, that the man was not "doomed to deviance" (Maruna, 2001, p. 165) and that he could carve a different identity for himself. His ability to shed a violent identity was proof that he had strength and resilience. This exchange reminded him of his existing skills and communicated a belief that he could change, when in the moment he felt hopeless about his future. The suggestion of agency was something he could take forward and reflect on (and that was followed up with a letter, see above), with the hope that he might draw on these ideas outside of professional contact.

Promoting agency also involves genuine belief in an individual's capacity to make choices that enable a meaningful, fulfilling and crime-free life, even when the current circumstances suggest it is impossible. We hold hope that people can build a life worth living when they doubt that or when they have never had the capacity or stability to think about this. For some individuals a life worth living feels impossible. Some fundamentally believe they are not worthy or deserving of building a positive and connected life. Some have lived their entire lives in survival mode, unable to think outside of their immediate circumstances. In these situations, we can be the reminder of hope of an alternative way. Linehan (1993) discusses the inherent capacity of the individual to change, and this is what we are referring to here. Even when the current circumstances look like proof they will never make it, we continue to believe there is a chance they will. So when a man said recently, "if this release doesn't succeed, that will be it for me, I can't do it again", our response was clear: "We believe you can succeed this time, but if it doesn't work, we will reset and try again". The role of the team is central here. At any point in someone's desistance journey, one professional may feel disheartened and hopeless. Having other supportive professionals around you who remind you that this is a hurdle to overcome, it is part of the journey, and it does not mean the person will never make it, is central to maintaining hope and continuing to communicate belief in someone's inherent capacity to succeed. This sense of remaining hopeful was noticed by Luke when he described what he had needed to succeed:

> You not giving up on me. Everyone has always given up on me, whenever I make mistakes. Everyone just walked away and left me, but you never have. You have always been there when I made mistakes and believed in me, which has helped me believe in myself. It has taken time, but I now believe in myself, I believe I can make a success of being in the community. I think until you really believe you can really do it; it will never happen.

This reflection suggests that Luke is beginning to find his inner sense of agency.

It is also worth mentioning the challenges of being hopeful and promoting of agency when working within a system that tends to look backwards, focus on risk and impose external controls. There is a general view that risk assessment should be more future focused and strengths based (Barnett & Mann, 2011) and this is certainly more consistent with the communication of hope and agency. However, current systems remain largely backwards looking and risk focused, which is experienced as disheartening by men in prison: "You spend so long looking at the bad that you forget there ever was any good" (Shingler et al., 2018). It can also be challenging to be communicating a message of hope and inherent capacity for change when things are seemingly going wrong and risk is escalating. To truly hold hope and believe in agency means being able to sit with this discomfort, outside of a collective view of a person as hopeless and doomed to deviance (based on a thorough understanding of their risks and needs, of course). To continue to hold hope does not equate to underestimating risk or colluding with denial or harmful behaviour. It means being prepared to imagine that things could be different. A range of perspectives are needed in order to guard against bias (Baker & Wilkinson, 2011), and that includes holding a hopeful perspective in the midst of hopelessness.

Some approaches to promoting agency and hope include:

- Frequently and clearly communicate belief that people can make it, that they can succeed (Orpwood & Ryan, 2022). This can be done in writing, or verbally, whenever the opportunity arises.
- Promote agency by promoting choice. Ultimately, each person is responsible for their own choices, so by providing actual choices, we can support better decision making. Ideally, this should start with services being voluntary rather than mandated (Canton, 2022; McNeill, 2006). Mandated treatment can trigger issues about control and autonomy that people may have battled all their lives – consequently refusal of mandated services may reflect a refusal to be controlled rather than a refusal to acknowledge problems or a lack of motivation to change.
- Another way to promote choice/agency is to co-produce intervention plans. Discuss and share goals, priorities and concerns; discuss and agree pathways to achieving goals (Shingler & Mann, 2006). For example, our intervention plans starts with a summary entitled "What is important to me". The aim of psychological and occupational therapy intervention in community resettlement is to support people to build a life with meaning and value that draws them away from offending pathways. Therefore, their priorities are a central consideration.
- Try to give as much choice as possible about the structure of services. For example, where possible, negotiate times, dates and locations of appointments and try to fit around people's lives, routines and families. For one man, the choice about how services were introduced made the difference between engagement and rejection. He chose to meet with us alongside his probation officer initially, with whom he already had a trusting relationship. He decided when he was ready to meet with us individually, at a point where he felt sufficient trust and confidence had been built.
- Use "language of agency" (Maruna, 2001, p. 77); Maruna gives the example of desisters preferring to talk about "recovery" rather than "rehabilitation", because "recovery" implies active involvement and agency in the journey, whereas "rehabilitation" implies being "done to" by professionals. For example, draw attention to people's choice to engage with services, and compare this favourably with the past, e.g., "Two years ago you wouldn't have sat in a room with me telling me why you had used heroin. You would have made an excuse, not turned up, avoided the discussion. Now you are prepared to have it". Notice and reflect back expressions of choice and agency.
- It is worth a word here about what being promoting of agency is *not*, and in our view it does not involve pushing people towards a narrative in which they "take responsibility" for their offending. Our view is that agency is about taking responsibility for the future (Ware & Mann, 2012), and this is our focus.

Be accepting of the individual in their context

Different people need different things from services as they transition from prison to the community, and it is important that we *meet people where they are* in their own personal journey. Providing what individuals need to feel safe and contained within their own unique context is an important part of trauma-informed care (Orpwood & Ryan, 2022). For some, this means therapy; for others, it means regular phone calls to support processing of the emotional burden of release. For some, the primary task in the early days of release (and beyond) is relational, "a process of relating to and 'being with'" (Orpwood & Ryan, 2022, p. 324) that enables the person to begin to build a more steady foundation from which to step out into the world. This approach can make the difference between engagement and disengagement with services, as people feel efforts are being made to understand them as individuals, and listen to what they need to succeed.

At the point of release, people have either come to the end of the custodial element of their sentence, or their release has been directed by the Parole Board. Therefore, our opinion of that release decision is irrelevant and it is our job to work with people wherever they are in their journey. Communicating an acceptance of a person's place in their journey is important in communicating our values: we are there to work with them to build a life worth living, that does not cause harm to others or to themselves, and that we will work with them wherever they are already on that pathway. It does not mean we overlook risk, or ignore it, or minimise it. We hope that this approach removes some of the pressure to perform that people experience in other contacts with criminal justice professionals. Other authors have reflected on the sense of second-guessing what professionals are thinking in order to get the answers right and therefore be permitted to take the next step towards progress (Crewe, 2012; Shingler et al., 2020). Accepting people where they are and working with that means there are no right or wrong answers, and no evaluated performances.

Another way of representing the value of acceptance is to make efforts to understand people within their context. Beckley (2011) discusses the importance of placing an individual's offending within their developmental context via psychological formulation. We also believe that we need to formulate barriers to resettlement within the context of someone's developmental and custodial experiences. We steer away from the "fundamental attribution error" (Jones & Nisbett, 1971) of seeing problems as entirely located within the individual, and towards a contextual understanding of someone, understanding them within the context of their life, their experiences, their imprisonment and their ongoing sentence, if relevant. This is particularly salient for people serving indeterminate sentences whose sentences remain a part of their lives indefinitely. Recognising the impact that an indeterminate sentence continues to have on someone, even when they are released from prison is an essential part of being contextually sensitive in community professional relationships. For example, one man felt unable to show any frustration or disagreement with professionals, several years into his release, for fear it would be seen as evidence of hostility that could lead to his recall. Naming and validating this in context enabled him to make progress towards expressing an opinion and making a choice about professional contact.

Finally, with acceptance of where the person is comes an ability to make our work more future focused. Research has indicated that the constant focus on the past (and in particular on painful recollection of offences) is demoralising, demotivating and can lead to feelings of hopelessness and despair (Attrill & Liell, 2007; Shingler et al., 2020; Ward & Fisher, 2006). It can lead to people feeling judged and condemned to a life of deviance. When supporting people to transition from prison into the community, the focus must be on "making good" (Maruna, 2001) and looking forward. We specifically explore strengths and abilities; interests and hobbies. We reflect on someone's sense of self: who are you, who do you want to be? This enables us to build a relationship from a place of acceptance, with an eye on building a life worth living. Linehan (1993) discusses the balance between acceptance and change when working with people who have long and traumatic histories of maladaptive coping behaviours (including self-harm, substance misuse, violence). Linehan's view is that acceptance of where someone is in the here and now is central to the process of change. She argues that many therapists focus entirely on change, and when therapists push too hard for change, people feel invalidated, misunderstood, blamed. People cannot change if no one takes the time to understand where they are and how they got there. Criminal justice settings are characterised by prioritising change: violent people must become less violent; angry people must learn to manage their anger. Whilst this approach has a place, the ability to accept someone where they are provides a different footing for the building of relationship.

Summary and conclusions

This chapter has focused on the therapeutic values of connectedness, humanity, agency and acceptance, and discussed how these values can be communicated via behaviour and approach. This is partly because we believe that values hold the key to effective practice, and partly because any attempt to "manualise" the therapeutic relationship is doomed to failure. The general view is that following guidance on what to do to build relationships results in robotic, reductionist practice (Marshall, 2009; Shingler et al., 2018) that is almost certainly inconsistent with the value of humanity. In fact, Schön (1983) specifically notes that "skilful action often reveals a, 'knowing more than we can say'" (p. 51). It is also true to say that human interactions are complex and unpredictable, and it is impossible to provide guidance on how to respond effectively to every interpersonal encounter.

Our aim is to embody the values we discuss in all aspects of our work, and at times, our priorities are purely to communicate these values. So much correctional psychological practice is functional, for example, meeting with someone to conduct a risk assessment, or to engage in a structured programme of intervention. By the nature of prison work, relationships are rarely enduring, and it is unusual for the relationship, for trust, connection and humanity, to be the goal in itself. Yet the therapeutic relationship is the cornerstone of effective practice. It is what brings people into services and enables them to remain engaged in services. The relationship is the ideal vehicle for exploring and addressing ambivalence about change and can "facilitate the formation of a non-criminal identity" (Burnett, 2004, p. 169). Therefore, as professionals, prioritising our attitude and approach to our relationships with the people we work with is the single most important thing we can do to effect change.

Notes

1 Release on Temporary License – usually from Open Prison, and comprising either day release to a town local to the prison, or overnight release usually to the planned resettlement area.
2 https://www.emailaprisoner.com/. The additional benefit of the "email a prisoner" service is that it allows people to reply at no cost to themselves, providing a useful opportunity for reciprocal communication.
3 We recognise that for some people working in prisons this approach might seem fraught with danger. We are clear to protect information about ourselves that sits outside of our personal and professional limits. We are also realistic that boundaries have to be different in the community, as we are sharing the same physical and geographical space. People see us getting into and out of our cars; they can see the direction from which we arrive for an appointment; we might bump into each other in the street. This creates a different basis for relating and for sharing information.

References

Alexander, S., Shilts, L., Liscio, M., & Rambo, A. (2008). Return to sender: Letter writing to bring hope to both client and team. *Journal of Systemic Therapies*, 27(1), 59.
Andrews, D. A., & Bonta, J. (2010). *The psychology of criminal conduct* (5th ed). New Jersey: Andersen Publishing.
Ansbro, M. (2008). Using attachment theory with offenders. *Probation Journal*, 55(3), 231–244.
Arcaya, J. M. (1978). Coercive counseling and self-disclosure. *International Journal of Offender Therapy and Comparative Criminology*, 22(3), 231–237.
Attrill, G., & Liell, G. (2007). Offenders' view on risk assessment. In N. Padfield (Ed.), *Who to release? Parole, fairness and criminal justice* (pp. 191–201). Cullumpton, Devon: Willan Publishing.
Baker, K., & Wilkinson, B. (2011). Professional risk taking and defensible decisions. In H. Kemshall, and B. Wilkinson (Eds.), *Good practice in assessing risk: Current knowledge, issues and approaches* (pp. 13–29). London: Jessica Kingsley.
Barnett, G. D., & Mann, R. E. (2011). Good lives and risk assessment: Collaborative approaches to risk assessment with sexual offenders. In H. Kemshall, and B. Wilkinson (Eds.), *Good practice in assessing risk: Current knowledge, issues and approaches* (pp. 139–154). London: Jessica Kingsley.

Beckley, K. (2011). Therapeutic style and adapting approaches to therapy. In P. Willmott & N. Gordon (Eds). *Working positively with personality disorder in secure settings* (pp. 115–126). Chichester: Wiley.

Blagden, N., Winder, B., & Hames, C. (2016). "They treat us like human beings" – Experiencing a therapeutic sex offenders prison: Impact on prisoners and staff and implications for treatment. *International Journal of Offender Therapy and Comparative Criminology*, 60(4), 371–396.

Burnett, R. (2004). To reoffend or not to reoffend? The ambivalence of convicted property offenders. In S. Maruna & R. Immarigeon (Eds). *After Crime and Punishment: Pathways to Offender Reintegration* (pp 152–180). Cullumpton, Devon: Willan Publishing.

Butler, M. (2008). What are you looking at? Prisoner confrontations and the search for respect. *The British Journal of Criminology*, 48(6), 856–873.

Canton, R. (2022). After-care, resettlement and social inclusion: The role of probation. *Probation Journal*, 69(3) 373–390.

Crewe, B. (2011). Depth, weight, tightness: revisiting the pains of imprisonment. *Punishment and Society*, 13(5), 509–529.

Crewe, B. (2012). *The prisoner society: Power, adaptation and social life in an English prison.* Oxford: Oxford University Press.

Croft, J. & Winder, B. (2018). License conditions … don't stop you committing offences and they don't protect the public, they're just there to make you feel worse: A qualitative analysis of the experiences of individuals who have served prison sentences for a sexual offence and been recalled to prison. Unpublished research paper.

di Viggiani, N. (2006). Surviving prison: exploring prison social life as a determinant of health. *International Journal of Prisoner Health*, 2(2), 71–89.

di Viggiani, N. (2007). Unhealthy prisons: exploring structural determinants of prison health. *Sociology of Health and Illness*, 29(1), 115–135.

Dowden, C., & Andrews, D. A. (2004). The importance of staff practice in delivering effective correctional treatment: A meta-analytic review of core correctional practice. *International Journal of Offender Therapy and comparative criminology*, 48(2), 203–214.

Fitzalan Howard, F. (2019). The experience of prison recall in England and Wales. *The Howard Journal of Crime and Justice*, 58(2), 180–201.

Gillespie, A. (2011). Concluding comment: Contact without transformation: The context, process and content of distrust. In I. Marková & A. Gillespie, (Eds.) *Trust and conflict: Representation, culture and dialogue* (pp. 201–216). Abingdon, Oxon: Routledge.

Graham, G. H. (2003). Role preparation in brief strategic therapy: the welcome letter. *Journal of Systemic Therapies*, 22(1), 3–14.

Hanson, R. K., Bourgon, G., Helmus, L., & Hodgson, S. (2009). The principles of effective correctional treatment also apply to sexual offenders: A meta-analysis. *Criminal Justice and Behavior*, 36(9), 865–891.

Hulley, S., Crewe, B., & Wright, S. (2016). Re-examining the problems of long-term imprisonment. *British Journal of Criminology*, 56(4), 769–792.

Jacobson, J., & Hough, M. (2010). *Unjust Deserts: Imprisonment for Public Protection.* London: Prison Reform Trust.

"James" & Sainsbury, L. (2011). One patient's therapeutic journey. In P. Willmott & N. Gordon (Eds). *Working positively with personality disorder in secure settings* (pp. 147–156). Chichester, West Sussex: Wiley.

Jarvis, D., Shaw, J., & Lovell, T. (2022). Service user experiences of a psychologically enhanced resettlement service [PERS] in an English open prison. *The Journal of Forensic Practice* (ahead-of-print).

Jewkes, Y. (2005). Loss, liminality and the life sentence: Managing identity through a disrupted lifecourse. In A. Liebling & S. Maruna (Eds.) *Effects of imprisonment* (pp. 366–388). Cullompton, Devon: Willan Publishing.

Jones, E. E., & Nisbett, R. E. (1971). *The actor and the observer: Divergent perceptions of the causes of behaviour*. Morristown, NJ: General Learning Press.

Kennealy, P. J., Skeem, J. L., Manchak, S. M., & Eno Louden, J. (2012). Firm, fair, and caring officer-offender relationships protect against supervision failure. *Law and Human Behavior*, 36(6), 496.

King, N., & Crisp, B. (2021). Conceptualising 'success' among Imprisonment for Public Protection (IPP) sentenced offenders with personality-related difficulties. *Probation Journal*, 68(1), 85–106.

Lambert, M. J., & Barley, D. E. (2001). Research summary on the therapeutic relationship and psychotherapy outcome. *Psychotherapy: Theory, Research, Practice, Training*, 38(4), 357.

Landy, J., Piazza, J. R., & Goodwin, G. (2016). *When it's bad to be friendly and smart: The desirability of sociability and competence depends on morality*. Manuscript submitted for publication. Retrieved from http://eprints.lancs.ac.uk/79801/1/Contingency_Rev2_SUBMITTED.pdf.

Liem, M., & Kunst, M. (2013). Is there a recognizable post-incarceration syndrome among released "lifers"? *International Journal of Law and Psychiatry*, 36(3–4), 333–337.

Linehan, M. M. (1993). *Cognitive-behavioural treatment of borderline personality disorder*. New York: The Guilford Press.

Lowenkamp, C. T., Holsinger, A., Robinson, C. R., & Alexander, M. (2014). Diminishing or durable treatment effects of STARR? A research note on 24-month re-arrest rates. *Journal of Crime and Justice, 37*(2), 275–283.

Lown, N., & Britton, B. (1991). Engaging families through the letter writing technique. *Journal of Systemic Therapies*, 10(2), 43.

Marshall, W. L. (2009). Manualization: A blessing or a curse? *Journal of Sexual Aggression*, 15(2), 109–120.

Marshall, W. L., Ward, T., Mann, R. E., Moulden, H., Fernandez, Y. M., Serran, G., & Marshall, L. E. (2005). Working positively with sexual offenders: maximising the effectiveness of treatment. *Journal of Interpersonal Violence* 20(9), 1096–1114.

Maruna, S. (2001). *Making good: How ex-convicts reform and rebuild their lives*. Washington: America Psychological Association.

Maruna, S., Immarigeon, R. & LeBell, T. P. (2004). Ex-offender reintegration: theory and practice. In S. Maruna & R. Immarigeon (Eds). *After Crime and Punishment: Pathways to Offender Reintegration* (pp. 3–26). Cullumpton, Devon: Willan Publishing.

McNeill, F. (2006). A desistance paradigm for offender management. *Criminology & Criminal Justice*, 6(1), 39–62.

Moules, N. J. (2002). Nursing on paper: Therapeutic letters in nursing practice. *Nursing Inquiry*, 9(2), 104–113.

Moules, N. J. (2003). Therapy on paper: Therapeutic letters and the tone of the relationship. *Journal of Systemic Therapies*, 22(1), 33–49.

Needs, A. (2016). Rehabilitation – writing a new story. *The Psychologist*, 29, 192–195.

Needs, A. (2022). Change must engage a person's sense of identity, meaning, control and belonging. *The Psychologist*, 35, 28–33.

Orpwood, K. & Ryan, S (2022). Trauma-informed community services. In P. Willmot & L. Jones (Eds.). *Trauma-informed forensic practice* (pp. 316–329). Abingdon, Oxon: Routledge.

Rennie, A., & Crewe, B. (2022) 'Tightness', autonomy and release: The anticipated pains of release and life licencing. *The British Journal of Criminology*.

Rex, S. (1999). Desistance from offending: Experiences of probation. *Howard Journal of Criminal Justice*, 38(4), 307–318.

Sainsbury, L. (2011). Attachment theory and the therapeutic relationship in the treatment of personality disorder. In P. Willmott & N. Gordon (Eds). *Working positively with personality disorder in secure settings* (pp 93–114). Chichester, West Sussex: Wiley.

Schinkel, M. (2014). *Being imprisoned: punishment, adaptation and desistance.* London: Palgrave Macmillan.

Schön, D. A. (1983). *The reflective practitioner: How professionals think in action* (Vol. 5126). Aldershot: Ashgate.

Shingler, J. (2019). *Understanding psychological risk assessment: Exploring the Experiences of Psychologists*, Indeterminate Sentenced Prisoners and Parole Board Members (Unpublished doctoral dissertation). Hampshire: University of Portsmouth.

Shingler, J., & Mann, R. E. (2006). Collaboration in clinical work with sexual offenders: treatment and risk assessment. In W. L. Marshall, Y. M. L. Fernandez, L. E. Marshall, & G. A. Serran (Eds). *Sexual offender treatment: Controversial issues* (pp. 225–239). Chichester, West Sussex: Wiley.

Shingler, J., Sonnenberg, S. J., & Needs, A. (2018). Risk assessment interviews: Exploring the perspectives of psychologists and indeterminate sentenced prisoners in the United Kingdom. *International Journal of Offender Therapy and Comparative Criminology*, 62(10), 3201–3224.

Shingler, J., Sonnenberg, S. J., & Needs, A. (2020). Psychologists as 'the quiet ones with the power': Understanding indeterminate sentenced prisoners' experiences of psychological risk assessment in the United Kingdom. *Psychology, Crime & Law*, 26(6), 571–592.

Sim, J. (1994). 'Tougher than the rest?' Men in Prison. In T. Newburn & E. Stanko (Eds.), *Just boys doing business: Men, masculinities and crime.* Abingdon, Oxon: Routledge.

Sykes, G. M. (1958). *The Society of Captives: A study of a maximum security prison.* Princeton, NJ: Princeton University Press.

Townsend, K. C., & McWhirter, B. T. (2005). Connectedness: A review of the literature with implications for counseling, assessment and research. *Journal of Counseling & Development*, 83(2), 191–201.

Tyler, T. R., & Huo, Y. J. (2002). *Trust in the law: Encouraging public cooperation with the police and courts.* New York: Russell Sage Foundation.

Ward, T., & Fisher, D. (2006). New ideas in the treatment of sexual offenders. In W. L. Marshall, Y. M. L. Fernandez, L. E. Marshall & G. A. Serran (Eds.), *Sexual offender treatment: Controversial issues* (pp. 143–158). Chichester, West Sussex: Wiley.

Ware, J., & Mann, R. E. (2012). How should "acceptance of responsibility" be addressed in sexual offending treatment programs? *Aggression and Violent Behavior*, 17(4), 279–288.

Warr, J. (2008). Personal reflections on prison staff. In J. Bennett, B. Crewe & A. Wahidin, (Eds.) *Understanding prison staff* (pp. 17–29). Cullumpton, Devon: Willan Publishing.

Willmot, P. & Tetley, A. (2011). What works with forensic patients with Personaloty Disorder? Integrating the literature on Personality Disorder, correctional programmes and psychopathy. In P. Willmott & N. Gordon (Eds). *Working positively with personality disorder in secure settings* (pp. 35–48). Chichester, West Sussex: Wiley.

10 "They spoke to me like I was a human, so I behaved like a human"

Mattering, Hope and Release from Prison

Jennifer Stickney and Joe Lowenstein

Imagine returning to your home town after a long time away. Also imagine that when you return, no one cares, no one notices, no one is interested. You settle in and start trying to build a life again but who do you tell, no one is concerned about your progress, no one is there to enjoy the wins with you or console you when you are struggling. No one is coming to you for help or advice either, no one needs your input or is attentive to your views. You are essentially invisible to those around you. You do not matter to anyone... How do you feel right now?

The scenario above is not entirely fictitious. Up and down the United Kingdom individuals will be released from prison and face this experience to a greater or lesser degree. This chapter examines the concept of mattering in the context of offending behaviour and release from custody. In particular it discusses the link between mattering and hope. Finally, it provides recommendations for enhancing a sense of mattering and developing and maintaining hope as a person progresses through prison to resettle in the community.

What is mattering?

The concept of mattering emerged from Rosenberg and McCullough's (1981) work on self-esteem. It is defined as "a person's need to feel significant in the eyes of other people" (Flett, 2018, p. 31). Mattering is a developing concept that is currently thought of as having seven key components (Maslach, Stapp & Santee, 1985; Rosenberg, 1985; Rosenberg & Mccullough, 1981; Schlossberg, 1989):

1 Importance: feeling significant to others
2 Attention: feeling others are taking notice of what we are doing
3 Dependence: feeling important because others are relying on us
4 Ego extension: feeling that others are emotionally invested in us and that what happens to us also affects them
5 Noted absence: feeling missed by someone
6 Appreciation: feeling valued by others
7 Individuation: feeling special as a unique person in your own right

DOI: 10.4324/9781003308171-13

Mattering can be relevant to a specific person (friend, partner, children), group (family, work colleagues), a wider community or society as a whole. There is limited direct research regarding the development of mattering in childhood, but it has been suggested that the roots of mattering are closely linked with attachment (Bowlby, 1969). Charles and Alexander (2014) have suggested that the strength and quality of the attachment are the foundation from which a sense of mattering develops. This is supported by research that has demonstrated that feelings of mattering are negatively associated with both anxious and avoidant attachment (Flett, Burdo & Nepon, 2021; Raque-Bogdan, Ericson, Jackson, Martin & Bryan, 2011) and positively associated with secure attachment (Flett et al., 2021). Mattering has also been found to be negatively associated with reports of emotional maltreatment and emotional neglect (Flett et al., 2016).

It makes intuitive sense that an individual with a secure attachment to a parental figure will form the strongest sense of mattering at an early stage and this will perpetuate throughout the individual's life. It also follows that individuals with ambivalent, avoidant, or disorganised attachments (Ainsworth, Blehar, Waters, & Wall, 1978) will be unlikely to form a view of themselves as mattering in the world. Consequently, future relationships will be modelled on this, causing feelings of being unwanted or unloved (Elliott, 2009).

Prilleltensky (2020) identifies that mattering is a fundamental psychological need and recognises the vital importance it has on the health, wellbeing and success of individuals across societies.

> Failure to meet that need results in significant suffering to the person, and potential damage to the people and communities surrounding that individual.
>
> (p. 17)

However, it is not something that is evenly distributed: some have too little whilst others have too much. Prilleltensky (2020) notes that the latter can also manifest pathologically such as behaving in ways that excessively draw attention to themselves at the expense of others, thriving on adulation and being unable to tolerate criticism.

In terms of impact across the lifespan, multiple research studies have reported a relationship between perceived mattering and mental health. For example, low levels of mattering are associated with delinquency, depression, anxiety and stress levels (Dixon & Robinson Kurpius, 2008; Dixon, Scheidegger & McWhirter, 2009; Flett et al., 2021; Rosenberg & McCullough, 1981). Conversely, those who report higher levels of mattering also report better general mental health and self-acceptance (Raque-Bogdan et al., 2011; Taniguchi, 2015), wellbeing (Dixon Rayle, 2005; Marshall, 2001) and self-esteem (Dixon & Robinson Kurpius, 2008; Elliott, Colangelo & Gelles, 2005; Marshall, 2001; Rosenberg & McCullough, 1981) and are less likely to experience suicidal ideation (Elliott et al., 2005).

The concept of "anti-mattering" has been defined as a feeling of not mattering (Flett, 2018), feeling invisible and insignificant to others (McComb, Goldberg, Flett & Rose, 2020). However, anti-mattering is not just construed as the opposite of mattering but actually a negative internalised stance on mattering (Flett et al., 2022; France & Finney, 2009). John describes this in his account of being in prison:

> I was up for parole, I had done all the courses I needed to do, I had done everything that I had been told that I had to do on my sentence plan to get out. Then when it came to parole, they said I needed to "consolidate" my skills. I lost it then. I thought they don't care about me; I won't care about me either. So, I stopped caring about me, about everything. I was so angry, I trashed everything around me. I completely trashed by cell, so they shipped me out.

John highlights that anti-mattering is not just about feeling invisible, it is also the active process of behaving in ways that reinforce to self and others that they do not matter and do not care about anything including the consequences of their actions. The construct of anti-mattering is in its infancy and has had less research attention than mattering. However, it is proposed that an individual who demonstrates high levels of anti-mattering holds an orientation geared towards defending themselves and a desire for protection from adverse interactions compared to individuals who score highly in mattering (Flett et al., 2022).

Mattering and offending behaviour

There have been specific links made between mattering and offending behaviour. For example, adolescents with lower levels of mattering were more likely to engage in antisocial behaviour (Rosenberg & McCullough, 1981; Marshall, 2004), aggressive acts such as fighting or damaging property (Marshall, 2004) and more serious violence (Chiodo et al., 2012; Edwards & Neal, 2017; Elliott, 2009; Elliott, Cunningham, Colangelo, & Gelles, 2011; Jasko, Lafree, & Kruglanski, 2016; Kruglanski et al., 2013; Lewis, 2017). It has been suggested that a low sense of mattering should not only be thought of as a risk factor for offending (e.g., having nothing to lose) but rather it should be considered as a potential driver to violent offences (Lewis, 2017). For example, it has been proposed that violence can be an attempt to achieve a sense of feeling that one matters in the world (Billingham & Irwin-Rogers, 2021; Elliott, 2009). This can be understood through David's reflection.

> I tried for ask for help but no one listened, I even went to the police and told them if someone didn't help me, I was going do something. Nobody listened. When I did what I did I felt relief … at last people were noticing me and listening.

A study of 1,500 perpetrators of violence concluded that "the use of violence can be in part predicted by a set of conditions that evoke a common psychological state of personal insignificance" (Jasko et al., 2016, p. 13). Billingham and Irwin-Rogers (2021) highlight that young people who feel as though they increasingly do not matter to their families are commonly led to some "doom-laden inevitability into the most murky or criminal undergrounds" (p.17) This was experienced by Luke who identified that:

> As a child I never felt important. Mum always put her partners before me. She never showed me any love and was never interested in what I did. When I was 12, I was taken into care. There were older boys there, they were really kind to me, and I got on well with them. I thought they liked me and would look after me. They told me they understood when I felt sad, and they could give me something that would make me feel better … I really thought that they were looking after me. That was the first time I took any drug, it was heroin. That was the start of me becoming addicted to heroin and led to me starting to commit crime.

Luke's feeling of being invisible, of anti-mattering, was eased by the pleasure he gained from feeling cared for and understood. This blinded him to noticing he was being led into a life of deviancy and criminal behaviour. It illustrates how the concept of mattering can be linked directly with an offending trajectory.

Mattering in custody

Within the custodial setting, a sense of mattering has been identified as absent in men who have self-harmed. Male prisoners reported feeling that staff did not genuinely care about them or resented looking after them. They also perceived a sense of not mattering to the wider organisation citing the perceived lack or inconsistency of specialist support across the prison estate as an example of this (Fitzalan Howard & Pope, 2019). Conversely, amongst prisoners attempting to stop using substances in custody, positive interactions with staff created a feeling of importance and of mattering which could benefit their recovery (Wakeling & Lynch, 2020). Neil spoke about his experience of coming off methadone.

> I met with SMS {Substance Misuse Service} and I thought we agreed a plan. I wanted to come off methadone fast, but they told me to slow down, so I did… and that was it. They never followed me up, never responded to my apps[1]. I was on my own feeling shit … so decided to just stop taking it, to go cold turkey. Then I got an appointment slip through to see them … but this wasn't about me… they just didn't want a death on their hands.

Neil's view was that the positive work he was doing went unnoticed and only when the prison felt there was a risk of him dying, did they respond to his needs reinforcing to him that he did not matter. It demonstrates that the prison environment plays a significant role in influencing whether someone feels important, significant, of value (that they matter) or invisible, unwanted, unneeded (that they do not matter). John describes a turning point in his prison pathway:

> Things changed for me when I got kicked out of [name of prison] having totally trashed my cell. I arrived at [name of prison] with nine nickings.[2] When I arrived, I went to see the Governor who told me that he was wiping all the nickings but he didn't want to hear my name being mentioned negatively in the prison. I was told that if I kept my head down for six months and did not get into any trouble, I would be given a place on a PIPE.[3] This made me feel like I had a chance to change, that someone believed I could change and they were willing to give me the chance to … I kept my head down and six months to the day when I was told I would have a place on a PIPE I was transferred.

John's reflection highlights the significance that one member of staff can make to an individual in prison feeling significant, worth taking a chance with; consequently, making them feel that they matter. The Good Lives Model (Ward, 2010) construes offending partly as a faulty means of achieving basic human goods (such as intimacy, a sense of mastery, control). Therefore, inversely in order to reduce recidivism, a person needs to feel capable and skilled. The Good Lives Model promotes a focus on building strengths and capabilities rather than purely focusing on removing risk factors (Ward, 2010). Using the Good Lives Model as a basis for intervention in custodial settings, and focusing on a person's interests, abilities, and aspirations can be instrumental in supporting the development of opportunities to develop a sense of mattering.

Fitzalan Howard and Pope's (2019) study refers to a small group of people in prison having access to a specialist psychological unit. Whilst not overtly identified in this report it suggests it could be a prison PIPE where people are accommodated on a specific wing with staff who have advanced knowledge of self-harm and emotional dysregulation. People can access additional support including psychological input and occupational therapy to assist in developing skills in meaningful and trusting relationships, in an environment that feels safe. An extract from this study highlights the importance of simple caring human interaction on supporting a sense of mattering "staff … talk to you like you're a human… that matters a lot" (p.18). Relatedly, there is evidence that this human approach of taking time to listen and get to know someone (i.e., demonstrating by your behaviour as a professional that they matter) can alleviate some of the pains of psychological risk assessment for men serving indeterminate prison sentences (Shingler, Sonnenberg & Needs, 2018).

The people that we support in their pathway out of prison to the community (and sometimes back following recall) have generally experienced significant childhood trauma. This impacts on their sense of self, their sense of worth and ultimately on their sense of mattering. They commonly enter prison having either "burned such bridges" with family and friends when they became consumed with crime and drugs (LeBel & Maruna, 2012, p. 667) or formed misaligned relationships with people, that provided them with a false sense of importance and mattering. Many people do not have any form of social contact whilst they are in prison. This lack of social connection whilst in prison, including social support from significant others (Holt-Lunstad, Smith & Layton, 2010) compounded with being invisible to the outside world, commonly increases the feeling of not mattering. This in turn can lead to loss of hope. Ryan reflected that:

> Before I went to prison, I had loads of friends. Lads I had known since school – we did everything together. We had time for each other, I was a big personality, I was liked, I was funny and confident. I thought they would always be there; we would always be part of each other's lives. Then I came to prison. They dropped me; I haven't heard from any of them since I came in. I hear some of them have got kids, most of them are married or with a partner…. And I'm here, stuck, left behind.

The experience of feeling part of something in the community, where Ryan felt valued, needed, wanted and visible, gave him a clear identity and a belief that he mattered to those around him. The impact of both his offence and incarceration left him feeling abandoned, rejected and without hope that he would ever feel included in the world again. Humans are social beings who have a strong need to belong (LeBel & Maruna, 2012). However, this can be difficult to achieve in prison. Feelings of being forgotten, unimportant and invisible can impact on a person's motivation to change. Neil's account demonstrates the damage not mattering can have on hope for now and hope for the future:

> Nobody is interested in me, not my brother, not anyone here. I have tried so hard. I put in app after app to see my POM [Prison Offender Manager], no response, I put in an app to see healthcare, no response – but others who put an app in after me get seen, I put in an app to see my substance worker, no response, I put in an app for work – nothing. I now think why bother… what's the point …. I will just see my sentence through and get out and go back to the life I know on release.

Interactions between staff and those in prison can be instrumental in supporting a change in the course of a person's prison journey (Liebling et al., 2019). John's reflection of his interaction with a prison governor above and his reflection below of being on a PIPE wing both demonstrate the power of relationships with prison staff. These show the impact relationships can have on a person feeling visible, important and of sufficient value that they start to believe they can be in control of their journey through prison in a positive way rather than through engaging in anti-mattering behaviours.

> The PIPE unit gave me an opportunity to be someone different. They did not judge me for my past but took me for who I had become. On the main wing in prison, in my view, it doesn't feel as though they are there to help you. There are too many prisoners. The only interaction between staff and prisoners was negative. On the PIPE it feels as though you are someone, that you are important and that helps you start making better decisions about who you are and what you do. They spoke to me like I was a human, so I behaved like a human. I was in prison 8 years before I went to the PIPE, I was on the PIPE for 17 months then got released. It shows you that it is the environment that makes the difference.

However, the relationship between prison staff and prisoners is complex, primarily due to the significant power imbalance (Crewe, 2011). Supportive relationships with prison officers can provide the steppingstones for those in prison who have no social connections to start to positively connect with others, sowing the seed that they do matter and can matter to others moving forward. As clinicians we have heard many people recall the impact of positive relationships they have had with prison staff. Sometimes the simplest act of kindness sticks with those in a position of having no power or control for many years. Luke telephoned us to thank us for the first birthday card he had received in years. Receiving this allowed him to recognise his birthday and with this, others were able to celebrate with him in prison, something he had not done for a long time. Through the nature of prison life, and chronic understaffing within some establishments, relationships with prison staff can equally be damaging to prisoners (Crewe, 2011). Inconsistent or forgotten appointments with prison staff, lost belongings and personal items when prisoners are moved reinforce the sense of being invisible and not mattering. This can trigger negative feelings and unhelpful behaviours.

Release and mattering

The scenario first described at the start of this chapter paints a stark picture of how release can feel. As an alternative to this visualise the following:

> Imagine returning to your home town after a long time away. Also imagine that when you return, you feel lonely. However, you have a number of people who you feel are invested in you, who notice you, who are interested in you, who feel like they genuinely care. You settle in and start trying to build a life again and you talk about how hard it is with those around you. You describe some of the positive things and some of the setbacks. After a short time, you are linked in with a group of other people who are newly released. You feel able to provide them with some advice. It feels like a small thing but you are glad you can help in some way. How do you feel right now?

The second scenario paints a much more hopeful picture of the future and the success around release feels more likely. Having someone holding you in mind and valuing your place in the world, allowing you to contribute to supporting others and sharing in your successes and struggles are all simple yet protective approaches.

Commonly the primary focus for release is being able to meet a person's immediate needs and ensure that some of the practical skills required for resettlement are supported (see Chapters 2 and 7). For those being released from prison following long sentences, the concept of mattering is largely overlooked. Most people we work with do not have supportive relationships in the community, and often significant work has to go into developing plans to manage unhelpful community relationships. Neglecting mattering on release can risk missing a fundamental human need. This could impact on the success of re-entry and resettlement. Humans want intimacy (to feel connected to others), diversity (to contribute to the lives of others), to be useful (to be valued by others), and to belong (to be accepted by others), to gain a sense of who they are, where they fit in and how to make a life for themselves (Sarason, 1988; Walton & Wilson, 2018). To achieve success in these four areas requires a set of complex skills, which can be challenging for those coming out of prison having served long sentences. Additionally, the stigma attached to having been in prison can further hinder a person developing a sense of mattering within the community.

Darren who had been in prison for over 30 years wanted to feel as though he belonged in the community immediately on release. However, the impact of such a long sentence had left him unskilled in meeting people who would be a positive influence to him. He struggled with knowing who he was in the community, and how to positively socially interact with people. His desire to belong, to feel accepted and successfully resettle was so intense that he started mixing with people who took advantage of his vulnerabilities. His wish to matter to this group was such that he showed mistaken loyalty to them. He was unable to see the negative impact they were having on him, resulting in him making poor decisions, becoming emotionally dysregulated and ultimately being recalled to prison.

Darren's strong desire to matter, and the loss of skills that would support him in developing social connections impacted on his ability to effectively resettle in the community. For people who have experienced significant childhood trauma, being able to understand hidden agendas behind others behaviours can be impacted by their inherent need to matter.

Mattering and hope

Hope can be significantly influenced by a person's sense of mattering. Snyder et al. (1991) identifies that "hope is fuelled by the perception of successful agency related to goals" and "is influenced by the perceived availability of successful pathways related to goals" (p. 570). For hope to be actualised, a person needs to believe that their goals are achievable, will be noticed and valued by others and that they have support to achieve them: in essence a person needs to feel as though they matter to enable them to have legitimate hope. Ruddell, Broom and Young (2010) highlight the impact community in-reach workers had on instilling hope to men being released on life licence, supporting goal planning prior to release.

Strong social bonds and community connections are important to both community resettlement and desistence from crime (Laub, Nagin & Sampson, 1998; Wolff & Draine, 2004). They can support feelings of value, importance and social inclusion. For those in prison, connection with the outside world provides hope: hope that at some point the person will be back out in the community, living a free life. Van Ginneken (2015) identifies that hope and optimism support people being persistent in trying to achieve goals. For those serving shorter-term sentences, working toward meaningful goals to support release, it is easier to keep hope alive. For those serving long or indeterminate sentences, holding hope for a better future can be challenging, if not at times impossible (Wainwright, Harriott & Saajedi, 2019). People who are serving long prison sentences, whether this is determinate, life or IPP[4] commonly lack family or other social support in the community or choose to disconnect from support (Codd, 2008; Haney, 2003; Schinkel, 2014). Contact can also be an unbearably painful reminder of what has been lost. Many experience being exiled from families and communities, leaving a sense of being lost, not mattering and hopelessness about the future (Schinkel, 2014). Julian recalled:

> Growing up my Mum didn't want me; I was a mistake. When I was born, she left me with my Grandma and Grandad and never came back for me. I was a handful, I found learning hard and did not like school so got into a lot of trouble. I found making friends really hard, I still do, I've never really had any. Mum went and got married and had more kids, who stayed with her. She wanted them, not me. My Grandma was very strict, and I wasn't very nice to her, she died when I was still young, and I still feel bad about how I treated her. I was bought up by Grandad who did not want me there, so I was looked after by other people a lot, some of them weren't nice to me and hurt me, nobody listened to me about this. I went to prison and now I don't have any family, friends or anyone, I feel lonely but have to just get on with it.

Julian's experience highlights how mistrust has affected his ability to build relationships, connect with others, build social capital[5] and develop a sense of mattering. Julian's narrative describes the impact that feeling that you do not belong anywhere or matter to anyone has on hope in later life. The messages that Julian took from his childhood were that he was unwanted, unimportant and didn't have a voice worth hearing. These messages impacted on him as he grew up, influencing his behaviour towards both himself and others. He engaged in activities that drew negative attention to himself by shouting at people who he perceived had caused him hurt in the past, regardless of who he was with or where he was. He did not experience positive interactions, resulting in a belief that any interactions that made him feel visible were better than being unnoticed. On release from prison Julian's hope for a better life felt unreachable, he found living hard, had no positive social support and felt stuck and lacked any hope that life could be different.

Enhancing hope and mattering

Understanding the concept of mattering is essential when considering a person's pathway through prison and into the community. Additionally, understanding how a sense of anti-mattering can drive offending behaviour through an attempt to gain power or self-esteem is vital. As we discussed earlier, many individuals who have offended will have internalised lifelong messages that they are not important, do not have a place in the world, hold no value or cannot contribute anything positive. Counteracting this is a significant challenge. Charles and Alexander (2014) describe three simple actions to take to enhance mattering:

1   Show people that they exist as valid and unique
2   Demonstrate that they are important to us
3   Give these two messages consistently and reliably

The idea of repeating this positive message and being patient regarding the impact is also highlighted. Below we look at some general principles to support mattering regardless of where a person is in their pathway through the criminal justice system.

The power of an enabling and supportive environment

The austereness and size of prisons can make them impersonal and soulless. Whilst little can be done to change the structure of prisons, enabling people to have their own space within them to gain and hold a sense of self can start to sow the seeds that they are someone with their own identity who matters. Liebling et al. (2019) emphasise the value of having a community spirit within a prison, where there are clear and consistent boundaries that support the development of trust between staff and prisoners. Tait (2011) describes the value of people in prison having "sociable and respectful relationships with staff, feeling understood and listened to, having requests for help followed through, and being given reassurance and encouragement" (p.449), whilst Liebling et al. (2019) highlight the importance of using peoples' preferred names in prison, reminding those in prison that they are human and that their feelings matter. Getting someone's name right is a small but significant step in having them know they matter.

As clinicians we work closely alongside Approved Premises (AP)[6] prior to a person's release, to identify important environmental needs that will assist the person when they arrive at the hostel. This is particularly important for people who have specific health or social care needs, to ensure they arrive at the accommodation with the appropriate means to manage their needs safely and effectively.

Within probation offices, the culture, environment and experience of individuals under probation has been highlighted as an area of development (His Majesty's Prison and Probation Service (HMPPS), 2021). Making environments more welcoming, warmer and investing in them so they are in a good state, are all likely to improve the experience of those that attend by demonstrating that they matter enough to deserve a decent environment.

The importance of relationships

Supportive relationships enable people to develop their identity and connect with others with whom they have things in common and who can be mutually supportive. This is a valuable starting point in supporting people in feeling as though they matter in prison.

Where possible, we start to in reach into prisons at least six months prior to release, to start to form and build relationships to assist in the transition process from prison to the community. This in reach work varies from face-to-face prison visits to video calls, letters, emails and telephone calls. A combination of these provides the starting point to building a relationship, showing the person being released that we are interested in them, that they matter, that they are important to us. In preparation for release, we start to support the formation of community connections, identifying community-based organisations that can offer a sense of belonging in line with each person's interests, beliefs and skills. As highlighted earlier, positive community connections, where an individual can engage in activities that enable them to gain a sense of self-worth, value and importance, all contribute to achieving a sense of mattering.

Tromanhauser (2003) identifies the importance of people recently released from prison having "a significant other or believer, to support them, …someone to turn to when things seem hopeless" (p. 93). Within the community we maintain regular and consistent contact with those recently released. Within the realms of an individual risk assessment, we might prioritise going to the person's home or meeting them in the community to support engagement in a project or face a particular challenge. This creates a sense of flexible working and not just "fitting them in" to a slot. We have found that the simple act of providing mobile numbers has been effective so that individuals can call us or send and receive text messages (often a preferred means of communicating). This has enabled individuals to more effectively reach out when they are struggling and have a response that shows they matter. Equally they are able to contact us when something positive happens and we can share in their celebrations. Acknowledging good times and being there for the challenging times provides a clear message that the person matters.

For those who have been recalled back to prison we make contact with them as soon as possible after recall. This provides a light touch point to show we know where they are, acknowledge the challenges they must be facing and remind them of our contact details if they wish to get in touch. This contact also provides a sense of the person being visible, that they matter. We can offer guidance and support to enable people to start to make connections with others in a similar position for peer support. We link in with the community accommodation providers from where they have been recalled, ensuring important paperwork and documents are safe. For people who have no one in the community to collect their belongings, we negotiate personal items being sent into prison. At times of great distress, this simple consideration of personal possessions is symbolic of caring for and holding them in mind particularly when they are likely to be expecting a more punitive response. Finally, we link in with appropriate agencies within prison to ensure that, where needed, they are aware of health and social care needs and environmental adaptions required. This sense of being understood and visible is important in the early days following recall.

Valuing lived experience

The best people to help prisoners can be prisoners themselves. They have the benefit of lived experience, which can bring enormous value to service developments and to supporting people in their journey from custody to the community. We aspire to employ someone with lived experience, as Frank stated:

> Having someone with lived experience offering support would help in developing connection. Knowing someone else has made it [successfully into the community] makes it feel that it can be done, and gives you hope that it could work for me as well.

We involve people with lived experience in many ways including: co-producing a monthly newsletter giving people the voice to write about topics they wish to share thoughts on; running an annual creative arts exhibition to encourage people to showcase creative work that reflects their experiences of the criminal justice system. Where possible we encourage peers to contribute to group sessions, where attendees share their experiences and learning. We have people with lived experience on interview panels and engaged in committee meetings to offer their experiences and views to drive forward better service delivery. Drawing on peoples' lived experience acknowledges the skills they have and the value they bring to others, which in turn reflects how much they matter.

Taking a strengths-based approach

Prison in reach work enables us to build up a strengths-based picture of a person. We notice what they have achieved in their past and what they are doing in the present. We show interest in what they are good at and what they aspire to accomplish. This allows us to demonstrate our view of the person as someone who can contribute positively to the world and succeed, showing each person that they are important and that they matter.

Enabling a person to understand their own skills and strengths can be challenging for individuals coming out of prison. This type of discussions can often be unfamiliar, as conversations in prison tend to focus on risks. Therefore, this work is done gradually so is non-intrusive, non-threatening and feels a natural development in conversations. With the collection of skills and strengths (as well as needs), we are able to identify places in the community that will support each person in being able to use their skills and develop themselves further. Jake was the prison's "unofficial" barber. Through conversations with him he identified that on release he would like to do a barbering course at college. We discussed this with his Community Probation Practitioner, and taking into account his risk management plan, we were able to support him gaining a place on this training shortly following release. Supporting people to access training routes that may have felt unobtainable in the past has been effective in reducing the temptation to fall back into old habits (e.g., using substances).

For those recalled back to prison we encourage them to reflect on the positives they gained from the time they spent in the community. The aim of this is to assist them to look at the skills and strengths that they used to navigate the complex world of the wider community. This reflection can then be invaluable in the preparation for their next release when the time comes. It provides good reference points of the skills someone has shown in the community, and how these can be used again to support a more successful resettlement. It can show the person that their time in the community was noticed, was important and there is hope for the future.

Holding hope and making plans

Prior to release we support individuals to set achievable release plans for the first few days and weeks in the community. Careful consideration goes into this planning phase to ensure people are able to make realistic plans that are achievable within the context of their values. Emphasis is placed on slowing things down (see Chapter 2) and recognising feelings of being overwhelmed (see Chapter 5). This planning stage is important to reinforce to people being released that they will be supported, that shared plans for release are in place and that they will be visible; all aspects to support a person feeling as though they matter at a vulnerable time.

As the individual's time in the community grows, the challenges undoubtedly evolve. The individual may suffer setbacks when applying for accommodation moves, further education or employment. Continuing to check in on progress and ensuring that space is provided to reflect on challenges or obstacles experienced is beneficial. Advocating for the individual appropriately at this stage and more importantly, encouraging them to be able to advocate assertively for themselves continues to reinforce that they "have someone in their corner". In addition, it is important to validate any negative emotions about life in the community being hard and acknowledge that sometimes an offending life can seem like the easier route.

For those who have been recalled, capacity for hope is more challenging. People in this position commonly experience feelings of hopelessness and despair, feeling that they have failed and cannot succeed. They fear that by being back in prison they will become invisible, be overlooked and not matter (Fitzalan Howard and Pope, 2019). Our roles in this situation are usually to hold hope for the person who has been recalled. Holding hope is temporarily shifting the balance of hope from the person feeling hopeless to the person supporting them. Flaskas (2007) suggests this is a shift from feeling hopeless to "doing hope" (p.190). "Doing hope" entails us showing we are still there, holding the person in mind, and showing we have not given up on them. Luke commented

> Just knowing you hadn't given up on me, like everyone else always has, showed me that I could not just give up.

We hold this hope until a time where the person can take it back to start setting their own goals to move forwards.

General recommendations

In summary there are a number of simple principles that can be embedded within services to enhance a sense of mattering.

Hold hope

Holding hope for people during times of despair is central. We remind them of our hope for them, and allow a vision for their future. We continue to reiterate the message that change is always possible and that the individual can contribute something positive to the world. Show them you still believe that they can succeed.

Enable individuals to have a voice

We facilitate people to sit on committees and in meetings, influencing and supporting change in their own lives and those of others. We encourage individuals with lived experience to be part of the service in all possible capacities. This could include recruitment and strategy. Enabling people to have opportunities for meaningful contribution, to suggest things and be heard, to make decisions that are listened to, to offer support that helps others are all examples of giving voice.

Help other professionals to see the wider context

Challenge/be curious about any simplistic views of an individual as "an offender" or "an addict". The sharing of a wider formulation may be useful here to understand the context behind the person's behaviour and why they may have taken the path they did in life. Encourage others to think what it might be like to be the individual for a day. By promoting an alternative perspective of the individual, others might feel more compassionate and be motivated have more nurturing interactions, ultimately enhancing mattering.

Keep the person in mind

Your relationship is the foundation of any work and can influence real change. Being genuinely interested in an individual's wellbeing, successes and failures will be noticed. Be responsive to communications and try to really attend to and listen to the individual you work with. Holding someone in mind when not physically present (through letters, cards, phone calls etc.) is a very powerful statement that they matter to you outside of your appointment times.

Embed a sense of mattering within your service at all levels

Every interaction is crucial and, if consistent, this will go some way towards gently challenging the individuals' views of themselves. Be aware of the services you signpost to/routinely use and how they interact with the individual you work with. What is the individual's experience of these services likely to be? If you referred them to a third party then you may well be held accountable for how they treat the individual. Perhaps testing out services before you refer individuals may be a way to mitigate this risk.

Conclusion

The concepts of mattering and anti-mattering and the impact of not mattering are crucial components in understanding offending behaviour and the support and approaches people need as they transition through the criminal justice system to resettlement. As clinicians we recognise the importance in individuals, within criminal justice services, feeling and being of value and valued by others, including friends, family, the community in which they live and professionals working with them. The principles recommended within this chapter suggest some practical ways that services can promote mattering, which in turn can lead to the development of hope for successful transitions from prison to the community.

Notes

1 "App" abbreviation using within the prison system for an application.
2 "Nicking" also known as an adjudication, a breach of a prison rule.
3 PIPE – Psychologically Informed Planned Environment – a wing in a prison designed to support identified individual screened into the Offender Personality Disorder Pathway.

4 IPP – Imprisonment of Public Protection – an indeterminate sentence that was designed to protect the public from serious offenders but was used too widely and inconsistently than intended. IPP was abolished in 2012, but its legacy remains.
5 Social Capital is a concept that recognises the value of social networks, where people with shared values form relationships enabling that society to function effectively.
6 Approved Premise hostel –24 hour supervised accommodation run by probation staff for identified people released from prison to resettle in the community.

References

Ainsworth, M. D. S., Blehar, M. C., Waters, E., & Wall, S. (1978). *Patterns of attachment: A psychological study of the strange situation*. New Jersey: Lawrence Erlbaum.
Billingham, L., & Irwin-Rogers, K. (2021). The terrifying abyss of insignificance: Marginalisation, mattering, and violence between young people. *Oñati Socio-Legal Series*, 11(5), 1222–1249.
Bowlby, J. (1969). *Attachment and loss* (Vol. 1). New York: Basic Books.
Charles, G., & Alexander, C. (2014). Beyond attachment: Mattering and the development of meaningful moments. *Relational Child and Youth Care Practice*, 27(3), 26–30.
Chiodo, D., Crooks, C. V., Wolfe, D. A., McIsaac, C., Hughes, R., & Jaffe, P. G. (2012). Longitudinal prediction and concurrent functioning of adolescent girls demonstrating various profiles of dating violence and victimization. *Prevention Science*, 13(4), 350–359.
Codd, H. (2008). *In the shadow of prison: families, imprisonment and criminal justice*. Cullompton, Devon: Willan Publishing.
Crewe, B. (2011). Soft power in prison: Implications for staff–prisoner relationships, liberty and legitimacy. *European Journal of Criminology*, 8(6), 455–468.
Dixon Rayle, A. (2005) Adolescent gender differences in mattering and wellness. *Journal of Adolescence*, 28(6), 753–763.
Dixon, A. L., Scheidegger, C., & McWhirter, J. J. (2009) The adolescent mattering experience: Gender variations in perceived mattering, anxiety, and depression. *Journal of Counselling and Development*, 87(3), 302–310.
Dixon, S. K., & Robinson Kurpius, S. E. (2008). Depression and college stress among university undergraduates: Do mattering and self-esteem make a difference? *Journal of College Student Development*, 49(5), 412–424.
Edwards, K. M., & Neal, A. M. (2017) School and community characteristics related to dating violence victimization among high school youth. *Psychology of Violence*, 7(2), 203–212.
Elliott, G. C., Colangelo, M. F., & Gelles, R. J. (2005). Mattering and suicide ideation: Establishing and elaborating a relationship. *Social Psychology Quarterly*, 68(3), 223–238.
Elliott, G. C. (2009). *Family matters: The Importance of mattering to family in adolescence*. Chichester, West Sussex: John Wiley & Sons.
Elliott, G. C., Cunningham, S. M., Colangelo, M., & Gelles, R. J. (2011). Perceived mattering to the family and physical violence within the family by adolescents. *Journal of Family Issues*, 32(8), 1007–1029.
Fitzalan Howard, F., & Pope, L. (2019). *Learning to cope: An exploratory qualitative study of the experience of men who have desisted from self-harm in prison*. Ministry of Justice analytical series. London: HMPPS.
Flaskas, C. (2007). Holding hope and hopelessness: Therapeutic engagements with the balance of hope. *Journal of Family Therapy*, 29, 186–202.

Flett, G. L., Goldstein, A. L., Pechenkov, I. G., Nepon, T., & Wekerle, C. (2016) Antecedents, correlates, and consequences of feeling like you don't matter: Associations with maltreatment, loneliness, social anxiety, and the five-factor model. *Personality and Individual Differences*, 92, 52–56.

Flett, G. L. (2018). *The psychology of mattering: Understanding the human need to be significant*. London: Academic Press.

Flett, G. L., Burdo, R., & Nepon, T. (2021). Mattering, insecure attachment, rumination, and self-criticism in distress among university students. *International Journal of Mental Health and Addiction*, 19, 1300–1313.

Flett, G. L., Nepon, T., Goldberg, J. O., Rose, A. L., Atkey, S. K., & Zaki-Azat, J. (2022). The Anti-Mattering Scale: Development, psychometric properties and associations with well-being and distress measures in adolescents and emerging adults. *Journal of Psychoeducational Assessment*, 40(1), 37–59.

France, M. K., & Finney, S. J. (2009). What matters in the measurement of mattering? A construct validity study. *Measurement and Evaluation in Counseling and Development*, 42(2), 104–120.

Haney, C. (2003). *The psychological impact of incarceration: Implications for post-prison adjustment*. US department of health and human services "From home to prison the effect of incarceration and re-entry on children, families and communities" Conference. Bethesda, MD.

His Majesty's Prison and Probation Service (HMPPS) (2021). The Target Operating Model for probation services in England and Wales. Retrieved from: www.gov.uk/guidance/strengthening-probation-building-confidence#related-documents.

Holt-Lunstad, J., Smith, T. B., & Layton, J. B. (2010). Social relationships and mortality risk: a meta-analytic review. *PLoS Medicine*, 7(7), 1–20.

Jasko, K., Lafree, G., & Kruglanski, A. (2016). Quest for significance and violent extremism: The case of domestic radicalization. *Political Psychology*, 38(5), 815–831.

Kruglanski, A. W., Belanger, J. J., Gelfand, M., Gunaratna, R., Hettiarachchi, M., Reinares, F., Orehek, E., Sasota, J., & Sharvit, K. (2013). Terrorism: A (self) love story: Redirecting the significance quest can end violence. *American Psychologist*, 68(7), 559–575.

Laub, J. H., Nagin, D. S., & Sampson R. J. (1998). Trajectories of change in criminal offending: Good marriages and the desistance process. *American Sociological Review*, 63, 225–238.

LeBel, T., & Maruna, S. (2012). Life on the outside: Transitioning from prison to the community. In Petersilia, J., & Reitz, K. R. (Eds.). *The Oxford handbook of sentencing and corrections* (pp. 657–683). Oxford: Oxford University Press.

Lewis, D. M. (2017). A matter for concern: Young offenders and the importance of mattering. *Deviant Behavior*, 38(11), 1318–1331.

Liebling, A., Laws, B., Lieber, E., Auty, K., Schmidt, B. E., Crewe, B., Gardom, J., Kant. D., & Morey, M. (2019). Are hope and possibility achievable in prison? *The Howard Journal*, 58(1), 1–23.

McComb, S. E., Goldberg, J. O., Flett, G. L., & Rose, A. L. (2020). The double jeopardy of feeling lonely and unimportant: State and trait loneliness and feelings and fears of not mattering. *Frontiers in Psychology*, 11, 1–8.

Marshall, S. K. (2001). Do I matter? Construct validation of adolescents' perceived mattering to parents and friends. *Journal of Adolescence*, 24(4), 473–490.

Marshall, S. K. (2004). Relative contributions of perceived mattering to parents and friends in predicting adolescents' psychological well-being. *Perceptual and Motor Skills*, 99(2), 591–601.

Maslach, C., Stapp, J., & Santee, R. T. (1985). Individuation: Conceptual analysis and assessment. *Journal of Personality and Social Psychology*, 49, 729–738.

Prilleltensky, I. (2020). Mattering at the intersection of psychology, philosophy, and politics. *American Journal of Community Psychology*, 65(1–2), 16–34.

Raque-Bogdan, T. L., Ericson, S. K., Jackson, J., Martin, H. M., & Bryan, N. A. (2011). Attachment and mental and physical health: Self-compassion and mattering as mediators. *Journal of Counseling Psychology*, 58(2), 272–278.

Rosenberg, M. (1985). Self-concept and psychological well-being in adolescence. In R. L. Leahy (Ed.), *The development of the self* (pp. 205–246). London: Academic Press.

Rosenberg, M., & McCullough, B. C. (1981). Mattering: Inferred significance and mental health among adolescents. *Research in Community and Mental Health*, 2, 163–182.

Ruddell, R., Broom, I., & Young, M. (2010). Creating hope for life-sentenced prisoners. *Journal of Offender Rehabilitation*, 49, 324–341.

Sarason, S. B. (1988). *The psychological sense of community: Prospects for a community psychology*. Cambridge, MA: Brookline.

Schinkel, M. (2014). *Being imprisoned: punishment, adaptation and desistance*. London: Palgrave Macmillan.

Schlossberg, N. K. (1989) Marginality and mattering: Key issues in building community. *New Directions for Student Services*, 48(1), 5–15.

Shingler, J., Sonnenberg, S. J., & Needs, A. (2018). Risk assessment interviews: Exploring the perspectives of psychologists and indeterminate sentenced prisoners in the United Kingdom. *International Journal of Offender Therapy and Comparative Criminology*, 62(10), 3201–3224.

Snyder, C. R., Harris, C., Anderson, J. R., Holleran, S. A., Irving, L. M., Sigmon, S.T., Yoshinobu, L., Gibb, J., Langelle, C., & Harney, P. (1991) The will and the ways: Development and validation of an individual-differences measure of hope. *Journal of Personality and Social Psychology* 60, 570–585.

Tait, S. (2011). A typology of prison officer approach to care. *European Journal of Criminology*, 8(6), 440–454.

Taniguchi, H. (2015). Interpersonal mattering in friendship as a predictor of happiness in Japan: The case of Tokyoites. *Journal of Happiness Studies*, 16(6), 1475–1491.

Tromanhauser, E. (2003). Comments and reflections on forty years in the criminal justice system. In J. I. Ross & S. C. Richards (Eds.), *Convict criminology* (pp. 81–94). Belmont, CA: Wadsworth.

Van Ginneken, E. (2015). The role of hope in preparation for release from prison. *Prison Service Journal*, 220, 10–15.

Wainwright, L., Harriott, P., & Saajedi, S. (2019). *What do you need to make the best use of your time in prison?*London: Prison Reform Trust.

Wakeling, H., & Lynch, K. (2020). *Exploring substance use in prisons: A case study approach in five closed male English prisons*. Ministry of Justice analytical series. London: HMPPS.

Walton, G. M., & Wilson, T. D. (2018). Wise interventions: Psychological remedies for social and personal problems. *Psychological Review*, 125, 617–655.

Ward, T. (2010). The good lives model of offender rehabilitation: Basic assumptions, etiological commitments, and practice implications. In F. McNeill, P. Raynor, & C. Trotter (Eds.), *Offender supervision: New directions in theory, research and practice*. Cullompton, Devon: Willan Publishing.

Wolff, N., & Draine, J. (2004). The dynamics of social capital of prisoners and community re-entry: Ties that bind? *Journal of Correctional Health Care* 10(3), 457–490.

11 Afterword

Breaking down barriers to resettlement: Acknowledging and overcoming the 'them and us' mindset

Ian C

I have first-person lived experience of community reintegration and the complex issues that an individual faces upon release from detention. Books of this nature are very useful informative tools for services providing support. They explain the mental and social aspects faced by a prison leaver and give the reader an almost first-hand insight of how and why a prison leaver is feeling and acting the way they are. In my experience the onus is usually on risk management and box-ticking, however this book highlights the need to look at the prison leaver with a more therapeutic mindset. Just something as simple as understanding technologies and institutional processes can evoke anxieties and self-sabotaging behaviour. This can easily be seen as somebody reverting to type and being unwilling to engage with services, when in fact the true reality is that they are self-sabotaging due to adverse effects of previous trauma amplified by their prison experience and the emotional upheaval of release and resettlement.

In my personal opinion books like this are also useful to individuals during incarceration and when close to release. This kind of book can help the individual understand the psychological responses that they are experiencing and the highs and lows in mood. Overall, this kind of literature being available can only promote a better, more therapeutic approach to release. In my own 10 years of incarceration at various institutions across England, I don't think I met one individual who was not witness to some form of trauma. In the case of these individuals most responses to authority are the result of the "them and us mindset" that they have been exposed to during their detention, coupled with these early traumas. Non-engagement with services is usually a coping strategy or way of feeling safe and protected.

In my own personal experience, I gained resilience and strength through many things such as my family and this kept me moving forward. I also had children who needed me to stay on course and keep being the best version of myself, this became part of my motivation. Their mother was still living a chaotic life and they needed one of us to be stable. Once I decided this, my mind was made up and I put myself through a cold turkey from class A drugs, prescription drugs and alcohol.

I did this alone without rehab or NA meetings. I decided it was time to change and be the parent my kids deserved – it really was as simple as that with

DOI: 10.4324/9781003308171-14

my drug use. However, even though I had achieved so much, I still did not feel like I was part of society. Many prison leavers do not have this support or motivation. This is where services can step in and be more therapeutic and understanding. This is how services helped me to feel like I belonged in the community and that people would accept me despite my past.

In my opinion if you want to reach an individual who is a product of the system you have to break down the "them and us mindset" in order to create real trust and engagement in services. If services can do this, they will create a better support network for the individual and help them develop more resilience for coping with resettlement, it is what worked in my case.

Coming from a prison environment and having the label "ex-con", can really make you feel like you don't fit in, just as this book reports. Admittedly sometimes this is created by your own self monologue, but it has to be recognised that being a convicted criminal or being released from prison comes with stigma. Personally, this made me feel very isolated and the draw of my old cohorts was always very strong and inviting. This made me long for the security of my old life when things were not going well for me. I knew that they would accept me and not judge me, I knew I would fit in. They were all I knew, and everyday society was an unforgiving environment. However, I never gave up, I had found my inner resilience. I had genuine support and humanity.

Now I am through the other side, I can see how this was again mostly my own self monologue. And that I had created a place of isolation for myself. This hindered me socially and in terms of personal growth. It reinforced my anxieties and restricted my momentum in terms of resettlement. I didn't want to reoffend and I knew that hanging out with the people that I used to use drugs and offend with would lead to this, but it was where I felt accepted and comfortable. I did not give up but I had created another prison for myself mentally. I was metaphorically trapped, psychologically marooned on a self-imposed island. On one side was integration and uncomfortable situations. And on the other side my peers and comfort zone of past behaviours and ways I had grown used to. I had manifested this myself with my own inner monologue and distorted self-perception. I never reoffended but I had a few wobbles.

At times like this when my resilience was wavering, services were there to pick me up and helped to strengthen my resilience. The kind, genuine interactions with services and practitioners showed me trust and really helped with my mistrust of services. Treating me like a person, accepting me, and showing me my self-worth, broke down the barriers and showed me how to recharge my own resilience. When you've been through trauma, trust is hard to build. Gaining it and having that with services really broke down that "them and us mindset" that the prison environment had conditioned within me. Once that was gone things clicked.

For any practitioners reading this, please be proactive and try to break down that "them and us mindset". This toxicity is one of the biggest obstacles to rehabilitation as far as I am concerned. It's a problem on both sides. Call out any judgemental or toxic colleagues, nurture a more therapeutic approach. Show you mean what you say and that you are reliable. The worst thing to encourage disengagement from me was flakiness and lack of conviction. Why should I be bothered if you aren't? Not trusting services was all I had known. Deception and brutality were my starting points, mentally, and the reasons why I built psychological barriers for protection. Disengagement was my armour, not a sign of contempt or lack of respect. Deep down, disengagement was a response to my own trauma. In my opinion, heal the trauma and you will rehabilitate the offender. I am over 20 years clean from all substance misuse. I went back to education after leaving school at 13. I have achieved a degree and diploma of higher education in psychology and never looked back. Your role is not pointless and it is possible to help people like I was.

To anyone in prison or just about to leave who wants to truly succeed and change your life, heal from your demons, embrace the therapies that work for you. Remember that only you can find out what works for you and try as many things as are available to you until something clicks.

But also remember that what you personally put in will determine what you get out. Use every available support. Don't bottle things up: talk even if it's to a third-party organisation like the Samaritans. Find someone or people that you can trust and seek that support. Be open when things are difficult.

Do not self-sabotage. Try and find strategies like exercise or hobbies to distract yourself when you are feeling down or negative: even when you don't want to. The more you practice doing things when you don't feel like it, the more your resilience will grow. It's hard, but try to remember the realisation you felt when you first landed in prison. The feelings of hopelessness and being out of control of your own freedom. To keep going has to be better than that, no matter how rubbish things feel. Then turn that into fuel to motivate yourself; remember how lucky you are and how much your freedom means.

Don't look at your detention in a negative way; change the narrative. Most people never get the chance you've had to truly understand their own freedom. You understand its true value, never give up, you got this!

Index

Page numbers in italics refer to figures. Page numbers in bold refer to tables.

For Product Safety Concerns and Information please contact our EU
representative GPSR@taylorandfrancis.com
Taylor & Francis Verlag GmbH, Kaufingerstraße 24, 80331 München, Germany

www.ingramcontent.com/pod-product-compliance
Lightning Source LLC
Chambersburg PA
CBHW070324270326
41926CB00017B/3754

9 7 8 1 0 3 2 3 1 1 1 5 9